Best Books

for kindergarten through high school

Revised edition of *Books for Christian Students*

 Bob Jones University Press
Greenville, South Carolina 29614

NOTE:
The fact that materials produced by other publishers are referred to in this volume does not constitute an endorsement by Bob Jones University Press of the content or theological position of materials produced by such publishers. The position of Bob Jones University Press, and the University itself, is well known. Any references and ancillary materials are listed as an aid to the reader and in an attempt to maintain the accepted academic standards of the publishing industry.

Best Books
Revised edition of *Books for Christian Students*

Compiler:
Donna Hess

Contributors:

June Cates	Wade Gladin
Connie Collins	Carol Goodman
Stewart Custer	Ronald Horton
L. Gene Elliott	Janice Joss
Lucille Fisher	Gloria Repp

Edited by Debbie L. Parker
Designed by Doug Young
Cover designed by Ruth Ann Pearson

© 1994 Bob Jones University Press
Greenville, South Carolina 29614

ISBN 0-89084-729-0

15   14   13   12   11   10   9   8   7   6   5   4   3   2

Contents

Preface iv

Kindergarten—Grade 3 1

Grade 3—Grade 6 89

Grade 6—Grade 8 117
    Books for Analysis and Discussion 125

Grade 8—Grade 12 129
    Books for Analysis and Discussion 136

Biographies and Autobiographies 145

Guidelines for Choosing Books 157

Author and Title Index 167

Preface

"Live always in the best company when you read," said Sydney Smith, a nineteenth-century clergyman. But how does one determine what is "best" when choosing books for young people? Good books, like good companions, should broaden a student's world, encourage him to appreciate what is lovely, and help him discern between truth and falsehood. These three concepts undergird the choices we have made for *Best Books*. The works listed in the general bibliographies are intended for recreational reading and focus on the first two ideas. The two sections titled **"Books for Analysis and Discussion,"** one for grades 6-8 and another for grades 8-12, focus on the third concept and are included for the distinct purpose of helping students develop discernment. The annotated bibliographies as well as the final section, "Guidelines for Choosing Books," will provide valuable insight and help clarify how the works in these two sections might be used.

Kindergarten - Grade 3

Aardema, Verna. *Why Mosquitoes Buzz in People's Ears*. Illus. Leo Dillon and Diane Dillon. 1975. In this 1976 Caldecott Medal winner, Mosquito starts a tall tale that is passed to Iguana, Python, Rabbit, and finally to Mother Owl. Through this experience, Mosquito learns never to tell tales. Instead she adopts a habit that lingers with us today.

Adelson, Leone. *All Ready for Summer*. Illus. Kathleen Elgin. 1956. An information/concept book about spring, a time when animals, plants, and people prepare for summer.

Adoff, Arnold. *Eats: Poems*. Illus. Susan Russo. 1979. This delightful book is full of clever poetry, all about food. Children will enjoy the humor and unusual arrangement of some of the poems.

Agostinelli, Maria Enrica. *I Know Something You Don't Know*. 1970. In this intriguing picture book, partially seen objects become unexpected surprises when the whole picture is revealed. Young children will find this book especially delightful.

Allamand, Pascale. *The Little Goat in the Mountains*. Trans. Michael Bullock. 1977. This fanciful tale relates the story of a little goat who goes in search of some beautiful alpine flowers. He intends to decorate the necks of all the goats, hoping that the townspeople will then admire them as much as they admire the flower-laden cows.

Allen, Gertrude E. *Everyday Animals*. 1961. This information book reveals fascinating details about the cottontail rabbit, chipmunk, white-footed mouse, striped skunk, porcupine, and gray squirrel.

———. *Everyday Turtles, Toads, and Their Kin*. 1970. Young readers will find this book informative and enjoyable as they learn about turtles, lizards, snakes, salamanders, toads, and frogs.

Allen, Jeffrey. *Mary Alice, Operator Number Nine*. Illus. James Marshall. 1975. A simple story about a duck named Mary Alice who is a responsible and efficient telephone operator. When Mary Alice gets sick, the other animals find that none of them who try to take her place can do the job quite as well as she does.

Allen, Judy. *Usborne Guide to Stamps and Stamp Collecting.* 1981. Colorful illustrations of stamps make this an informative source for the young stamp collector.

Alston, Eugenia. *Come Visit a Prairie Dog Town.* Illus. St. Tamara. 1976. This intriguing book describes the activities in a prairie dog town. The black-and-white illustrations show great attention to detail.

Andersen, Hans Christian. *The Ugly Duckling.* Illus. Johannes Larsen. Translated by R. P. Keigwin. 1955. This story, one of Andersen's most endearing, teaches the timeless theme of self acceptance.

Anderson, C. W. *Billy and Blaze.* 1962. Billy, a young boy who loves horses, receives a beautiful bay pony for his birthday. Billy's adventures with his new pony begin in this first book of the *Billy and Blaze* series.

————. *Blaze and the Forest Fire.* 1962. Billy and Blaze discover a forest fire and set out to find help before the fire destroys the farmers' lands.

————. *Blaze and the Gray Spotted Pony.* 1968. Tommy, like Billy, loves horses and dreams of having a gray spotted pony. This is the story of how his dream is fulfilled.

————. *Blaze and the Indian Cave.* 1964. While on a camping expedition in the hills, Billy and Blaze set up camp in an Indian cave. During the night Blaze disappears, and an old Indian offers to help Billy discover what has happened to his pony.

————. *Blaze and the Lost Quarry.* 1966. While on one of their riding adventures through the countryside, Billy and Blaze discover a lost quarry. This discovery leads to other interesting discoveries.

————. *Blaze and Thunderbolt.* 1955. This is the story of Billy's attempt to befriend a beautiful, wild horse named Thunderbolt.

————. *Blaze Finds Forgotten Roads.* 1970. Billy and Tommy ride their ponies, Blaze and Dusty, into the hills to do some exploring. This is a story of the treasures they find on their expedition.

————. *Blaze Shows the Way.* 1969. Billy and Tommy decide to enter their horses in a show. But they soon discover that Dusty, Tommy's horse, is afraid of jumping. Billy and Blaze determine to help Tommy teach Dusty to overcome that fear.

————. *Pony for Three.* 1958. Spot, a pony, is given to three children who love him dearly. One day Spot steps into a woodchuck hole and hurts his foot. The children determine that it is up to them to nurse Spot back to health.

————. *The Rumble-Seat Pony.* 1971. One day while riding in a rumble-seat car, three children see a dirty pony for sale. They buy the pony and take him home. To their delight they find that buried under all the dirt is a beautiful pony.

Anderson, LaVere. *Svea: The Dancing Moose.* Illus. Richard Amundsen. 1978. Svea, a tamed female moose, is sent to Denmark to prevent the Dane's moose herd from becoming extinct. But Svea enjoys people and finds her way back to town no matter where she is placed. The entertaining moose makes friends of all the children and many of the adults.

Anderson, Lonzo. *Ponies of Mykillengi.* Illus. by Adrienne Adams. 1966. Rauf and Egli protect themselves and their pony near her foaling time in the midst of an earthquake and storm in Iceland.

Anglund, Joan Walsh. *A Friend Is Someone Who Likes You.* 1958. A charming concept book on the value of friendship.

————. *Animal Counting Book.* Illus. Moritz Kennel. 1974. Adapting the old nursery rhyme "Over in the Meadow," this book uses poetry to teach children about the activities of animals.

————. *The Brave Cowboy.* 1959. This is a fanciful book about a young boy who imagines himself a cowboy.

Appell, Clara, and Appell, Morey. *Glenn Learns to Read.* Photographer Suzanne Szasz. 1964. A simple story about Glenn, a first-grader, who learns to read and eventually gets his own library card and the chance to choose his own books.

Arnold, Caroline. *A Walk in the Desert*. Illus. Freya Tanz. 1990. The simple text describes plants and animals that live in the desert, including cactuses, lizards, and jack rabbits. The full-page illustrations are vivid and colorful.

————. *Who Works Here?* Photographer Carole Bertol. 1982. The book describes how diverse jobs add to the vitality of a community.

Ayres, Pam. *When Dad Fills in the Garden Pond*. Illus. 1988. A child describes the virtues of the family pond, without which life would not be nearly so much fun.

Baba, Noboru. *Eleven Cats in a Bag*. 1988. Eleven naughty cats learn the importance of obeying instructions on signs after an encounter with a laughing monster.

Bailey, Carolyn Sherwin. *Flickertail*. Illus. 1962. Because he is different, Flickertail, a squirrel with a golden tail, can find no friends among the Nutting family of squirrels. Forced to look elsewhere, Flickertail makes friends with Bear, Coon, the Beaver family, and Skunk. When a fire destroys the mountain, Flickertail becomes a hero, and the Nutting family begins to realize their mistake in shunning Flickertail.

Baker, Eugene. *I Want to Be a Forester*. Illus. Darrell Wiskur. 1969. Dan, a city boy, loves being a "trail blazer." His Uncle Joe takes him to see the forest where he works as a forester. Dan learns about conservation, how to protect forests, and how to become a forester. He has fun logging and camping. Children would gain much from this information book about forestry and camping.

————. *I Want to Be a Service Station Attendant*. 1972. A boy traveling with his father sees firsthand the job of a service station attendant and the workings of a service station.

Balian, Lorna. *The Aminal*. 1972. Patrick finds his Aminal while on a picnic and later describes it to a friend. This friend describes it to another friend, and so on. The descriptions of the animal become more and more fantastic and "monster-like." Eventually all of Patrick's friends decide they must warn and protect him, but when they arrive, they are surprised to discover the true identity of Patrick's "monster."

————. *I Love You, Mary Jane*. 1967. A simple story about some children and their favorite dog, Mary Jane. Mary Jane's birthday party provides the setting in which the children show their love for this big, shaggy dog.

Bancroft, Henrietta. *Down Comes the Leaves*. Illus. Nonny Hogrogian. 1961. Changes in trees are caused by the changes in weather. This information book not only identifies the leaves of many common trees but also explains the service that leaves perform for the trees.

Bancroft, Henrietta, and VanGelder, Richard G. *Animals in Winter*. Illus. Gaetano di Palma. 1963. This information book explains how some animals hibernate during winter while others find their food under the snow.

Bannon, Laura. *The Gift of Hawaii*. 1961. An endearing story about a little boy and his pet myna bird who look for a gift for Mama's birthday. Both the story and charming illustrations give interesting details about Hawaii.

Barner, Bob. *The Elevator/Escalator Book*. 1990. Simple text describes elevators, escalators, and other forms of transportation, while fanciful color pictures illustrate the text and tell a story of their own.

Barr, Cathrine. *Gingercat's Catch*. 1970. When it is time to return to the United States, Tom and Jennifer must find a home in India for their cat. They take Gingercat to the village state office to try to get him a job catching mice.

Barr, Jene. *Good Morning, Teacher*. Illus. Lucy Hawkinson and John Hawkinson. 1957. The children will enjoy this primer, which is all about beginning school days.

————. *Mr. Zip and the U.S. Mail*. Illus. Helen Fulkerson. 1964. This information book gives a good summary of the mailman's role in the mail system. It also gives a very thorough, yet simple, explanation of how the whole system works.

Barrett, Judi. *Benjamin's 365 Birthdays*. Illus. Ron Barrett. 1974. A dog named Benjamin discovers how he can have a birthday every day.

Bartlett, Margaret Farrington. *The Clean Brook*. Illus. Aldren A. Watson. 1960. This beginning science reader shows how fish and screens of rocks and sand help clean the brook.

————. *Where the Brook Begins*. Illus. Aldren A. Watson. 1961. Rain forms pools which build brooks or streams. In this simple information book the author rhythmically describes how this phenomenon occurs.

Bartoli, Jennifer. *In a Meadow Two Hares Hide*. Illus. Takeo Ishida. 1978. This informative story about two snowshoe rabbits (hares) shows how they survive in a meadow, how they change with the seasons, and how these changes protect them from predators.

Bauer, Judith. *What's It Like to Be an Airline Pilot?* 1990. This information book describes the work of an airline pilot as he gets his plane into the air, completes the scheduled flight, and lands. Colorful illustrations and captions are included.

————. *What's It Like to Be a Nurse?* 1990. This simple book describes the work of a nurse as she makes her rounds and sees to the needs of children that have different medical conditions. Simple but colorful pictures enhance the text.

Beales, Joan. *Travel by Land*. 1968. The interesting book includes a wealth of information about early-to-modern methods of travel, including the transportation of goods to market.

Beatty, Hetty Burlingame. *Little Wild Horse*. 1949. When Peter was seven years old, he moved with his family to a western ranch. This is the story of how he finds and tames a wild horse. Brightly colored drawings enhance the quiet charm of the book.

Behrens, June. *I Can Be a Nurse*. 1986. This informative book describes the different kinds of nurses, their duties, and the places they work. The simple text is enhanced by many full-color photographs.

————. *Soo Ling Finds a Way*. 1965. A new laundromat opens near Soo Ling's grandfather's hand laundry. Fearing for her grandfather's job, Soo Ling suggests that he stand at the window and iron so that people will notice his work. The people do notice, and so does the new laundromat owner.

————. *Where Am I?* Photographer Austin Anton. 1969. This information book, written in riddle form, describes the helpers found in the community.

Behrens, June, and Brower, Pauline. *Colonial Farm.* Photographs complied by P. Brower. 1976. The text and photographs of this picture book present life on a farm in colonial Virginia.

Beim, Jerrold A. *Andy and the School Bus.* Illus. Leonard Shortall. 1947. Andy, who is not yet old enough to go to school, dreams of the day when he will ride the school bus. Eventually, his dream comes true.

————. *Country School.* Illus. Louis Darling. 1955. This is a story of a young boy named Tony and how he overcomes his fear by helping another child.

————. *The Smallest Boy in the Class.* Illus. Meg Wohlberg. 1949. Jim, the smallest boy in the class, is nicknamed Tiny. Despite his size, however, Tiny makes the loudest noise and tells the biggest stories. By the end of the story, we also learn that he has the biggest heart.

Bell, Gina. *Andy and Mr. Wagner.* Illus. George Wilde. 1957. Andy is a little boy who always wanted a dog. This is a charming story of how this dream comes true.

Bemelmans, Ludwig. *Madeline.* 1939. Madeline, a small and often mischievous child in Mrs. Clavel's charge, has an emergency appendectomy. This rhymed story reveals the fun she made of the situation.

Benchley, Nathaniel. *The Deep Dives of Stanley Whale.* Illus. Mischa Richter. 1973. Fanciful story of a young whale who bravely saves his uncle's life. Includes many pictures and details about the habits of whales.

————. *Oscar Otter.* Illus. Arnold Lobel. 1966. This story is about a young otter who disobeys his father and finds himself in danger.

————. *Sam the Minuteman.* Illus. Arnold Lobel. 1969. This is the story of a young boy named Sam and his reluctance to fight with his father at the battle of Lexington. Circumstances, however, soon change his mind. This easy-to-read story, told from a young boy's viewpoint, provides helpful information about life during the days of the Revolution.

————. *The Several Tricks of Edgar Dolphin.* Illus. Mamoru Funai. 1970. Edgar Dolphin, a trickster, disobeys his mother and finds himself captured by some underwater divers. He must then use his ingenuity to try to escape.

————. *The Strange Disappearance of Arthur Cluck.* Illus. Arnold Lobel. 1967. Arthur's unusual habit of riding on other animals' heads causes him to get lost. The wise old owl helps Arthur's mother find her missing son.

Bennett, Rainey, and Preston, Edna M. *The Secret Hiding Place.* Illus. Rainey Bennett. 1960. This is a charming story about a little hippo who seeks out a secret hiding place where he can be alone, but not too alone.

Berenstain, Michael. *The Lighthouse Book.* 1979. This is a simple book with readable text and intriguing illustrations which describe several well-known lighthouses, various methods of illumination, and the automated structures used today.

Berg, Jean Horton. *The Little Red Hen.* Illus. Mel Pekarsky. 1963. This is an excellent book for beginning readers, a charming story which teaches some very timely lessons about the value of diligence.

Bergman, Thomas. *Seeing in Special Ways.* 1976. Interviews with blind children reveal their feelings and the ways they use their other senses. The book includes remarkable photographs.

Berson, Harold. *A Moose Is Not a Mouse.* 1975. Victor, a small city mouse, will never be a moose, but he does grow to be a large, brave mouse.

————. *Henry Possum.* 1973. In this imaginative story, Henry's mother tries to teach him to roll over and play dead. While mastering this skill, he learns some others as well.

————. *Raminagrobis and the Mice*. 1965. This is a fanciful story about a family of mice who live in an abandoned tower. The disobedience of the youngest son, Grignotin, leads to a dangerous encounter for the entire family with their terrible enemy Raminagrobis.

Beskow, Elsa Maartman. *Pelle's New Suit*. Trans. Marion Letcher Woodburn. 1929. This is a tender story about a young boy who uses the wool from his lamb to have a new blue suit made for him.

Bishop, Claire Huchet, and Wiese, Kurt. *The Five Chinese Brothers*. 1938. In this nonsense tale, five Chinese brothers repeatedly escape execution in the most unusual ways.

Bix, Cynthia Overbeck. *Ants*. Photographer Satoshi Kuribayashi. 1982. Detailed text and remarkable photographs describe the characteristics and behavior of ants.

Bloome, Enid. *The Water We Drink!* 1971. This simple text and numerous black-and-white photographs explain our need for water, the problem of pollution of water, and the responsibility we have for preserving this resource.

Bolognese, Don. *Once Upon a Mountain*. 1967. In this fanciful tale, a shepherd boy leaves his flock and climbs a mountain to look for a lost lamb. His mountain climb begins an amusing adventure for him, for his king, and for all the townspeople as well.

Bond, Michael. *A Bear Called Paddington*. 1958. This fanciful tale is about a charming bear from "Darkest Peru" who lands in London as a stowaway.

Bond, Susan. *The Manners Zoo*. Illus. Sally Trinkle. 1969. This charming rhyming book describes different animals who have been placed in a zoo because of bad manners. The comparison between these animals and bad-mannered people provides some good entertainment and valuable lessons.

Bongiorno, Mary M. and Gee, Mable. *How Can I Find Out?* Illus. Lucy Hawkinson and John Hawkinson. 1963. Timmy goes to the library to find out about ants for a class report. He ends up telling his class not about ants but about how he found out about ants. This is a good book to use as an introduction to the library.

Bonsall, Crosby. *The Case of the Cat's Meow.* 1965. Wizard, Tubby, Skinny, and Snitch are "private eyes" who set out to find Snitch's cat Mildred and end up finding a good deal more.

―――. *The Case of the Hungry Stranger.* 1963. Wizard and friends team up again; this time they are trying to find the thief who stole a neighbor's blueberry pie.

―――. *Tell Me Some More.* Illus. Fritz Seibel. 1961. Andrew takes his friend Tim to a special place he has found where they can find all kinds of interesting animals and do the most interesting things.

Borack, Barbara. *Grandpa.* Illus. Ben Shecter. 1967. This is a charming story about a young girl and her grandfather.

Brandenberg, Aliki. *My Five Senses.* 1962. Children will find this well-illustrated information book about the five senses both informative and interesting.

―――. *My Hands.* 1962. This is an attractively illustrated beginning science book about the many ways we use our hands.

Brandenberg, Franz. *Fresh Cider and Pie.* Illus. Aliki Brandenberg. 1973. In this nonsense story the spider decides to give the fly he has just caught his last wish before he eats him. The fly's favorite dish is apple pie with a glass of cider.

Brandt, Keith. *What Makes It Rain?* Illus. Yoshi Miyake. 1982. This information book follows the journey of a raindrop through the water cycle and briefly discusses the characteristics and importance of water.

Branley, Franklyn Mansfield. *The Big Dipper.* Illus. Ed Emberley. 1962. Young children will learn how to find the Big Dipper and will learn some of the legends about this constellation. No adult help is necessary to make this simply-written book understandable.

―――. *Big Tracks, Little Tracks.* Illus. Leonard Kessler. 1960. The book describes the myriad, interesting tracks people and animals make when it snows.

―――. *Flash, Crash, Rumble, and Roll.* 1964. In this delightful book, Branley explains the wonder of thunder and lightning.

————. *Floating and Sinking*. Illus. Robert Glaster. 1967. Branley discusses how and why objects float or sink. Simple experiments are described to illustrate the concept.

————. *Gravity is a Mystery*. Illus. Don Madden. 1970. While no one really understands what gravity is, some facts about gravity can be made clear for children. Lively illustrations complement the text.

————. *The Moon Seems to Change*. Illus. Helen Borten. 1960. This book illustrates simple science concepts concerning the moon.

————. *North, South, East, and West*. Illus. Robert Galster. 1966. This book explains to young children how to tell directions simply by looking at the sun. Using a compass is also discussed.

————. *The Planets in Our Solar System*. Illus. Don Madden. 1981. This book uses illustrations, simple explanations, and easy-to-do experiments to give the young child a good understanding of the vastness and wonder of our solar system.

————. *Rain and Hail*. Illus. Borten Crowell. 1963. This concept book discusses how rain and hail form and fall to the earth.

————. *Rockets and Satellites*. Illus. Bill Sokol. 1961. Simple language is used to explain what a rocket and a satellite are and what they can do.

————. *Snow Is Falling*. Illus. Helen Stone. 1963. This informative book shows the benefits and the hardships that are caused by snow.

————. *The Sun: Our Nearest Star*. Illus. Helen Borten. 1961. This simple concept book discusses the sun and how it helps us.

————. *What Makes Day and Night*. Illus. Helen Borten. 1961. The beginning reader can learn from this text why we have sunrise and sunset.

————. *What the Moon Is Like*. Illus. Vladimir Bobri. 1963. Some important questions about the moon are answered in this book. Questions like the moon's size and its light and dark spots are discussed.

Breinburg, Petronella. *Shawn's Red Bike*. Illus. Errol Lloyd. 1976. This is a story of a small boy named Shawn who saves his money to buy a new red bicycle only to find that the bicycle is too large for him. Shawn perseveres until he overcomes this obstacle as well.

Bridwell, Norman. *Clifford, the Small Red Puppy*. 1985. A fanciful story about Emily's dog, which grows to immense size. The book has a simple but engaging text and excellent pictures.

Brierley, Louise. *King Lion and His Cooks*. 1981. King Lion has five cooks, each with a specialty, but one weekend, he takes matters into his own hands. The book has detailed, colorful illustrations.

Bright, Robert. *My Red Umbrella*. 1959. A little girl starts out with her umbrella on a sunny day. When it begins to rain, she finds that several little animals come to join her under her bright umbrella.

Brinckloe, Julie. *Gordon Goes Camping*. Illus. Julie Brinckloe. 1975. After a bear named Gordon reads a book about camping, he decides he wants to try it. A turtle named Marvin suggests all the camping supplies Gordon will need. Gordon finds, however, that he cannot possibly carry everything. Marvin helps him solve this problem too.

Broekel, Ray. *Fire Fighters*. 1981. This information book uses simple text and numerous photographs to discuss the work of firefighters and to describe a variety of fire trucks.

———. *Police*. 1981. The book is an introduction to the training, equipment, and duties of police officers.

Brothers, Aileen, and Holsclaw, Cora. *Just One Me*. Illus. Jan Balet. 1967. This is a simple story showing the value of individuality.

Brown, Marc. *Pickle Things*. 1980. Through simple humorous verse, the author describes what a pickle is not.

———. *Your First Garden Book*. 1981. How-to-do-it text suggests gardening projects such as sprouting seeds and growing sun flowers. Illustrations are colorful and humorous, with simple captions, riddles, and comments that children will enjoy.

Brown, Marcia. *The Bun: A Tale from Russia.* 1972. This is a familiar folktale about a proud bun who is outsmarted by a fox.

————. *How, Hippo!* 1969. Little Hippo usually stays close to his mother, but one day he ventures away and meets a crocodile.

Brown, Margaret Wise. *The Country Noisy Book.* Illus. Leonard Weisgard. 1940. A simple story about a dog named Muffin and his visit to the country.

————. *Fox Eyes.* Illus. Garth Williams. 1977. A fox causes concern among all the animals who think he is spying on them to learn their secrets. They soon learn, however, that the fox has a secret of his own.

————. *Goodnight Moon.* Illus. Clement Hurd. 1947. This is a charming picture book illustrating the coming of night.

Brown, Margaret Wise, and Gergely, Tibor. *The Noisy Book.* 1939. A blindfolded dog uses his sense of hearing to recognize the things around him.

————. *The Summer Noisy Book.* 1951. Muffin, a little black dog, hears all kinds of interesting sounds in the course of a summer's day. Accompanying the simple text are bright, bold illustrations.

————.*Wheel on the Chimney.* 1954. This delightful book describes the storks leaving Europe and flying to Africa then returning north again in the spring.

Brown, Myra Berry. *Pip Camps Out.* Illus. Phyllis Graham. 1966. When his sister goes on a camping trip, Pip decides to camp out in his own back yard, but he finds that all the night noises make it harder to fall asleep than he anticipated.

Bruna, Dick. *Little Red Riding Hood.* 1966. Simple illustrations and text are used to present the traditional story of "Little Red Riding Hood."

Brustlein, Janice. *Little Bear Learns to Read the Cookbook.* Illus. Marian Foster Curtiss. 1969. Unlike the other animals, Little Bear cannot seem to do anything worthwhile until a baker gives him a cookbook.

————. *Michael Is Brave.* Emily McCully. 1971. Michael is afraid to use the slide, but, by helping a little girl who is also afraid, he discovers that he can be brave.

Buckley, Helen E. *The Little Pig in the Cupboard.* 1968. An excellent story about a piggy bank that a little boy watches and wonders about. Soft line drawings help convey the mood of the text.

Budd, Lillian. *The People on Long Ago Street.* Illus. Marilyn Miller. 1964. This intriguing book recounts interesting customs in America before radio, television, automobiles, and electricity.

Budney, Blossom. *A Kiss is Round.* Illus. Vladimir Bobri. 1954. Light verse and bright illustrations describe several objects that are round.

Buff, Mary, and Buff, Conrad. *Forest Folk.* 1962. The activities of all the forest animals are pictured in their woodland habitat throughout the four seasons.

Bulla, Clyde Robert. *The Moon Singer.* Illus. Trina Schart Hyman. 1969. Torr attracts the attention of the queen with his beautiful singing. But the queen soon realizes that in bringing Torr to the palace, she would destroy the gift she admires in him.

————. *New Boy in Dublin.* Illus. Jo Polseno. 1969. Coady, who goes to Dublin to work as a page in a hotel, is overcome by homesickness until he meets a younger page whom he is able to befriend and whose job he endeavors to protect.

————. *Star of Wild Horse Canyon.* Illus. Grace Paull. 1953. While Danny and his family are searching for his horse, Star, Danny discovers a young neighbor boy who has been missing. The boy then aids Danny in solving the mystery of Star's disappearance.

————. *A Tree Is a Plant.* Illus. Lois Lignell. 1960. Using an apple tree as an example, Bulla traces the life cycle of a tree, from seed to flower to fruit.

Bunting, Eve. *Winter's Coming.* Illus. Howard Knotts. 1977. This is a delightful portrait of how one family prepares for the coming of winter.

Bunyan, John. *Pilgrim's Progress.* 1939. Retold for modern readers by Mary Godolphin. Illus. Robert Lawson. 1967. In this adaptation of Bunyan's classic, the tone of the original text and the spiritual lessons it presents are made accessible to children. The vivid illustrations of Pilgrim's encounters also create dynamic adventure for children.

Buxbaum, Susan Kovacs, and Rita Golden Gelman. *Splash! All About Baths.* Illus. Maryann Cocca-Leffler. 1987. Before he takes a bath, Penguin answers questions such as "What shape is water?" and "Why do soap and water make you clean?" Humorous illustrations enhance the simple text.

Bruningham, John. *Cannonball Simp.* 1982. An abandoned dog finds a circus and climbs into a cannon. Later he is admired for his talent and for his daring acts as a circus performer.

————. *cluck baa.* n.d. Whimsical illustrations and simple text that consists only of sound words will delight the young reader.

Burton, Jane. *Animals Keeping Safe.* 1989. Photographs and text depict how animals use teeth, claws, horns, camouflage, poison, and other ways to protect themselves from their enemies. Both common and uncommon animals and insects are featured.

————. *Buffy the Barn Owl.* 1989. Read-aloud text and excellent photographs depict a barn owl as it feeds, grows, and learns to fly during the first year of its life.

Burton, Virginia Lee. *Choo Choo.* 1937. A little locomotive gets tired of dutifully pulling train cars every day and decides to go off by herself. Through her adventures, she soon learns the value of contentment.

————. *Katy and the Big Snow.* 1943. In this simple story Katy, a red crawler tractor, helps a town hit by a big snowstorm.

————. *The Little House.* 1942. A well-loved story that describes the changes imposed by civilization on a small house. Simple text and superbly detailed, full-color illustrations are used in this classic.

————. *Mike Mulligan and His Steam Shovel.* 1939. Mike Mulligan uses his steam shovel to dig the foundation of the town hall in Popperville. But this proves to be only the beginning of their contribution to the people of Popperville.

Busch, Phyllis S. *Once There Was a Tree*. Photographer Arline Strong. 1968. The development and demise of a tree is explained with the help of excellent black-and-white photography. Good illustrations also show the potentially harmful forms of life to the tree such as fungi, tent caterpillars, and lichens.

Byars, Betsy. *Go and Hush the Baby*. Illus. Emily A. McCully. 1971. In this amusing and realistic story, a little boy devises various ways of amusing the baby in the family.

Calhoun, Mary. *Euphonia and the Flood*. Illus. Simms Taback. 1976. This simple story teaches that whatever is worth doing is worth doing well. Euphonia has only a broom, a pig, and a boat. But one day when it begins to rain and the water comes up to the house, she uses what she has to save the animals.

————. *The Traveling Ball of String*. Illus. Janet McCaffery. 1969. This fanciful tale tells how a widow's ball of string performed a good deed and became a hero.

Cameron, Elizabeth. *The Big Book of Real Trains*. Illus. George J. Zaffo. 1963. This information book identifies and describes different train cars, their operations, and the responsibilities of the workers.

Caple, Kathy. *The Biggest Nose*. 1985. Eleanor the elephant worries about having a big nose. Her classmates even tease her about having the biggest nose in school, but she eventually solves her problem.

Carême, Maurice. *Mother Raspberry*. Illus. Marie Wabbes. 1969. Mother Raspberry lives alone in her little white cottage in the woods. Each year, late in the summer, the village children come to help pick and preserve her berries. The children cannot visit Mother Raspberry during the bad weather of winter, but every day they can see the smoke curling up from her chimney. But one day there is no smoke, and the children prepare to make the difficult journey to see what happened to their friend.

Carle, Eric. *The Tiny Seed*. 1970. This intriguing information/concept book uses vivid illustrations and a simple, concise text to teach children about seeds.

————. *Do You Want to Be My Friend?* 1971. This picture book about a lonely mouse is good for stimulating children's individual storytelling and expressive language skills.

————. *The Mixed-Up Chameleon.* 1975. This story, which has a very brief text, is about a chameleon who wishes he could be like each of the animals he sees in the zoo. He finds it really is best to be himself.

————. *The Very Busy Spider.* 1989. An easy-to-read, simple story about a spider spinning its web. The text is highlighted by excellent illustrations.

————. *The Very Hungry Caterpillar.* 1969. This cleverly illustrated book teaches concepts not only about caterpillars but also about days of the week, foods, and numbers. (This book uses the term "cocoon" instead of the correct term "chrysalis" for a butterfly stage.)

————. *The Very Quiet Cricket.* 1990. This charming story about a little cricket trying to learn how to sing is enhanced by unique, colorful illustrations and a wonderful surprise ending.

Carlisle, Jane. *Balloon.* Illus. Jane Miller. 1968. An easy-to-read text about the experiences of a boy and his "pet" balloon.

Carlisle, Norman and Madelyn. *Rivers.* 1982. Simple text describes how a river begins, the many ways people use rivers, and the importance of keeping them unpolluted.

Carrick, Donald. *The Deer in the Pasture.* 1976. A lonely deer joins Mr. Wakeman's herd of cows. When hunting season comes, however, Mr. Wakeman must find a way to frighten the deer back into the woods for its own protection.

Casey, Denise. *The Friendly Prairie Dog.* 1987. Simple text and large, colorful photographs introduce the physical characteristics, habits, and natural environment of the prairie dog.

Catherall, Ed. A., and Holt, P. N. *Working with Water.* 1969. This book presents simple, interesting activities to do with water.

Caudill, Rebecca. *The Best-Loved Doll.* 1962. Illus. Elliott Gilbert. Betsy has a difficult time deciding which of her dolls to take to her friend's party. Prizes are to be given for the oldest doll, the best-dressed doll, and the doll who can do the most things. Betsy decides to take her favorite, old, much-played-with Jennifer, despite the fact that she fits none of the prize categories. But Betsy is pleasantly surprised when she reaches the party.

————. *Did You Carry the Flag Today, Charley?* 1966. This is an enjoyable book which teaches young children the importance of learning and doing what is right at school. The pen and ink sketches enhance the simple story.

————. *A Pocketful of Cricket.* Illus. Evanline Ness. 1964. An engaging story about a boy and his cricket.

Cavanah, Frances. *Abe Lincoln Gets His Chance.* Illus. Don Sibley. 1959. This biography covers the early years of Lincoln's life, including his financial problems, the death of his mother, the abandonment by his father, and his marriage to Mary Todd. It is she who encourages Abe in ways that eventually prepare him for his service to America.

Cave, Ron Joyce. *What About Trucks?* 1982. This information book describes a different type of truck on each page. Application questions follow each new description.

Chald, Dorothy. *Poisons Make You Sick.* 1984. In this information book simple, instructive text and bright illustrations help children understand the danger of some substances.

————. *Stop, Look, and Listen for Trains.* 1983. Simple text tells about types of train cars and gives tips for safety at railroad tracks and crossings. Colorful illustrations are included.

Chandler, Edna Walker. *Cowboy Sam and Big Bill.* Illus. Jack Merryweather. 1960. Big Bill goes to work on a ranch as a cook. The other cowboys give Bill a cookbook so that he can make new things to eat, and he eventually wins first prize for his pie in a baking contest.

————. *Cowboy Sam and Porky.* Illus. Jack Merryweather. 1961. Porky, Big Bill's horse, has a reputation on the ranch for eating but not working. But Porky's reputation changes one day when a cowboy who is hurt needs his help.

————. *Cowboy Sam and Shorty.* Illus. Jack Merryweather. 1962. This is the story of how some cowboys on a western ranch find a needed watchdog for their ranch.

Chandoha, Walter. *A Foal for You.* 1967. This concept book discusses a foal as it grows.

Chapin, Cynthia. *Wings and Wheels.* Illus. Kevin Royt. 1967. Mike and Mary explore the uses of wheels and wings in everyday life.

Charles, Donald. *Calico Cat Meets Bookworm.* 1978. Calico Cat is bored until Bookworm introduces him to all the exciting books found at the library.

Child, Lydia Maria. *Over the River and Through the Wood.* Illus. Brinton Turkle. 1974. This book illustrates the traditional song "Over the River and Through the Wood."

Claverie, Jean. *The Three Little Pigs.* 1989. This book is a happy retelling of the traditional nursery rhyme, featuring the pigs and the wolf in modern clothes and providing a most satisfactory ending.

Coatsworth, Elizabeth. *The Dog From Nowhere.* Illus. Don Sibley. 1958. John grows despondent waiting and hoping for his dog Pal to return until one evening he discovers a weakened, large black dog at his door. Inky, as John names him, is not claimed by anyone and so becomes John's new friend. But Inky's loyalty is put to a real test when the true owner appears.

Coles, Peter, and Kincaid, Doug. *Ears and Hearing.* 1983. In this book colorful photographs and lively text involve the reader and help him develop basic concepts relating to sound.

————. *Taste and Smell.* 1983. An easy-to-read story with bright pictures and intriguing activities that explore the senses of taste and smell.

————. *Touch and Feel.* 1983. A well-illustrated read-and-do book with simple vocabulary and activities that use the sense of touch to develop concepts of shape, size, and texture.

Collier, Ethel. *Hundreds and Hundreds of Strawberries.* Illus. Honoré Guilbeau. 1969. Tim is able to help a sick, elderly man with his roadside market by picking fruit and gathering eggs. He finds he still has a job even after the old man gets better.

————. *Who Goes There in My Garden?* Illus. Honoré Guilbeau. 1963. A little boy waits patiently for the right weather to come so that he can plant his seeds. The day arrives, he plants his seeds, and the sun and the rain cause his beans to grow. His friend from France helps him to know which insects and bugs are helpful to his garden.

Compere, Mickie. *Thomas Alva Edison, Inventor.* Illus. Jerome B. Moriarty. 1964. This brief account of Edison's life mentions only the most significant of his inventions: the light bulb, the movie camera, and the phonograph. Children will come to understand much of Edison's frustration and great effort with these inventions.

Conford, Ellen. *Impossible, Possum.* Illus. Rosemary Wells. 1971. Randolph cannot hang by his tail as all possums seem to be able to do. However, Randolph's smart (and smart-alecky) sister uses a trick which bolsters his confidence and enables him to hang by his tail with the other possums.

Conklin, Gladys. *Elephants of Africa.* Illus. Joseph Cellini. 1972. This book gives many facts about elephants' daily habits.

————. *Lucky Ladybugs.* Illus. Glen Rounds. 1968. This concept book traces the development of the ladybug and its usefulness to man.

————. *When Insects Are Babies.* Illus. Artur Marokvia. 1969. In this book, children enjoy discovering baby insects and watching them grow up to be adult insects.

Craft, Ruth. *The Winter Bear.* Illus. Erik Blegvad. 1975. This rhyming story tells of two boys and their sister who go outside for a walk on a winter day. It takes them a while to get ready. They count birds, gather a winter bouquet, pat a cow (who has her winter coat on), and the smaller boy finds a stuffed bear stuck in the top of a bush. He takes the bear out of the bush and goes home to find him "something to wear."

Craig, Janet. *Now I Know What's Under the Ocean.* Illus. Paul Harvey. 1982. Brief text and big, colorful pictures introduce animals and plants that live in the ocean.

Crawford, Mel. *The Cowboy Book.* 1968. This is a simple informative book about the West which illustrates and explains various cowboy gear and discusses the many experiences in the day of the cowboy. The pictures are realistic and colorful.

Credle, Ellis. *Down, Down the Mountain.* 1961. A brother and sister from the mountains raise turnips in order to buy themselves new shoes. Hard work and generosity are rewarded in this simple tale.

Cretan, Gladys. Y. *Ten Brothers with Camels.* Illus. Piero Ventura. 1975. This is a rhyming and counting book about ten brothers who come to a feast, each bringing a camel to sell in the East.

Cristini, Ermanno. *In My Garden.* 1981. An appealing picture book that invites the reader to discover and discuss the creatures pictured on each page.

Curry, Nancy. *A Beautiful Day for a Picnic.* Illus. Harvey Mandlin. 1968. A simple story about a teacher and her students preparing for a class picnic.

———. *Do You Suppose Miss Riley Knows?* Photographer Harvey Mandlin. 1967. Rudy wonders if his teacher, Miss Riley, knows that it is his birthday.

———. *The Littlest House.* Illus. Jacques Rupp. 1968. An interesting book about a boy who tells of his life in a trailer.

Dalgliesh, Alice. *The Bears on Hemlock Mountain.* Illus. Helen Sewell. 1952. Jonathan safely crosses Hemlock Mountain to get a big iron kettle, but his trip back home is delayed, forcing him to walk in the dark.

———. *The Courage of Sarah Noble.* 1954. This is the story of an eight-year-old girl, Sarah Noble, whose courage and strength help her endure the difficult trek she and her family must make to move out west.

———. *The Little Wooden Farmer.* Illus. Anita Lobel. 1930. This delightful tale reveals how the little wooden farmer and his wife collect animals to complete their little wooden farm.

———. *The Thanksgiving Story.* Illus. Helen Sewell. 1954. This is the story of the Pilgrims sailing to America and their first year in the new country.

Dallinger, Jane. *Spiders.* 1981. Text and striking color photographs describe how a variety of spiders produce silk and use it for making webs, trapping insects for food, and other purposes.

Darby, Gene. *Becky, the Rabbit.* Illus. Edward Miller. 1964. This story about rabbits is from an animal adventure series for beginning readers. After the story there is a brief informative section about rabbits.

————. *Pudgy, the Beaver.* Illus. Edward Miller. 1963. A beaver makes a new home for his family in the woods. Before the story there is a brief informative section about beavers.

————. *Sandy, the Swallow.* Illus. Edward Miller. 1964. This book about the habitat and habits of swallows is another in the animal adventure series. After the easy-to-read story, there is a brief informative section about swallows.

————. *Squeaky, the Squirrel.* Illus. Edward Miller. 1963. This book for beginning readers tells a simple story about a squirrel family whose winter home is burned, requiring them to build a summer nest elsewhere.

————. *What Is a Turtle?* Illus. Lucy Hawkinson and John Hawkinson. 1959. This book discusses turtles, including both land and sea turtles.

Darros, Arthur. *Follow the Water from Brook to Ocean.* 1991. This information book explains how water flows from brooks and streams to the ocean. Beautiful, detailed illustrations enhance the text.

Daugherty, James. *Andy and the Lion.* 1938. Andy checks out a book about lions from the library and becomes so absorbed with his thoughts about lions that his imagination creates a fanciful adventure.

D'Aulaire, Ingri, and Parin, Edgar. *Foxie, the Singing Dog.* 1969. A friendly man finds Foxie and gives her a home. The man already has a cat and a rooster whom he taught to play instruments, sing, and do tricks. Foxie soon learns enough to join the animal show, but on the night of her first performance, Foxie hears the voice of her former owner from the audience.

Davidson, Margaret, *Louis Braille.* Illus. Janet Compere. 1971. This biography about Louis Braille is written for the young reader and includes the Braille alphabet on the back cover.

Davis, Mary Octavia. *Rickie.* Illus. Dutz. 1955. Rickie is a greedy little rooster who eats so much and becomes so fat that his tail feathers pop off. Only after he learns to share and be kind does his tail grow back.

Davis, Tim. *Mice of the Herring Bone.* Bob Jones University Press, 1992. Two brave mice decide to rescue the Queen's treasure from pirate sea dogs.

Day, Jennifer W. *What Is a Bird?* Illus. Tone Chen. 1975. This book provides a general introduction to several different kinds of birds, including songbirds, tropical birds, and birds of prey.

De Brunhoff, Laurent. *Babar Loses His Crown.* 1967. As Babar's family tours Paris, Babar discovers that the flutist in the orchestra has accidentally taken the bag which carries Babar's crown and left his flute bag in its place. The story tells how Babar retrieves his crown and returns the flute.

DeLeeuw, Adele. *George Rogers Clark.* Illus. Russ Hoover. 1967. This biography shows the leadership that George Rogers Clark provided this country. Clark, one of the most famous Indian fighters on the frontier, also made several daring efforts to capture English forts during the American Revolution.

Delton, Judy. *Two Good Friends.* Illus. Giulio Maestro. 1974. In this simple tale, Duck and Bear learn the value of good friends.

Dennis, Wesley. *Flip.* 1941. This is a fanciful story about a pony named Flip and his desire to jump the brook.

———. *Flip and the Morning.* 1951. Flip, the pony, has one habit that bothers all the other animals on the farm; he likes to get up early. This is an amusing story of how Willie, the goat, tries to do something about Flip's early rising.

DePaola, Tomie. *Andy.* 1973. Andy's friends take the letters of his name and use them to form words.

————. *Charlie Needs a Cloak*. 1973. This is the story of how Charlie, a shepherd who needs a new coat, shears his sheep, washes and cards the wool, spins it into yarn, weaves and dyes the cloth, and finally sews it into a beautiful new red cloak.

————. *The Cloud Book*. 1975. This information book introduces common kinds of clouds and the sayings that have been inspired by their shapes. Lively, attractive illustrations accompany the text.

————. *Watch Out for the Chicken Feet in Your Soup*. 1974. Joey develops a new appreciation for his grandmother when he takes his friend to meet her.

DeRegniers, Beatrice Schenk. *The Shadow Book*. Photographer Isabel Gordon. 1960. Imaginative text and superb photographs explore the many things that a child and his shadow can do together.

Dempsey, Michael W., and Angela Sheehan. *Water*. 1970. This simple information book explains the sources and uses of water.

Devlin, Wende, and Devlin, Harry. *How Fletcher Was Hatched!* 1969. Fletcher, a large hound dog, is jealous because his owner Alexandra is so busy hatching baby chicks that she seems to have forgotten him. Two animal friends, Beaver and Otter, help Fletcher solve his problems in a most unusual and fanciful way.

Dickinson, Terence. *Exploring the Sky by Day*. 1988. Detailed text and colorful pictures describe different kinds of weather.

Dillon, Ina K. *About Policemen*. Illus. Robert Bartram. 1957. This concept book shows the different kinds of policemen and describes their responsibilities.

Dixon, Annabelle. *Wool*. 1990. This book describes how sheep's wool is made into a sweater. The weaving and wool dying are illustrated with many colorful photographs.

Dolch, Edward W., and Dolch, Marguerite P. *In the Woods*. Illus. Robert P. Borja. 1958. These easy-to-read true stories about caring for woodland animals will appeal to the young reader.

————. *I Like Cats*. Illus. Pauline Adams. 1959. This collection of nine easy-to-read short stories is about cats.

————. *On the Farm.* Illus. Don Robertson and Midge Robertson. 1958. This is a collection of eleven easy-to-read short stories about animals on the farm.

————. *Some Are Small.* Illus. Larry Kettlekamp. 1959. These easy-to-read stories are about animal pets such as squirrels, rabbits, raccoons, foxes, and skunks.

————. *Tommy's Pets.* Illus. Dee Wallace. 1958. This collection of twelve easy-to-read short stories is about a little boy's pets.

Domanska, Janina. *King Krakus and the Dragon.* 1979. The people of Krakow are being terrified by a dragon, but the shoemaker's apprentice, a young boy named Dratevka, thinks of a way to destroy the dragon.

DuBois, William Pène. *Otto in Africa.* 1961. Otto is a giant dog. In this exciting make-believe adventure Otto and his master, Duke, save a small African city from an attack by bandits.

Dugan, William. *The Truck and Bus Book.* 1966. This informative book discusses the different trucks and buses used for different jobs.

Duvoisin, Roger. *Donkey-donkey.* 1940. A fanciful story about a donkey who wants to change his ears.

————. *Periwinkle.* 1976. A giraffe and frog become friends when they learn they need to mind their manners by listening.

————. *Petunia, I Love You.* 1965. Petunia, a clever goose, manages to avoid all of Raccoon's attempts to eat her. Eventually the two become friends.

————. *Veronica and the Birthday Present.* 1971. This is a fanciful tale of how a kitten named Candy and a hippopotamus named Veronica become good friends.

————. *Veronica's Smile.* 1964. Veronica, a hippopotamus, is bored because she feels she has nothing useful to do. However, her boredom vanishes when she finds herself involved in one good deed after another.

Eberle, Irmengarde. *Beavers Live Here*. 1972. This book is a thorough, informational book about the life and habits of beavers in their natural habitat.

Eisler, Colin. *Cats Know Best*. 1988. Simple text and beautiful illustrations present basic concepts about cats. Also included on the copyright page is a list of cats' names.

Elkin, Benjamin. *Six Foolish Fishermen*. Illus. Katherine Evans. 1957. This story is based on the folktale in Ashton's chap-books of the eighteenth century. Six brothers go fishing and fear that one has drowned because each forgets to count himself each time one of the brothers counts. But a small boy comes along and eventually dispels their fears.

Emberley, Barbara. *Drummer Hoff*. Illus. by Ed Emberley. 1967. This is a short, rhythmic folk song that young boys will especially enjoy. The illustrations are bold, and colorful figures from cardboard cut prints lend a whimsical feel to the story.

Emberley, Ed. *Ed Emberley's Great Thumbprint Drawing Book*. 1977. An imaginative source book for making a wonderful variety of shapes and figures using thumbprints and simple lines.

————. *Rosebud*. 1966. Little Turtle is not happy being a plain turtle living in a muddy pond. She tries to disguise herself as a furry creature and then a feathered creature, but each time she ends up back in her murky pond. One day she is captured in a big net, scrubbed clean, and has a rosebud painted on her back before being displayed in a pet shop. Little Turtle is very pleased to end up in a new home with white pebbles, water, and a lettuce leaf for lunch every day.

Emberley, Rebecca. *Jungle Sounds*. 1989. The only words in this colorful picture book are the sounds made by jungle animals.

Emert, Phyliss Raybin. *Guide Dogs*. 1985. This information book describes dogs that are trained to help the blind.

Epstein, Sam, and Epstein, Beryl. *George Washington Carver*. Illus. William Moyers. 1960. This is the story of George Washington Carver, a black man who must overcome many difficulties to emerge as a creative, ingenious professor at Tuskegee Institute in Alabama.

Esbensen, Barbara Juster. *Swing Around the Sun*. Illus. Barbara Fumagalli. 1965. Children will enjoy these poems about the signs and activities of the four seasons.

Ets, Marie Hall. *Automobiles for Mice*. 1964. While Johnny is in bed, the mice decide to play with Johnny's toys. They soon decide, however, that it would be wise to stay away from such "dangerous" objects.

————. *In the Forest*. 1944. In this imaginative story, a small boy goes for a walk in the forest carrying his new horn. His music causes all of the animals he meets to follow him. Eventually, he leads them to a place made for picnics and games.

————. *Just Me*. 1965. In this fanciful tale, a little boy pretends that he can do what the animals do.

————. *Play with Me*. 1955. A little girl goes to the meadow and tries to make friends with the animals, but they run away until she sits quietly.

Evans, Eva Knox. *Sleepy Time*. Illus. Reed Champion. 1962. A woodchuck prepares to settle down for his winter nap but is interrupted by several other animals who come to join him before the first snow of the season.

Fairclough, Chris. *Take a Trip to Holland*. 1982. Easy text describes many aspects of life in Holland.

Farley, Walter. *Little Black, a Pony*. Illus. James Schucker. 1961. A pony named Little Black is sad because he cannot do all the things that Big Red, a horse, can do. However, one day Little Black discovers something even Big Red cannot do.

The Farmer in the Dell. Illus. Diane Zuromskis. 1978. This is an illustrated story of the traditional American singing game.

Fatio, Louise. *The Happy Lion*. Illus. Roger Duvoisin. 1954. One day the Happy Lion finds his door unlocked and decides to visit the city. He discovers that everyone is afraid of him, everyone except François.

————. *The Happy Lion's Treasure*. Illus. Roger Duvoisin. 1971. François, the zookeeper's son, learns the secret treasure of the Happy Lion.

————. *Hector Penguin*. Illus. Roger Duvoisin. 1973. Hector Penguin finds himself in a forest where none of the other animals have ever seen a penguin.

Fatio, Louise, and Duvoisin, Roger. *Marc and Pixie and the Walls in Mrs. Jones's Garden*. Illus. Roger Duvoisin. 1975. Mr. Angelo enjoys building stone walls in Mrs. Jones's garden because it makes a happy place for the chipmunks to live and play. But one day a Siamese cat appears and tries to change this tranquil atmosphere.

Felder, Eleanor. *X Marks the Spot*. Illus. Marylin Hafner. 1972. This intriguing book shows many things that the letter *X* is used to represent.

Fenton, Edward. *The Big Yellow Balloon*. Illus. Ib Ohlsson. 1967. Roger, who is taking a big yellow balloon home, soon finds himself followed by a cat, a dog, a dogcatcher, a lady, a thief, and a policeman. The adventure created by the yellow balloon turns out to be quite surprising.

Ferris, Helen. *Favorite Poems Old and New*. 1957. A valuable collection of favorite childhood poems.

Firmin, Peter. *Basil Brush Finds Treasure*. 1979. While vacationing at the seashore, a happy fox named Basil and his mole friend Harry decide to go on a treasure hunt.

Fisher, Aileen. *Animal Houses*. Illus. Jan Wills. 1973. A beautifully illustrated book with rhymed text describing different kinds of animal homes.

————. *Feathered Ones and Furry*. Illus. Eric Carle. 1971. This whimsical collection of poems is about animals that have feathers or fur.

————. *In the Middle of the Night*. Illus. Adrienne Adams. 1965. This collection of poems is about the sights and sounds of the night.

————. *Like Nothing at All*. Illus. Leonard Weisgard. 1962. Using rhythm and rhyme, the author takes the reader for a walk through the woods during the change of the seasons.

————. *My Mother and I*. Illus. Kazue Mizumura. 1967. Fisher's poetry creates a warm setting for this story about a young girl who was planning a special afternoon with her mother; the girl discovers that her mother has been called away on a special errand. On a walk by herself that afternoon, she discovers something that makes the return of her mother even more special.

————. *Once We Went on a Picnic*. Illus. Tony Chen. 1975. On their way to the park for a picnic, the children notice all kinds of insects, birds, and other animals. There is a map at the end of the book listing the animals and plants the children saw. The rhythm of this poetic narration will delight children.

————. *Where Does Everyone Go?* Illus. Adrienne Adams. 1961. This book, written in poetic narration, tells where all the animals go in the autumn to get ready for the first snowfall.

Fisher, Leonard Everett, illustrator. *The Seven Days of Creation*. 1981. This is a beautiful picture book with simple text retelling the Bible account in Genesis.

Flack, Marjorie. *Angus and the Cat*. 1931. Angus, a Scottie dog, is very lonely when he cannot find the cat.

————. *Angus and the Ducks*. 1930. Angus, the Scottie dog, escapes one day and chases the ducks. After talking together, the ducks decide to chase Angus home.

————. *Ask Mr. Bear*. 1932. In this fanciful tale Danny is searching for a birthday present for his mother. Finally he meets Mr. Bear, who gives him a good idea.

————. *The Story About Ping*. Illus. Kurt Wiese. 1933. When the goose Ping realizes that he will get a spanking for being the last one home, he decides not to go. But the adventures he faces make him question the wisdom of his decision.

————. *Walter the Lazy Mouse*. Illus. Cyndy Szekeres. 1937. Walter's family is moving, but Walter has been so lazy during packing that they forget about him when they finally get ready to move. Walter finally finds his way to his new home, but not before many changes occur.

Florian, Douglas. *A Carpenter*. 1991. Simple text describes a carpenter's daily work. Large, colorful illustrations enhance the text.

————. *Discovering Trees*. 1986. This information book describes the growth and reproduction of trees. It also shows different kinds of forests. The illustrations are realistic and bright.

Foster, Celeste K. *Casper, the Caterpillar*. 1958. Casper, the caterpillar, feels sorry for himself until a bee tells him what awaits him in the future.

Foster, Doris VanLiew. *A Pocketful of Seasons*. Illus. Talivaldis Stubis. 1961. Andy and his neighbor, the farmer, experience the four seasons. At the end of the year, Andy finds that he has a "pocketful of seasons."

Fox, Charles Philip. *When Winter Comes*. Photographs by the author. 1962. This book tells how the animals prepare for the long winter season.

Fradin, Dennis B. *Alaska in Words and Pictures*. 1977. This book provides a brief introduction to the geography, history, natural resources, and people of Alaska.

————. *Moon Flights*. 1985. Easy text and colorful photographs are used to describe the *Eagle* landing on the moon and the later moon walks in Project Apollo.

————. *Olympics*. 1983. This book briefly traces the history of the modern Olympic games.

François, Paul. *The Good Friends*. Illus. Gerda. Adapted by Fang Yi-K'iun. 1966. This is a charming story of how animals share with their good friends.

Freeman, Don. *Bearymore*. 1976. In this fanciful story a circus bear named Bearymore has a problem. He must think up a new act for the next season; however, it is time for him to hibernate. How can he do both?

————. *The Chalk Box Story*. 1976. This imaginative story is about eight sticks of chalk which hop out of their box and draw a picture on a piece of paper.

————. *Corduroy*. 1968. This charming story is about a small teddy bear named Corduroy who lives in a toy department but longs to be owned and loved. Unfortunately, a missing button on his overalls makes him a "poor purchase" until a little girl named Lisa comes along.

————. *Dandelion*. 1964. In this fanciful tale a lion named Dandelion is invited to an animal party. But when he arrives with a haircut and a new outfit, the hostess fails to recognize him and refuses to let him in. On the way home, Dandelion is caught in a thunderstorm and is forced to return to the party. He is surprised by the hostess's greeting on his second visit.

————. *Inspector Peckit*. 1972. A pigeon, named Inspector Peckit because of his clever detective escapades, retrieves a lost knit bag for a little girl. Because of his kind deed, the little girl rewards him with a ball of soft yarn to build a nest for his family.

————. *Quiet! There's a Canary in the Library*. 1969. This delightful story is about a little girl who goes to the library on a Saturday morning. While reading a book about a zoo, she daydreams about having a special library day when animals and birds may come to browse. Her daydreaming causes some unexpected problems.

————. *A Rainbow of My Own*. 1966. A little boy runs out to chase the rainbow but discovers that the rainbow is not where it should be. So he decides to have a rainbow of his own.

Freeman, Mae Blacker. *Do You Know About Stars?* Illus. George Solonovich. 1970. In this information book, young readers will learn to appreciate the size of stars, their distance from earth, and their temperature. The illustrations add clarity to the concepts.

Freschet, Berniece. *Bear Mouse*. Illus. Donald Carrick. 1973. This book describes the life of a bear mouse with four young mice to feed. It is set in the winter when food is particularly hard to find. An encounter with a hawk and a bobcat reveals some of the dangers for this mouse.

————. *The Flight of the Snow Goose*. Illus. Jo Polseno. 1970. This engaging picture book describes the migration of the wild snow goose, depicting a year in the life of Gander and his mate.

————. *Turtle Pond*. Illus. Donald Carrick. 1971. This concept book discusses pond animals and how they affect the turtle.

————. *The Web in the Grass*. Illus. Roger Duvoisin. 1972. Beautifully illustrated scenes from a meadow create interest in this story about the life of a spider.

Friskey, Margaret. *Birds We Know*. 1981. This book's full-color illustrations and line sketches help children understand how birds are equipped to fill their important place in the world.

————. *Chicken Little Count-to-Ten*. Illus. Katherine Evans. 1946. This book is a clever approach to teaching the numbers 1-10. Chicken Little cannot remember how he is supposed to drink. He asks one cow, two elephants, three camels, and so forth.

————. *Indian Two Feet and His Eagle Feather*. Illus. John Hawkinson and Lucy Hawkinson. 1967. Indian Two Feet proves his bravery by helping save his village when the dam breaks.

————. *Indian Two Feet and His Horse*. Illus. Katherine Evans. 1959. Because Indian Two Feet wants a horse more than anything else, he goes out to search for one. Growing weary of searching, he falls asleep. When he awakes, he finds an injured horse standing near him. He takes care of the horse, and it becomes his very own.

————. *Indian Two Feet and the Grizzly Bear*. Illus. John Hawkinson. 1974. Indian Two Feet tries to awaken the bear so that he can have his coat for a blanket. He returns home to find his mother has made him a wool blanket. He will get a bear coat when he is older.

Fritz, Jean. *Washington's Breakfast*. Illus. Paul Galdone. 1969. George W. Allen is proud of two things. He was born on George Washington's birthday and was even named for the first president. These facts make him want to learn everything there is to know about George Washington—even what he ate for breakfast.

Gág, Wanda. *The Funny Thing*. 1929. Bobo was a good little man that lived in the mountains. He fed the squirrels, birds, rabbits, and mice. One day a funny thing called an "aminal" came along. It liked eating dolls. The children will enjoy hearing how Bobo stopped the naughty "aminal" from eating dolls.

————. *Millions of Cats*. 1928. This is a charming story about an older couple who decides to find a cat for a pet. The old man indeed finds not one—but millions of cats—and cannot decide which to take home. The rollicking refrain which is part of the story will delight young readers.

Galdone, Paul. *The Old Woman and Her Pig.* 1960. This enduring folktale tells of the creative plan a little old woman must implement in order to coax her pig over a stile and to bring him safely home.

Gambill, Henrietta. *Are You Listening?* 1985. In this book, simple text explains the importance of being a good listener, especially when God speaks to us through His Bible and through the needs of others.

Gans, Roma. *Birds at Night.* Illus. Aliki. 1968. This easy-to-read book can help children understand God's creative power in an exciting, informative way. Topics covered will show children how swans sleep in the water, how feathers are constructed, and why a bird has three eyelids.

———. *Birds Eat and Eat and Eat.* Illus. Ed Emberley. 1963. This information book describes the different ways that birds obtain food. Also included are instructions for making a bird feeder.

———. *Hummingbirds in the Garden.* Illus. Grambs Miller. 1969. In this interesting book, children find answers to intriguing questions about the hummingbird's unique abilities. For example, how do these tiny birds hover over plants, get their food, dart quickly from flower to flower, or fly up or down, backward or forward? Children are also given ideas as to how they can observe hummingbirds by enticing them to artificial nectar.

———. *Icebergs.* Illus. Vladimir Bobri. 1964. The youngest readers will enjoy reading about how icebergs are formed, what happens to them, and the dangers they pose for ships. The bold illustrations help make this mysterious phenomenon understandable.

———. *It's Nesting Time.* Illus. Kazue Mizumura. 1964. This simple book explains the many different kinds of nests that birds build.

Garelick, May. *About Owls.* Illus. Tony Chen. 1975. This fascinating information book explains the various habits and general characteristics of small (Elf) owls, middle-sized (Barn) owls, and large (Great Horned) owls.

————. *Where Does the Butterfly Go When It Rains?* Illus. Leonard Weisgard. 1961. This simple book encourages children to observe nature, taking note of such occurrences as the mole who stays in its hole; the bee that goes to its hive; the bird that tucks its head under its wing; the cat that goes under the porch; or the snake that hides between the rocks.

————. *Who Likes It Hot?* 1972. This book's simple text and whimsical illustrations present different creatures that enjoy the sun's warmth.

Garten, Jan. *The Alphabet Tale.* Illus. Muriel Batherman. 1964. This concept book, using animals to teach the ABC's, gives clues by showing the tail of each animal on the previous page before giving the name of the animal.

Gauch, Patricia Lee. *Aaron and the Green Mountain Boys.* Illus. Margot Tomes. 1972. The redcoats are threatening to invade Aaron's hometown. Aaron searches for a way to join the Green Mountain Boys to help defend the Americans. But instead, Aaron plays a very important role at home.

Gay, Zhenya. *I'm Tired of Lions.* 1961. Little Leo the lion thinks he wants to be something other than a lion. But one day he sees his reflection in a puddle and decides he likes what he sees.

George, Jean Craighead. *All upon a Stone.* Illus. Don Bolognese. 1971. A mole cricket living below a stone begins to search for other mole crickets. His search is without success until he reaches the top of the stone.

Georgiady, Nicholas, and Romano, Louis. *Our Country's Flag.* Illus. Bill Barss. 1963. This colorful, informative book describes the many flags of our country since 1777.

Georgiou, Constantine. *The Nest.* Illus. Bathany Tudor. 1972. This simple book describes a robin who finds soft rabbit's fur and lamb's wool for the nest in which she will lay her eggs.

Gergely, Tibor. *The Parrot Book.* 1965. This is an informative book about parrots, macaws, cockatoos, parakeets, peacocks, toucans, and many other intriguing birds.

Giambarba, Paul. *The Lighthouse at Dangerfield.* 1969. The Dangerfield lighthouse on Cape Cod was built to warn sailors of the dangerous sandbars in the ocean. The book tells about the keeper's job and how he takes care of the lighthouse.

Gibbons, Gail. *Beacons of Light: Lighthouses.* 1990. This information book uses simple text and appealing water-color illustrations to provide an attractive survey of lighthouses, their history, and how they function.

————. *Catch the Wind!* 1989. When two children visit Ike's Kite Shop, they learn about kites and how to fly them.

————. *Department Store.* 1986. This book describes activities in a busy department store. The colorful illustrations show the whole story linked by escalators. The last page includes a history of marketing methods that preceded the department store.

————. *Farming.* 1988. In this book colorful pictures with captions introduce the work done on a farm throughout the seasons.

————. *The Missing Maple Syrup Sap Mystery.* 1979. A simple story about Mr. and Mrs. Mapleworth and their maple syrup. Beautiful, detailed illustrations enhance the text.

————. *Trains.* 1987. The simple text describes different kinds of trains, past and present. Large, brightly colored illustrations enhance the text.

Giff, Patricia Reilly. *Watch Out, Ronald Morgan.* Illus. Sussana Natti. 1985. Ronald has many humorous mishaps until he gets a pair of eyeglasses. The book includes a note for adults about eye problems.

Gilbert, Helen Earle. *Dr. Trotter and His Big Gold Watch.* Illus. Margaret Bradfield. 1948. Everyone in the village of Green Hill loves Doctor Trotter, especially the children. He has a special, round, old-fashioned gold watch with a striking alarm that can be set with a little gold key fastened to a gold chain. This watch captivates the interest of all the children and helps the doctor as well.

————. *Mr. Plum and the Little Green Tree.* Illus. Margaret Bradfield. 1946. Mr. Plum, a small-town cobbler working in the big city, does a kind deed for the mayor. In return the mayor decides to do something special for Mr. Plum.

Gilroy, Ruth G., and Gilroy, Frank. *Little Ego.* Illus. Lillian Obligado. 1970. This amusing story presents a little mouse named Ego who wants to be anything except a mouse until one day he saves the lives of thousands of animals from a stampede of elephants. He is given a banquet and presented a medal, and "to this day . . . elephants are still afraid of mice."

The Gingerbread Man. Illus. Carl Hauge and Mary Hauge. 1973. This traditional tale of the Gingerbread Man's race and capture is enhanced by the illustrations of Carl and Mary Hauge.

Glendinning, Sally. *Jimmy and Joe Get a Hen's Surprise.* Illus. Paul Frame. 1970. Jimmy and Joe take some Araucana hens to school for show-and-tell time. Their classmates find that the hens have some very interesting characteristics.

Goffstein, M.B. *Two Piano Tuners.* 1970. Debbie Weinstock wants to grow up to be a piano tuner like her grandfather, whom she loves very much.

Goldin, Augusta. *Ducks Don't Get Wet.* Illus. Leonard Kessler. 1965. This book covers a wide range of topics about ducks: their migration, feather preening, and how they acquire their food.

———. *Spider Silk.* Illus. Joseph Low. 1964. Pen-and-ink sketches with color wash effectively illustrate spiders spinning their webs. The text also explains how spiders hold their eggs in the webs, trap insects for food, and how the silk for the web is made.

———. *Straight Hair, Curly Hair.* Illus. Ed Emberley. 1966. Simple text, interesting activities, and humorous illustrations present basic facts about straight and curly hair.

———. *Where Does Your Garden Grow?* Illus. Helen Borten. 1967. Topsoil is described as necessary to the growth of any food we eat. The major component of topsoil is humus. A good description is given of what makes humus. Although limited in interest, the book provides a good explanation of the subject.

Goldman, Ethel. *I Like Fruit.* Illus. Sharon Lerner. 1969. Interesting text and bright pictures describe many kinds of fruit including oranges, apples, and plums.

Goodall, John S. *An Edwardian Summer.* 1976. This charming picture book portrays the early 1900's, including the dress, marketing, transportation, schools, and cooking methods.

Goor, Ron and Goor, Nancy. *Signs.* 1983. This photo essay shows more than fifty signs in similar settings. Most are signs that young children can read for themselves.

Goudey, Alice E. *The Day We Saw the Sun Come Up.* Illus. Adrienne Adams. 1961. Sue and her brother wake up early and discover the sun coming up. They watch their shadows throughout the day and find out how the earth moves around the sun. Using this book is an excellent way to teach solar concepts.

Graff, Steward, and Graff, Polly Anne. *Helen Keller: Toward the Light.* Illus. Paul Frame. 1965. This children's biography of Helen Keller creates admiration for one whose blindness and deafness struck when she was one and a half years old. It also shows Anne Sullivan's devotion to Helen for over fifty years. Helen's zeal for learning and helping others who were blind and deaf provides an excellent example for children.

Graham, Margaret Bloy. *Be Nice to Spiders.* 1967. Since Billy cannot take his pet spider to live with him in an apartment, he donates it to the zoo. The spider keeps the flies from bothering all of the animals in the zoo.

Graham, Mary Stuart. *The Pirates' Bridge.* Illus. Winifred Lubell. 1960. The little red schoolhouse once belonged to pirates. One day the pirates return, and the teacher refuses to take her students and leave. In this amusing sequence of events, the teacher teaches the pirates a lesson and acquires a much-needed new bridge to span the marsh to their schoolhouse.

Gramatky, Hardie. *Little Toot.* 1939. Little Toot is a tugboat who really does not take his work too seriously. One day when he helps save an ocean liner, Little Toot changes his attitude.

The Great Big Animal Book. Illus. Feodor Rojankovsky. 1982. This book tells about animal mothers and their babies.

Green, Ivah. *Where Is Duckling Three?* Illus. Lee Blanc. 1968. Mother Wood Duck takes care of her ducklings and teaches them how to survive in the forest.

Greene, Carol. *Astronauts.* 1984. Large-print text and photographs are used to describe what space travel is like and what astronauts do. The book is oriented toward the early years of space exploration.

————. *Shine, Sun!* 1983. Simple text and bright illustrations portray the effects of the sun.

Gregory, O. B. *Cotton.* Illus. Elsie Wrigley. 1981. Simple text and colorful pictures describe how and where cotton is grown and how it is processed into cloth.

————. *Cowboys.* 1982. Simple text and colorful illustrations describe the work of cowboys and how cattle get from ranch to market.

Guggenmos, Josef, and Lucht, Irmgard. *Wonder-Fish from the Sea.* Adapted from German by Alvin Tresselt. 1971. An artist's imagination transforms leaves into fish and birds. This book may be used to lead into a similar art activity for children.

Guilfoile, Elizabeth. *Have You Seen My Brother?* Illus. Mary Stevens. 1962. Andrew cannot find his brother Bobby anywhere. After asking several community helpers if they have seen his brother, Andrew finds him at the police station.

Gulick, Peggy, and Dresser, Elizabeth. *Hurrah for Maxie.* 1959. This is a fanciful story about four elephants who have a circus.

Hader, Berta, and Hader, Elmer. *The Big Snow.* 1948. This story shows the ways that many animals prepare for winter. The animals do not prepare enough food for the winter of the big snow, so a kind farmer and his wife give them food to help them live until spring.

Haley, Gail E. *The Post Office Cat.* 1976. A cat named Clarence does a good deed in a post office and finds a permanent home and occupation catching mice.

Hall, Donald. *Ox-Cart Man.* Illus. Barbara Cooney Porter. 1979. This lyrical story tells the everyday experiences of family life in early New England.

Hall, Lynn. *Barry: The Bravest Saint Bernard.* Illus. Gil Cohen. 1973. Deep in the Swiss Alps a group of monks and teams of St. Bernards rescue snowbound people. Many years ago Barry, the greatest of the Saint Bernards, risked his life on numerous occasions. Today only the greatest dogs at the monastery are named Barry in honor of this courageous dog.

Hamsa, Bobbie. *Your Pet Lion*. 1982. This humorous book provides many facts about lions.

Hankin, Rebecca. *I Can Be a Fire Fighter*. 1985. This simple book introduces the important work of fire fighters.

The Hare and the Tortoise. Illus. Paul Galdone. 1962. This is the most familiar and one of the most famous of Aesop's fables.

Hartelius, Margaret. *The Birthday Trombone*. 1977. This book without text tells the story of a monkey who gets a trombone for his birthday. The noise he makes creates quite a problem for the other jungle animals.

Harvey, Fran. *Why Does It Rain?* Illus. Lucy Hawkinson and John Hawkinson. 1969. Entertaining text and striking illustrations are used to explain the need for rain, its various forms, and its effects.

Hawes, Judy. *Shrimps*. Illus. Joseph Low. 1966. A good and simple explanation is given of the hatching of baby shrimps, their swimming to shallow water, and their travel back to the ocean to lay their eggs. Scientists cannot understand the fascinating speed with which a baby shrimp comes toward land, yet it cannot duplicate this when older.

————. *Watch Honeybees with Me*. Illus. Helen Stone. 1964. This is a concept book about the honeybee and his life and habits.

————. *What I Like About Toads*. Illus. James McCrea and Ruth McCrea. 1969. This beginning science book describes the life cycle of toads, their eating habits, their defense mechanisms, and their ability to help the farmer by eating dangerous insects.

Hawkinson, John, and Hawkinson, Lucy. *Little Boy Who Lives Up High*. 1967. Ricky lives up high in a skyscraper in the city.

Hawkinson, Lucy (Ozone). *All in One Day*. 1955. This book pictures common daily activities of children: walking, dressing, eating, reading, singing, playing, praying, and sleeping.

Hayes, Ann. *Meet the Orchestra*. Illus. Karmen Thompson. 1991. This information book describes the features, sounds, and role of each musical instrument in the orchestra. Full-age, imaginative illustrations portray animals as orchestra members.

Hayes, Geoffrey. *Bear By Himself.* 1976. "There are times when a bear has to be alone with himself."

Hays, Wilma Pitchford. *The Goose That Was a Watchdog.* Illus. Nelson McClary. 1967. Em, one of several geese purchased from a farm, becomes a pet for Tad Vogel. When Tad's landowners want to sell all the geese, Tad realizes he will lose Em. But Em becomes a hero by saving the chickens on the farm from some thieves, and Tad gets to keep him.

Hazen, Barbara Shook. *Where Do Bears Sleep?* Illus. Ian E. Staunton. 1970. This book deals with all types of farm and wildlife animals. The rhyming verse of the text and the pictures portray where each animal sleeps.

Hefter, Richard. *Noses and Toes.* 1974. This is a rhyming book of concepts showing spatial relationships.

Heide, Florence Parry, and VanClief, Sylvia W. *How Big Am I?* Illus. George Suyeoka. 1968. The little boy compares himself to many different objects both larger and smaller than he.

Heilbroner, Joan. *The Happy Birthday Present.* Illus. Mary Chalmers. 1962. Peter and his young brother Davy set out to search for a birthday present for their mother. Mother finds her "Happy Birthday Tree" the very best present she ever had.

Hein, Lucille. *My Very Special Friend.* Illus. Joan Orfe. 1974. While her mother is in the hospital, a five-year-old girl gets to know her great-grandmother.

Helmrath, Marilyn Olear, and Bartlett, Janet La Spiza. *Bobby Bear Finds Maple Sugar.* Illus. Marilue Johnson. 1968. Bobby Bear wakes up from his winter nap in time to see the men collecting and making maple syrup. With the hare he watches the process of making the syrup and decides to make some too. In this book the authors use rhyming words.

————. *Bobby Bear Goes Fishing.* Illus. Marilue Johnson. 1968. Bobby Bear goes fishing and catches a pretty sunfish.

————. *Bobby Bear in the Spring.* Illus. Marilue Johnson. 1968. Bobby Bear and his animal friends talk about the signs and activities of the different seasons of the year. In this book the authors use rhyming words.

————. *Bobby Bear's Rocket Ride.* Illus. Marilue Johnson. 1968. Bobby Bear takes a trip into space and visits the sun, moon, Mars, Mercury, Pluto, and Saturn.

Henriod, Lorraine. *I Know a Newspaper Reporter.* 1971. This information book uses detailed text and small but appropriate illustrations to describe the process of producing a newspaper.

Henry, Marguerite. *The Little Fellow.* Illus. Rich Rudish. 1975. A little foal named Chip is the darling of Chocolate, his mother, and all the other stable animals and personnel until a new foal, Strawberry Jenks, is born. Chip shows his jealousy in a number of ways before peace is restored to the pasture and stable.

Hill, Elizabeth Starr. *Evan's Corner.* Illus. Nancy Grossman. 1967. Evan's mother allows him to choose a corner in the cramped two-room house and fix it up for himself. Evan industriously earns money to buy his own pet and creatively adds little touches to his corner. However, he soon realizes that he has become selfish, and so he decides to help his younger brother Adam fix up his own corner.

Hoban, Julia. *Amy Loves the Rain.* Illus. Lillian Hoban. 1989. Very simple text tells how Amy and her mother drive through the rain to pick up Daddy. Colorful illustrations that look as if they were drawn with wax crayons enhance the text.

————. *Amy Loves the Sun.* Illus. Lillian Hoban. 1988. Easy-reader text describes how Amy picks flowers in the sunshine and takes them to her mother. Humorous, brightly colored pictures enhance the text.

Hoban, Russell. *Charlie the Tramp.* Illus. Lillian Hoban. 1966. Charlie decides he wants to be a tramp, not the hard-working beaver he should be. His parents agree to let him try. But his building instinct draws him to construct his own dam, which proves to be a splendid piece of architecture. Before long, Charlie gladly comes back to the life of a beaver.

Hoff, Syd. *Chester.* 1961. Chester, a horse, wants to be part of a ranch so that he can be loved and cared for.

————. *The Horse in Harry's Room.* 1970. Harry imagines he has a horse in his room. Even after his parents take him to the country and show him real horses, Harry keeps his imaginary horse. The horse wants to stay as much as Harry wants the horse to stay. This is a good reader for beginners.

————. *Sammy the Seal.* 1959. Sammy the Seal leaves his home in the zoo to see what the outside world is like. After many experiences, including a day in school, Sammy returns to the zoo, realizing that "there's no place like home."

————. *Thunderhoof.* 1971. Thunderhoof is finally caught when the drinking water dries up. Upon regaining his strength, he refuses to be tamed, and the ranchers let him go. Soon after his release, he misses the special treatment he had received and voluntarily goes back. Young readers will enjoy this book.

————. *When Will It Snow?* Illus. Mary Chalmers. 1971. Billy wonders when it will snow. One day, when the days become shorter and the wind blows, it begins to snow.

Hoffman, E.T.A. *The Nutcracker.* Trans. Ann King Herring; adapt. Magiochi Kushida; illus. Fumiko Hori. 1971. This book is a translation of Hoffman's story on which Tchaikovsky based the music for his ballet. It is about a little girl, Maria, who receives a nutcracker doll for Christmas.

Hoffman, Mary. *Zebra.* 1985. This information book uses simple text and many colorful photographs to describe the life and habitat of the zebra.

Hogrogian, Nonny. *One Fine Day.* 1971. When the fox drinks the old woman's milk, she cuts off his tail. After receiving help from several people and animals, the old woman sews his tail back on.

Holl, Adelaide. *The Runaway Giant.* Illus. Mamoru Funai. 1967. Several animals are concerned about the giant with the large hat and a thumping-stick. As each animal checks on the giant, it becomes smaller. The animals think they have successfully scared the giant away, but the pictures reveal that the disappearing giant is only a melting snowman.

Holland, Joyce. *Gertie Groundhog*. Illus. Lawrence Spiegel. 1963. Gertie Groundhog is afraid to come out of her hole, but one day Grandfather makes her go out. She finds that the "Big Black Thing" that scared her is just her shadow, which she sees in the spring and summer.

Holland, Rowena. *Farm Animals*. 1987. This book describes different kinds of farms and farm animals, including pigs, cattle, sheep, and goats, and more unusual ones such as camels and ostriches. The full-color photographs have helpful captions.

Holmgren, Virginia C. *Swallows Come Home*. Illus. Tom O'Sullivan. 1968. The swallows come to their home when spring arrives. Their nest is on the top of the train's red canopy.

Horwitz, Joshua. *Night Markets: Bringing Food to a City*. 1984. Lively text and black-and-white photographs are used to describe the nighttime activities of wholesale markets that supply New York City with meat, baked goods, and dairy products.

Hough, Charlotte. *Pink Pig*. 1975. At the beginning of this concept book, Little Pig does not like himself because he does not have spots or stripes. At the end he is glad to be a pink pig.

Howard, Milly. *Captive Treasure*. Bob Jones University Press, 1988. Carrie Talbot's family sets out on a long trip west in spite of the danger of Indian attacks.

————. *On Yonder Mountain*. Bob Jones University Press, 1989. Historical fiction set in the 1890s. Sarah Goodwin can hardly wait for her first year of school to begin, but when she reaches the one-room schoolhouse on Yonder Mountain, she finds nothing but boys.

————. *The Runaway Princess*. Bob Jones University Press, 1988. Princess Brenna tries to escape her ruthless uncle, Prince Zoran, who wants to rule her kingdom.

————. *The Treasure of Pelican Cove*. Bob Jones University Press, 1988. While everyone is scrambling for hidden treasure, Jimmy's dog, Blackie, disappears, and Jimmy is determined to find him.

Howe, Caroline Walton. *Teddy Bear's Bird and Beast Band.* 1980. Teddy Bear wants to lead the band, but his friend is too shy to help. Teddy goes to bed discouraged while his friend, remembering Teddy's birthday, plans an extra special birthday surprise. At last Teddy Bear can lead the band.

Humphrey, Jack W., and Altheide, Sandra. *Treat Truck and the Big Rain.* Illus. Jack Faulkner. 1974. The men are working in a hole by the playground when it begins to rain. The rain causes the slide to fall into the hole. Mike uses his Treat Truck to pull the slide out of the hole.

Hunter, Ilene and Judson, Marilyn. *Simple Folk Instruments to Make and to Play.* 1977. This information book describes the origin of folk instruments such as rhythm sticks, drums, and rattles. Also included are directions for constructing and playing the instruments.

Hurd, Edith Thatcher. *Johnny Lion's Bad Day.* Illus. Clement Hurd. 1970. Johnny has a bad cold and has to stay in bed and take medicine. He has many bad dreams, but Mother and Father Lion comfort him. He has a bad dream that night and crawls in bed with Mother and Father. The next morning he is well. This little story illustrates the principle of obedience to parents and also the importance of family love.

————. *Johnny Lion's Book.* Illus. Clement Hurd. 1965. This is a fanciful story about a little lion who obeys his mother and father. While his parents go out to hunt, Johnny stays home and reads a book about the adventures of another little lion who disobeyed his parents.

————. *Johnny Lion's Rubber Boots.* Illus. Clement Hurd. 1972. Johnny Lion has to stay indoors because it is raining, and he has no rubber boots to protect his feet. His father brings him home some boots, and Johnny goes out to play. When his parents cannot find him, they are concerned that a dog has gotten Johnny. Instead, he is safely tucked away in a box and waiting for the rain to stop.

————. *The Mother Owl.* 1974. This information book uses clear, interesting text and two-color illustrations to tell how a mother owl raises a nest full of owlets.

————. *Under the Lemon Tree.* Illus. Clement Hurd. 1980. A farmer thinks that his donkey is too noisy until he finds out that the donkey's noise protects the other farm animals from a fox.

Hurley, William. *Dan Frontier.* Illus. Jack Boyd. 1959. This story depicts frontier life in early America, emphasizing the hard work of the early pioneers. In this adventure Dan's horse, Star, rescues Dan who in turn rescues Jimmy and an injured dog from dangerous wolves.

————. *Dan Frontier and the Big Cat.* Illus. Jack Boyd. 1961. Jimmy and Bobby are lost in the woods and then are rescued by Dan Frontier.

————. *Dan Frontier, Trapper.* Illus. Jack Boyd. 1962. Depicting frontier life in early America, this book tells the adventures of Dan and his young friend Jimmy as they trap beaver for skins to sell at the trading post. Excitement comes after some robbers steal their furs. Dan and Jimmy, with the help of Indian friends, capture the robbers and retrieve the stolen furs for the frontier families.

Hutchins, Pat. *Goodnight Owl!* 1972. This charming story tells how all sorts of birds make too much noise for Owl to sleep during the day, so at night he does something about it.

————. *The Wind Blew.* 1974. In this clever rhyming book, the wind blows and snatches away an umbrella, a balloon, a hat, a kite, a shirt, a hanky, a wig, a postman's letters, a flag, new scarves, and newspapers. After mixing them up, it drops them and blows out to sea.

Ichikawa, Satomi. *A Child's Book of Seasons.* 1975. Children engage in different activities as the seasons change throughout the year.

Ipcar, Dahlov. *Bug City.* 1975. In fanciful Bug City the bugs carry on their daily activities.

————. *The Song of the Day Birds and the Night Birds.* 1967. Young children will enjoy this imaginative picture book about birds.

————. *Stripes and Spots.* 1961. A little striped tiger and a little spotted leopard have quite an adventure looking for food together one day in the jungle before their mothers come to rescue them.

Israel, Laurie, ed. *Poems for Weather Watching.* Illus. Gilbert Riswold. 1963. This book includes poems and illustrations for seasons and weather makers.

Jarrell, Randall. *A Bat is Born.* Illus. John Schoenherr. 1964. Poetic text and striking, imaginative photographs are used in this intriguing book about bats.

Jefferies, Madeleine Milner. *Katey.* 1961. Katey lives on a big Texas ranch in the early days of our country. She describes life in these isolated circumstances as she tells about her aunt who comes from Europe to visit.

Jennings, Terry. *Seeds.* Illus. David Anstey. 1988. Simple text and colorful illustrations convey basic facts about seeds and how they grow. Also included are directions for experiments and activities.

————. *Trees.* 1989. This information book provides an introduction to trees, including a description of their basic parts. Also included are suggestions for interesting activities.

————. *Weather.* 1988. This book introduces basic concepts about weather. Also included are activities that investigate rain, clouds, wind, and snow. The illustrations are clear and colorful.

Jennison, Keith W. *From This to That.* Illus. Kathleen Elgin. 1961. In telling what becomes of a little spruce tree, this book explains the progress of manufacturing paper.

Johnson, Crockett. *Upside Down.* 1969. Kangaroo's geography book confuses him by showing a picture of a globe with a boy and girl standing upright in the United States. A kangaroo is at the bottom, upside down, on the other side of the world. This scares Kangaroo into thinking all his world is upside down.

————. *Will Spring Be Early or Will Spring Be Late?* 1959. The groundhog comes out of his hole and tries to convince everyone that spring has arrived. He finds a red flower in bloom. Pig comes, destroys the bloom, and makes a prediction that it will snow. Winter returns, and the groundhog goes back into his hole.

Johnson, Gladys O. *Jimmie, the Youngest Errand Boy.* Illus. June Talarczyk. 1967. Jimmie feels sorry for himself. Since he is the youngest boy in the family, practically everything he gets is secondhand—even jobs. The hardware store has a bike in the window, and Jimmie wishes he could earn enough money to buy it. But the only jobs he gets are errands to run for his next-door neighbor. One day, while running an errand for Mrs. Beach, Jimmie finds a wonderful surprise.

Johnson, Hannah Lyons. *Let's Bake Bread.* Photographer Daniel Dorn. 1973. This book provides step-by-step instructions in the art of baking bread. Large black-and-white photographs enhance the text.

Johnson, Jean. *Police Officers, A to Z.* 1986. Each letter of the alphabet introduces a topic relating to police officers and their jobs. Clear, black-and-white photographs accompany the text.

Johnson, Margaret S. *Snowshoe Paws.* Morrow, 1949. A kitten named Lanny finds that becoming friends with a puppy named Impy is not easy. One day Lanny bravely rescues Impy from a big dog. His brave act earns him the right to live peacefully in Miss Abbott's home.

Johnson, Margaret S., and Johnson, Helen Lossing. *Joey and Patches.* Illus. Margaret S. Johnson. 1947. The funny escapades of two kittens are a delightful tale for young readers. Patches is a gentle kitten, but Joey constantly gets himself into trouble with his owners. One night the cries of one of the kittens awakens their owners to find a smoke-filled house. Their owners show their appreciation by allowing more house privileges for both of their kittens.

Johnson, Sylvia. *Wheat.* 1990. This information book describes the life cycle of wheat, how it is harvested, and its value as a food source. The colorful photographs and captions help clarify the text.

Johnston, Johanna. *Long Ago In Colonial Days.* Illus. Lauren Cooke. 1964. Simple text and colorful, appealing pictures are used to describe many aspects of colonial life that differ from modern times, including family custom, schooling, and transportation.

Jordan, Helene J. *How a Seed Grows.* Illus. Joseph Low. 1960. This book describes how seeds grow. It suggests seed-planting activities to observe seed growth.

————. *Seeds by Wind and Water.* Illus. Nils Hogner. 1962. This concept book tells how seeds are spread by wind, water, animals, humans, birds, and even by automobiles.

Joslin, Sesyle. *Brave Baby Elephant.* 1960. This book tells the story of a baby elephant and his solitary brave adventure.

Kahl, Virginia. *The Duchess Bakes a Cake.* 1955. A humorous tale about the experiences of a duchess who tries to bake a "lovely light luscious delectable cake."

Kandoian, Ellen. *Under the Sun.* 1987. Within the frame of a story, the reader is taken on a visual journey that follows the setting sun. Detailed, full-color illustrations enhance the text. Also included are directions for a science experiment using a globe and a flashlight to demonstrate day and night.

Kauffman, Lois. *What's That Noise?* Illus. Allan Eitzen. 1965. A little boy hears a noise in the night. He tries to discover the source of the noise, only to find that the noise was Dad's snoring.

Kaufmann, John. *Bats in the Dark.* 1972. This subject will intrigue many children. They will learn that bats have fur-covered leathery skin and that they are the only flying species of mammals. They will also learn about the exceptional hearing ability of bats.

Keats, Ezra Jack. *Peter's Chair.* 1967. Peter decides to leave home because his cradle and high chair are being painted pink for his baby sister. When he discovers that he no longer fits in his chair, he tells his father to paint it pink for baby sister.

————. *The Snowy Day.* 1962. Peter awakes to find snow covering the world. After breakfast he investigates the outdoors. He discovers all the fun a child can have in the snow.

————. *Whistle for Willie.* 1964. This is the story of a little boy who wants to learn to whistle. He keeps trying and finally manages the skill.

Kellogg, Steven. *Johnny Appleseed.* 1988. This is the story about the life of John Chapman, better known as Johnny Appleseed. The text admirably describes Johnny's love of nature, his kindness to animals, and his physical fortitude.

Kesselman, Wendy. *Time for Jody.* Illus. Gerald Dumas. 1975. This is an imaginative story of Jody, a little groundhog who moves to a distant field to carry out the duties of a resident groundhog.

Kessler, Ethel, and Kessler, Leonard. *All Aboard the Train.* 1964. This is a repetitious, patterned story about a train ride.

————. *Peek-a-boo.* 1956. A little boy plays a game of peek-a-boo with his family.

Kessler, Leonard. *Here Comes the Strikeout.* 1965. Bobby cannot hit the ball when he plays baseball. He asks a friend to help him with his hitting. His practice and hard work pay off when he hits a home run to win the game for his team in the last inning.

————. *Kick, Pass, and Run.* 1966. Some children are playing football. When the ball is kicked out-of-bounds, the animals of the field see it and wonder what is going on. After they watch the children play, they try to play the game themselves.

————. *Mr. Pine's Mixed-up Signs.* 1961. Mr. Pine, the sign painter, causes much confusion in his town when he loses his glasses and puts all the town's signs in the wrong places.

Kirkland, Wallace. *A Walk in the Woods.* 1971. Each page of this information book presents a clear black-and-white photograph of different animals, plants, and insects you might see as you walk through the woods.

Kirkpatrick, Rena K. *Look at Flowers.* 1978. This easy-to-read text describes various kinds of flowers. Colorful illustrations with helpful captions enhance the text.

Kishida, Eriko. *The Lion and the Bird's Nest*. Illus. Chiyoko Nakatani. 1970. All the animals of the forest are afraid of King Jojo, the lion king of the jungle. Jojo really is tired of being the fierce creature that the other animals think he is. One day Jojo is able to help a little bird, and the other animals realize how gentle Jojo really is.

Knight, David C. *Let's Find Out About Weather.* Illus. René Martin. 1967. The author presents a satisfying explanation of air's involvement in weather. The temperature of air affects wind. Explanation is given as to how we get rain, fog, snow, and clouds. Lightning, thunder, and rainbows are also briefly mentioned.

Knightly, Rosalinda. *The Farmer.* 1987. Brightly-colored, simple pictures and very brief text describe a farm and different jobs performed by a farmer and his family.

Krauss, Ruth. *The Carrot Seed*. Illus. Crockett Johnson. 1945. A little boy plants a carrot seed and patiently waters and weeds it until it grows.

Kuchalla, Susan. *Baby Animals.* 1982. A brief test and colorful illustrations introduce several baby animals and show how they play and learn.

Kuhn, Dwight. *The Hidden Life of the Forest.* 1988. Excellent color photographs and interesting text introduce animals, insects, and plants that make their homes in a forest.

Kumin, Maxine. *The Beach Before Breakfast*. Illus. Leonard Weisgard. 1964. This story is about an adult and a child who search the beach for treasures. They find different kinds of shells and animals. The child then finds his most wanted treasure, a rowboat, which he uses to find more treasures for breakfast—crabs and fish.

Kuskin, Karla. *Roar and More*. 1956. This is a rhyming book about animals and the sounds they make.

Lamont, Bette. *Island Time*. Illus. Brinton Turkle. 1976. This is the story of a young child's many experiences on a two-week camping trip on an island in Puget Sound.

Langner, Nola. *Dusty.* 1976. A little girl tells the story of Dusty, a stray cat which came to her back porch for food one summer.

Lasky, Kathryn. *Sugaring Time*. Photographer Chistopher G. Knight. 1983. This book tells how a family taps the sap from maple trees and processes it into maple syrup.

Leaf, Munro. *Boo*. Illus. Frances Tipton Hunter. 1948. Alexander, Boo's cat, helps him overcome his fear of the dark.

————. *Manners Can Be Fun*. 1958. The simple drawings in this book will amuse the young reader as he is reminded of the importance of good manners.

LeBar, Mary. *We Are Helpers*. Illus. Faith M. Lowell. 1950. Children help with various household chores.

Lee, Susan, and Lee, John. *Sam and John Adams*. Illus. Chuck Mitchell. 1974. This biography reveals significant differences between the two cousins, Sam Adams and John Adams. Yet both of them were great contributors to the cause of American independence and growth.

Lefèvre, Félicité. *The Cock, the Mouse, and the Little Red Hen*. Illus. Tony Sarg. n.d. In this old tale, the cock and the mouse learn not to grumble after their frightening experience with the bad fox.

Leister, Mary. *The Silent Concert*. Illus. Yoko Mitsuhashi. 1970. Each of the creatures of the forest wishes that he could make a beautiful sound like his neighbor. All at once "everyone at the same moment tried to make music the way the other fellow had been doing it." But there is no sound at all. The wise old owl hoots, "Let each one sing in his own special song in his own special way."

Lenski, Lois. *Cowboy Small*. 1949. Cowboy Small keeps his horse, Cactus, at the Bar S Ranch. He takes good care of his horse and the ranch. He rounds up cattle and brands them. Pictures of equipment are labeled for reference, and a glossary of cowboy terms is included. This book is full of action and teaches good principles of caring for animals and property.

————. *The Little Airplane*. 1938. Mr. Small goes up in his airplane. He has to execute a fast landing because his fuel line gets clogged. Quickly, he fixes the problem and finishes his happy ride.

————. *The Little Auto.* 1934. Mr. Small explains his car and describes his trip in it.

————. *The Little Fire Engine.* 1946. Fireman Small takes care of his fire engine and helps to fight the fires in his town. He is a good helper in his community.

————. *The Little Sailboat.* 1937. Mr. Small and his dog sail out to fish, and Mr. Small falls into the water. They sail home before the storm comes.

————. *The Little Train.* 1940. Engineer Small supplies the train with water and coal, then loads luggage, cargo, and passengers for the journey to the city. They pass through interesting countryside and arrive safely.

————. *Policeman Small.* 1962. The simple text describes a day in the life of a traffic policeman.

————. *Surprise for Mother.* 1962. Three little sisters, Niddy, Noddy, and Nancy, set out to make a surprise birthday cake for their mother. They want to show their appreciation for her love and care for them.

Lewis, Jean. *The Big Book of Dogs.* 1988. This is a reference book about dogs. Pictures and brief text describe the different breeds.

Le Tord, Bijou. *Picking and Weaving.* 1980. This simple book describes the process of how cotton is taken from the fields to the textile mill and finally to the store.

————. *Rabbit Seeds.* 1984. Simple text and line drawings depict the experiences of a rabbit as he tends his garden.

Liffring-zug, Joan. *Ray and Stevie on a Corn Belt Farm.* 1956. A description of life on the farm in the middle 1950s, seen from the perspective of two boys.

Lillegard, Dee. *I Can Be a Carpenter.* 1986. This book examines different kinds of jobs in the field of carpentry and points out the education and training necessary for each job. Colorful captioned photographs and drawings enhance the text.

Lindman, Maj. *Snipp, Snapp, Snurr and the Red Shoes.* 1936. Three boys learn that their mother wants a pair of red shoes lined with gold. They each find jobs that provide money enough to buy the shoes and present them to their mother as they sing "Happy Birthday."

————. *Snipp, Snapp, Snurr and the Seven Dogs.* 1959. Three young Swedish boys and their dog become friends with six neighborhood dogs. Because of its simple dialogue, this story is an excellent choice for new readers.

Linn, Margot. *Trip to the Doctor.* Illus. Catherine Siracusa. 1988. Simple question-and-answer format introduces the procedures, instruments, and routines involved in a visit to the doctor.

Lionni, Leo. *The Biggest House in the World.* 1968. This is a fanciful story about a little snail who wants to have the biggest house in the world but finds that some things are really better small.

————. *Fish Is Fish.* 1970. A minnow and a tadpole become friends in a pond. When the tadpole becomes a frog, the fish has a hard time understanding their differences. The fish feels he too should venture out of the pond so that he can see all the unusual things in the world that the frog tells him about.

————. *Inch by Inch.* 1960. A clever inchworm proves to a robin that he is useful and that he should not be eaten. The worm also proves that he can "inch" his way right out of a dangerous situation.

————. *Little Blue and Little Yellow.* 1959. This is a fanciful tale of two splotches of color, Little Blue and Little Yellow, who become friends and become green. This book could be correlated with an art activity on mixing tempera colors.

Lippman, Peter. *Busy Trains.* 1981. This information book presents different kinds of trains. Detailed, imaginative, colorful drawings accompany the simple text.

Littledale, Freya, and Littledale, Harold. *Timothy's Forest.* Illus. Rosalie Lehrman. 1969. Timothy lives in the city. Since there is no forest in the city, Timothy decides to make one. This book could be used to motivate children to make a collage art project.

Livingston, Myra Cohn. *Up in the Air.* Illus. Leonard Everett Fisher. 1989. Rhymed text and full-color, imaginative illustrations depict the sights and sensations of flying in an airplane.

Lobel, Arnold. *Frog and Toad Are Friends.* 1970. The first in a series of well-loved stories about the adventures of Frog and Toad, this book includes a chapter describing their experiences with receiving mail. The text is enhanced by the charming, detailed illustrations.

Longfellow, Henry Wadsworth. *Paul Revere's Ride.* Illus. Ted Rand. 1990. Beautiful, full-color illustrations portray Longfellow's famous narrative poem, recreating Paul Revere's famous midnight ride in 1775 to warn the people of the Boston countryside that the British were coming.

Lowitz, Sadyebeth, and Lowitz, Anson. *Mr. Key's Song.* 1967. This is an account of how our national anthem came to be written.

Lund, Doris Herold. *Attic of the Wind.* Illus. Ati Forberg. 1966. This haiku poetry fancifully takes a little girl up into the "attic of the wind" where many childhood treasures have drifted. These treasures include such things as umbrellas, balloons, bubbles, feathers, kites, hats, and papers.

McCain, Murray. *The Boy Who Walked off the Page.* Illus. Alvin Smith. 1969. Benjamin finds his favorite book one day when Miss Heath takes her whole class to the library. He cannot read the book, but the pictures of a clown named Jeremy make Benjamin want to grow up fast so that he can read the book all by himself.

McCall, Edith. *Butternut Bill and the Bear.* Illus. Darrell Wiskur. 1965. Bear causes many problems on the farm until one day he decides to be friends with all the other animals.

————. *Butternut Bill and the Bee Tree.* Illus. Darrell Wiskur. 1965. Butternut Bill gets honey from the beehive for Granny. This book is excellent for reinforcing sight words.

————. *The Buttons at the Zoo.* Illus. Jack Faulkner. 1960. The Button family visits the zoo.

McClintock, Marshall. *A Fly Went By.* Illus. Fritz Siebel. 1958. Different animals hurry past a little boy sitting by the lake. Each animal thinks it is being chased by the animal who is following. The repetition of this rhyming book, the suspense it arouses, and the reason for the animals' running will enchant the young reader.

McCloskey, Robert. *Blueberries for Sal.* 1948. This is a charming story with a smooth song-like rhythm that children will enjoy. The plot is about Sal, who goes out with her mother to pick blueberries. While out on this excursion, they encounter a mother bear and her cub also gathering blueberries for the coming winter.

————. *Lentil.* 1940. A boy named Lentil wants to make music; so he saves up enough pennies to buy a harmonica.

————. *Make Way for Ducklings.* 1941. Mr. and Mrs. Mallard (ducks) search for a site to raise a family. They decide to make their home on the island in the city park.

————. *One Morning in Maine.* 1952. Sal loses her first tooth and learns many interesting things about this exciting event.

————. *Time of Wonder.* 1957. The coming of a hurricane to their summer home on a Maine island provides anticipation and excitement and leaves treasures for the children to pack as they prepare to return to their home and autumn school days.

McClung, Robert M. *Possum.* 1963. Possum's life cycle is traced from the time she is seen hanging onto her mother's back until Possum has her own offspring.

————. *Ruby Throat: The Story of a Hummingbird.* 1950. This simple story of a year in a hummingbird's life is brilliantly illustrated with a picture on each page.

————. *Spike: The Story of a Whitetail Deer.* 1952. Young readers will learn about deer by personally getting to know Spike. Spike must face confrontations with man, animals, and nature.

————. *Stripe: The Story of a Chipmunk.* 1951. Stripe is born underground and is hardly the size of a bumblebee, but when he grows up, he easily takes care of himself. Stripe can build his own home, and find and carry his own food by making several trips. He can carry in one of his cheeks two acorns, five hazel-nuts, or fifteen kernels of corn.

MacDonald, Golden. *Little Frightened Tiger.* Illus. Leonard Weisgard. 1953. Little Tiger is frightened by everything. As his parents take him through the animal kingdom, the little tiger finds out that animals are frightened by him.

MacDonald, Golden, and Weisgard, Leonard. *The Little Island.* 1946. This intriguing book describes the singular beauty of island life. The appealing, full-color illustrations enhance the text.

MacGregor, Ellen. *Theodore Turtle.* Illus. Paul Galdon. 1955. Theodore cannot keep up with his things. He always loses something else, while finding what he had just lost. Yet all Theodore can see is how *clever* he is for remembering where he had left things.

Machentanz, Sara, and Machentanz, Fred. *Robbie and the Sled Dog Race.* 1964. Robbie and his well-trained dog team wait for the countdown at the Alaska snow fair. Suddenly they are off with shouts of encouragement ringing. A moose blocks the path, giving Robbie's team the chance it needs to by-pass the moose *and* its opponent.

McGovern, Ann. *Zoo, Where Are You?* Illus. Ezra Jack Keats. 1964. A little boy named Josh sets out to make a zoo for himself. He collects all kinds of beautiful junk in his search and ends up with a zoo full of junk.

MacLachlan, Patricia. *Sarah Plain and Tall.* 1987. This is a delightful story about a widower who places an ad in the paper for a wife, someone who will "make a difference" for his two children Anna and Caleb.

McMillan, Bruce. *The Alphabet Symphony.* Photographs by author. 1977. The photographs of the different instruments of the orchestra reveal the letters of the alphabet.

McPhail, David. *The Bear's Toothache.* 1972. One night a little boy hears a bear with a toothache howling outside his bedroom window. The boy tries to help him in many imaginative and amusing ways until finally he succeeds in pulling the bear's tooth.

Maestro, Betsy, and Maestro, Giulio. *Harriet Goes to the Circus.* 1977. Harriet the elephant is determined to be first in line at the circus.

————. *Snow Day.* 1989. Simple text describes the job of digging out after a major snowstorm, with particular emphasis on snow removal vehicles.

Margolis, Richard J. *Big Bear to the Rescue.* Illus. Robert Lopshire. 1975. Big Bear tries his best to rescue Mr. Mole, who has fallen into the well. He finds all the other animals too busy to help their friend.

Marino, Dorothy. *Buzzy Bear and the Rainbow.* 1962. Buzzy Bear searches for the end of the rainbow where he believes there is a pot of gold. He takes a pot with him and finds honey in a tree. He shares the honey with his friends and family.

————. *Buzzy Bear's Winter Party.* 1967. Buzzy Bear and his family decide to stay awake during the first snowstorm. Buzzy Bear and his mother set up a tree and decorate it for a winter party for Daddy Bear. After supper Buzzy Bear falls asleep and does not wake up until spring.

Martin, Dick. *The Fish Book.* 1964. Animals that live in or near the ocean are sailfish, crabs, sea gulls, flying fish, porpoises, sea horses, seals, sea turtles, starfish, whales, and kissing fish.

Martin, Patricia Miles. *The Lucky Little Porcupine.* Illus. Lee Smith. 1963. In an interesting succession of events, Mr. Patchett, Mrs. O'Leary, and the little porcupine become friends.

Martini, Teri. *Cowboys.* 1981. This book describes the clothing cowboys wear; their duties on the ranch, range, roundup; and their recreation at rodeos.

Massie, Diane Redfield. *Chameleon Was a Spy.* 1979. In this imaginative story, Chameleon becomes a spy in order to recover the world's best pickle formula, which has been stolen by a pickle scientist from The Pleasant Pickle Company.

Mayer, Marianna, and Mayer, Mercer. *Me and My Flying Machine.* 1971. A little boy begins to build a flying machine in an old barn full of great things. He has a fanciful dream about all the tremendous feats his machine will accomplish. But before he pulls it out of the barn, his flying machine falls apart. Still undaunted, he decides that the next day he will build a boat.

Mayer, Mercer. *Just Me and My Dad.* 1977. This humorous story, told from a child's viewpoint, describes a camping trip.

Meek, Pauline Palmer. *When Joy Came: The Story of the First Christmas.* Illus. Shannon Stirnweis. 1971. This gives a brief but accurate account of the birth of Christ and the appearance of the angels announcing the birth to the shepherds.

Mell, Jan. *Grand Canyon.* 1988. Beautiful photographs portray the history, geography, and plant and animal life of the Grand Canyon National Park.

Menken, John. *Grandpa's Gizmos.* Illus. Tim Davis. Bob Jones University Press, 1993. Grandpa Winslow has all kinds of fascinating gizmos in his back yard. One of them is so special that his grandson doesn't want to share it with anyone else.

Miklowitz, Gloria D. *The Parade Starts at Noon.* Illus. Don Madden. 1969. David's two favorite things in the world are his squirrel, Pest, and his brass tuba. On the day of a big parade, Pest gets stuck in the tuba, and David almost misses playing in the parade band.

Miles, Miska. *Apricot ABC.* Illus. Peter Parnall. 1969. Verse and pictures take the reader through meadowland, visiting creatures great and small. Each page features a letter of the alphabet.

———. *Kickapoo.* Illus. Wesley Dennis. 1961. In order to be a part of the local pony race, Howdie sells Kickapoo, his mule. However, Kickapoo becomes as "stubborn as a mule," and Howdie must buy the mule back. But he finds that he can legally enter the race with Kickapoo as his partner. Kickapoo makes Howdie proud when he wins the race.

———. *Mississippi Possum.* Illus. John Schoenherr. 1965. When the river begins to flood, the animals begin to look for higher ground. Rose Mary and Jefferson spot a possum, but they think he is dead. As the children sleep in the refugee tent, the possum moves in with them. The family develops a warm friendship with this wild creature which is illustrated in the book with vivid woodcuts.

———. *Noisy Gander.* Illus. Leslie Morrill. 1978. Combining realism and fantasy, this story is about a young gosling who is at first embarrassed by his father's loud honking but soon finds that the honking serves a useful purpose.

————. *Rabbit Garden.* Illus. John Schoenherr. 1967. A timid rabbit develops into a strong, confident one. Descriptions of the garden activities around him dominate the narrative.

————. *Swim, Little Duck.* Illus. Jim Arnosky. 1976. Little Duck promises to stay close to home, but instead she decides to see the world. Each animal that Little Duck sees thinks its own world is the best, and Little Duck agrees with them all.

————. *This Little Pig.* Illus. Leslie Morrill. 1980. The runt of a litter of pigs finds himself always being last. When he decides to go on a little trip, his brothers and sisters come to find him, fearing he is lost. Instead, they get lost and the runt pig temporarily becomes the leader.

Miller, Edna. *Mousekin's Christmas Eve.* 1965. Mousekin discovers his reflection in a Christmas ornament, and it scares him. But when he finds the nativity scene with the Babe lying in a manger and crumbs under the tree, Mousekin rests comfortably.

————. *Mousekin's Family.* 1969. Mousekin is caught in the rain, away from his hollow tree. When he returns, he finds his children missing. He finds one of them and tries to teach him to climb, but the mouse will only jump. This mouse child is not one of his own at all; so Mousekin must begin his search again for his family.

Miller, Natalie. *The Story of the Star-Spangled Banner.* Illus. George Wilde. 1965. This is the story of the dramatic events that led Francis Scott Key to write the national anthem.

————. *The Story of the Statue of Liberty.* Illus. Lucy Hawkinson and John Hawkinson. 1965. This is the amazing story of Auguste Bartholdi's development of the Statue of Liberty, symbol of friendship between France and the United States. The magnitude of the project is clearly presented so that children can grasp the size of the famed lady-statue.

Miller, Patricia K., and Seligman, Iran L. *Big Frogs, Little Frogs.* Illus. Lee Ames. 1963. This concept book is about the frog and its development.

————. *Joey Kangaroo.* Illus. Ed Renfro. 1963. This book describes the lives and habits of kangaroos.

————. *You Can Find a Snail.* Illus. Thomas M. O'Brien. 1963. This book gives some very interesting facts about snails.

Milne, A. A. *When We Were Very Young.* Illus. Ernest Shepard. 1961. The work of A. A. Milne delights both the young and old with poetry that depicts the whim, nonsense, and surprises of childhood. Shepard's illustrations charm the reader.

————. *Winnie-the-Pooh.* Illus. Ernest H. Shepard. 1926. Milne's classic collection of episodic tales are brought to life through Shepard's endearing pen-and-ink sketches of such delightful characters as Pooh, Eeyore, Piglet, Kanga, Baby Roo, Owl, and the boy Christopher Robin.

Minarik, Else Holmelund. *Little Bear.* Illus. Maurice Sendak. 1987. These four short stories about Little Bear will charm the young reader.

————. *Little Bear's Friend.* Illus. Maurice Sendak. 1960. This book contains four short stories about Little Bear and his new friend Emily. Little Bear is sad to see his friend Emily go back to school at the end of the summer. His mother teaches him to write so that he can write Emily a letter.

————. *Little Bear's Visit.* Illus. Maurice Sendak. 1961. Little Bear has a delightful time when he goes to visit his grandmother and grandfather in their little house in the woods.

Mizumura, Kazue. *The Emperor Penguins.* 1969. This beginning science book gives interesting facts concerning the life and habits of the emperor penguins.

————. *If I Were a Cricket.* 1973. Twelve "If I were a ____" are used to express kind things that animals, insects, or fish might do for somebody out of a generous heart. These include such things as a starfish becoming an ornament atop a Christmas tree or an oyster giving a gift of a pearl.

Mock, Dorothy. *Thank You, God, for Water.* 1985. This small book shows ways in which the young child may enjoy water, and it reminds him to thank God for creating it.

Montgomery, Elizabeth Rider. *Alexander Graham Bell*. Illus. Gray Morrow. 1963. This easy-to-read account reveals that Alexander and Melvin Bell as young boys constructed a "talking machine." Alexander soon dedicated all his energies to inventions. When he finally made the telephone, people did not realize its usefulness at first.

Moore, Lilian. *I Feel the Same Way*. Illus. Robert Quackenbush. 1976. This book is a collection of poems about some things we see and feel (sunshine, insects, rain, ocean, wind, and fog).

————. *Junk Day on Juniper Street and Other Easy to Read Stories*. 1969. This is a collection of easy-to-read stories that children will find entertaining.

————. *Little Raccoon and No Trouble at All*. Illus. Gioia Fiammenghi. 1972. A mother chipmunk gets Little Raccoon to babysit her two chipmunk children. The chipmunks try to play tricks on Little Raccoon until he takes the chipmunks to Mr. Beaver's dam so that they can taste the crayfish he is enjoying so much. There in the middle of the water, they are stuck and learn the lesson Little Raccoon wanted to teach them.

————. *Little Raccoon and Poems from the Woods*. Illus. Gioia Fiammenghi. 1975. This book of poems discusses different animals and woodland scenes. The illustrations include night and day scenes as well as seasonal scenes.

Moore, Lillian, and Fiammenghi, Gioia. *Little Raccoon and the Thing in the Pool*. Illus. Gioia Fiammenghi. 1963. Little Raccoon goes for the first time to get a crayfish out of the water by himself. Fear overcomes him when he sees an animal staring back at him from the water. Each time he picks up a stone or a stick as if to throw at the animal, the animal does the same thing. Finally, he tries smiling at the animal, who smiles back at him in return. This gives Little Raccoon the courage to go after the crayfish.

Morris, Robert A. *Seahorse*. Illus. Arnold Lobel. 1972. The text describes the fragile bodies of seahorses, which are subjected to many perils. They often hide among seaweed for protection. The unusual breeding habits are described, the male taking a more active role with the eggs than for most animals. The soft pastel illustrations greatly enhance this book.

Morrison, Bill. *Squeeze a Sneeze.* 1977. This humorous book suggests delightful combinations of rhyming words such as "stuff a goose and a moose in a tiny caboose." Children can enjoy writing some of their own rhymes, following the book's example.

Morse, Flo. *How Does It Feel to Be a Tree?* Illus. Clyde Watson. 1976. A child explores the idea of what it must be like to be a tree. This book of verse could be used to motivate an art activity in drawing trees or an exercise in simple role playing.

Morse, Samuel French. *All in a Suitcase.* Illus. Barbara Cooney. 1966. Using each letter of the alphabet, the narrator of this rhyming text names an animal that he will pack in his suitcase when he goes to Boston.

Mott, Evelyn Clarke. *Steam Train Ride.* 1991. A young boy takes a ride on a steam engine and learns how it works. Many colorful photographs enhance the text.

Myers, Bernice. *Herman and the Bears Again.* 1976. Herman is a little boy who goes into the woods to visit his bear friends. In this fanciful story, a scout leader and his troop try to rescue him from the bears but finally realize the bears are friendly.

Myller, Rolf. *How Big is a Foot?* 1962. The King decides to give the Queen a bed for her birthday. Since beds have not yet been invented, no one knows how big a bed should be. The King uses his foot as a means of measure.

Myrick, Mildred. *Ants are Fun.* Illus. Arnold Lobel. 1968. Don, the new neighbor, shows Jack and Jimmy his ant nest. Somehow it is broken, and Jack and Jimmy volunteer to help build a new one. The two boys learn things about ants they never knew—how they lay their eggs, how they fight, and what they eat.

Neigoff, Anne. *New House, New Town.* 1973. In this easy-to-read story, the construction of a family's new home is described step by step.

Newberry, Clare Turlay. *Mittens.* 1936. Richard is a six-year-old boy who has a new pet kitten named Mittens. One day Mittens runs away. Richard's father puts an ad in the newspaper, but not one of the kittens that people find is Mittens. Finally, a neighbor finds Mittens in a tree in his yard.

Nicholas, Charles. *The Elephant Book.* 1965. The biggest animals of the forest are the elephants. They eat leaves and grass, bathe in the river, and move heavy objects. The elephant's friends are the hippopotamus and the rhinoceros.

Niizaka, Kazuo. *Clouds.* Adapt. Henry Stanton. 1975. Mary, Tom, and Puff-the-dog lie on the green grass and watch the clouds go by. They think of animals and objects that the clouds resemble.

Numeroff, Laura Joffe. *The Ugliest Sweater.* 1980. Peter does not like the red, white, and blue sweater his grandmother gave him. He wears it to school anyway so that he will not hurt her feelings. Something happens at school to make him glad he has it after all. The teacher wants someone who is wearing red, white, and blue to go to the office to welcome their class visitor from France.

Oda, Hidetomo. *The Turtle.* 1986. This information book describes the life cycle and behavior patterns of turtles. Excellent color photographs with helpful captions accompany the text.

Odor, Ruth Shannon. *A Child's Book of Manners.* Illus. Robert Burchett. 1990. This illustrated book on good manners for home, school, and church includes many Bible verses to remind the children of the important rules from God's Book about being kind.

Oetting, Rae. *The Orderly Cricket.* Illus. Marilue Johnson. 1968. Kasper K. Crickett has a bad habit of trying to make all the other animals live just as he does. He finally learns "that everyone lives in his own special way!"

———. *Timmy Tiger's New Coat.* Illus. Vic Cantone. 1970. Timmy Tiger wants to have a new coat, one like the deer or snake. When he arrives home, his mother does not recognize him. He returns to the lake and washes off his new coat, deciding that a tiger coat is best for him.

Once in a Wood: Ten Tales from Aesop. Adapt. and Illus. Eve Rice. 1979. A collection of ten fables retold for the beginning reader, includes "The Fox and the Crow" and "The Lion and the Mouse."

O'Neil, Catherine. *Let's Visit a Printing Plant.* Photographer James W. Parker. 1987. This information book describes the processes of book production in a printing plant. Detailed, colorful photographs enhance the text.

O'Neill, Mary. *Hailstone and Halibut Bones*. Illus. Leonard Weisgard. 1961. Twelve children's poems make color come alive through the senses of sound, taste, smell, feel, and sight.

Oppenheim, Joanne. *Have You Seen Trees?* Illus. Irwin Rosehouse. 1967. Many kinds of trees are presented for young readers in rhythmic free verse.

Orlowsky, Wallace and Perera, Thomas Biddle. *Who Will Wash the River?* 1970. The problem of pollution and our need for clean water is told in simple story format with apt illustrations.

Panek, Dennis. *Catastrophe Cat*. 1978. The pictures and simple text of this amusing book reveal very clearly why a cat is called Catastrophe.

Pape, Donna Lugg. *King Robert the Resting Ruler*. Illus. Lola Edick Frank. 1968. The Queen offers a large reward to anyone who wakes her sleeping king. A poor farmer finally finds just the thing—a crowing rooster.

Parish, Peggy. *A Beastly Circus*. Illus. Peter Parnall. 1969. Each page of this alphabet book pictures an animal and contains one sentence with words beginning with the particular alphabet letter pictured. For example, "Amazing alligator acrobats amuse admiring animals."

————. *Too Many Rabbits*. Illus. Leonard Kessler. 1974. Miss Molly finds a rabbit and gives her a home. Mrs. Rabbit's family increases until Miss Molly can keep them no longer. She gives them to a man who has an island that needs animals on it.

Parr, Letitia. *When Sea and Sky Are Blue*. Illus. John Watts. 1971. The children sit on the sea wall and watch the ocean and animals in the sea.

Parson, Virginia. *Homes*. 1958. This book discusses homes of many animals and concludes that our home is the best.

Patent, Dorothy Hinshaw. *An Apple a Day*. Photographer William Munoz. 1990. The book tells about growing apples, from planting and harvesting them to getting them onto the grocery shelves.

————. *Humpback Whales*. Photographer Mark Ferrari. 1989. Simple text describes the physical characteristics and habits of humpback whales. Large, full-color photographs with helpful captions enhance the text.

Patterson, Geoffrey. *All About Bread.* 1984. Detailed text and excellent pictures tell this simple story.

Peck, Helen E. and Dearmin, Jennie T. *The Smiling Dragon.* Illus. Leon Sevillia. 1963. A Japanese boy named Taro wants to fly his dragon kite in a contest with his friend Ichiro. Ichiro becomes sick, and Taro gives his kite to his sick friend. Taro's sister Umi helps him make another kite—a bird kite. Ichiro insists Taro fly the dragon kite, and Umi flies the bird kite in the contest. Taro wins the contest for his sick friend.

Peet, Bill. *Randy's Dandy Lions.* 1964. Randy Monroe is a fine lion tamer, but his five big lions suffer from stage fright at every performance and are unable to perform their fantastic tricks. The chain of events that help Randy's lions to overcome their fear will delight the young reader.

Penny, Malcolm. *Let's Look at Whales.* 1990. Simple text describes the different types of whales, their behavior, and their habitat. Full-color illustrations enhance the text.

Peppé, Rodney. *The House That Jack Built.* 1970. This Mother Goose tale is about a dog being tossed in the air by the cow with the crumpled horn, a smug cat, a minister all shaven and shorn, and a maiden all forlorn.

————. *Odd One Out.* 1974. A little boy named Peter has a busy day. He eats breakfast, then walks to school, works hard at school, goes to the zoo, visits his aunt and uncle's farm, and returns home to bed. This book is unique because on every page the reader can find one thing out of place.

Perkins, Al. *The Ear Book.* Illus. William O'Brian. 1968. This rhyming book about sounds would be enjoyable with a tape to accompany the sounds mentioned—clock, popcorn, bells, and so forth.

Perry, Phyllis J. *Let's Look at the Birds.* 1965. An informal text and bright illustrations convey interesting information about birds and their nesting habits.

Petersham, Maud, and Petersham, Miska. *The Box with Red Wheels.* 1949. Some curious animals find a baby in a strange-looking box with red wheels. At first they are shooed away, but the understanding mother lets the animals in the gate to play with the baby when she realizes how sad they all are.

————. *The Circus Baby.* 1950. What happens when a circus elephant decides that her baby must learn to eat like circus people? This fanciful tale will amuse children.

Peterson, Hans. *When Peter Was Lost in the Forest.* Illus. Harald Wiberg. 1970. Peter, seeing hare tracks in a snowy forest, decides to follow them to see where they lead. While following them, he becomes distracted by all the other playful animals in the forest. Soon he becomes lost and cannot find his way home. He spends the night in an old farmhouse and is not afraid because of the friendly company of the animals.

Peterson, Willis, and Church, Jeffrey. *Nature's Lumberjack.* Photographer Willis Peterson. 1961. This story of Barnaby Beaver and his family portrays the habits and habitat of beaver colonies. It shows how conservation officers start a new beaver colony by moving Barnaby and some of his friends to a mountain stream to build a new dam to help with land conservation.

Pfloog, Jan. *The Bear Book.* 1965. Very young children will enjoy this informative simple book about various kinds of bears.

————. *The Fox Book.* 1965. This informational book is about various kinds of foxes: the red fox, the silver fox, the gray fox, and the arctic fox.

————. *Kittens Are Like That.* 1976. Washing, licking, splashing, hiding, sneaking, scratching, and climbing are all activities kittens engage in. This book pictures these activities for young and old to enjoy.

————. *Puppies Are Like That.* 1975. This adorable presentation of typical activities of puppies will interest any young child.

Piatti, Celestino. *The Happy Owls.* 1964. In this legend two happy owls tell the secret of their happiness to the barnyard fowl who do nothing but quarrel. This story gives an excellent opportunity to apply Christian principles.

Pierce, Robert. *The Day of the Wind.* 1969. Pete goes fishing, and the wind begins to blow. He takes shelter in a box and catches objects as they fly by. The wind blows him into the water, and he catches a fish.

Pinkston, William S., Jr. *With Wings as Eagles*. Bob Jones University Press, 1983. Ten-year-old Bob Duncan has the opportunity to spend the summer at a cottage in the Upper Peninsula of Michigan with his scientist father, observing a nest of bald eagles. A prowler in the woods threatens to spoil Bob's summer but winds up teaching him to obey and trust in the Lord. Bob learns that when he seeks to serve God, the Lord gives him strength so that he can "mount up with wings as eagles."

Piper, Watty. *The Little Engine That Could*. Illus. George Hauman and Doris Hauman. 1961. The little train has food and toys for the children on the other side of the mountain. The engine breaks down, and the passenger engine, freight engine, and rusty old engine will not help. The little blue engine pulls the loaded cars over the mountain. This book teaches children a good character trait.

Pitt, Valerie. *Let's Find Out About Names*. 1971. There is much interesting information and background about names in this attractively illustrated book.

Podendorf, Illa. *Animal Homes*. 1982. This book describes a variety of animal homes, including shelters constructed by man. The book also explains that some animals do not build homes.

————. *Color*. Illus. Wayne Stuart. 1971. This concept book is about the colors red, blue, yellow, green, orange, purple and brown.

————. *Many is How Many?* Illus. Jack Haesly. 1970. This book is about relative and comparative size concepts of big/small, long/short, and a lot/few/many. It pictures animals, vegetables, insects, and marbles. It concludes that many is not a certain number.

————. *Shadows and More Shadows*. Illus. Darrell Wiskur. 1971. This book explores the cause of shadows. Light is the source of all shadows, but children will be able to tell easily that the light affects an image differently and therefore will cause it to cast different-shaped shadows. It is very simple, readable text.

————. *Things to Do with Water*. Illus. Larry Winborg. 1971. Alex and Corky learn what it means to make inferences. They do this as they observe prints or tracks in the snow or as they try to guess what is in wrapped packages. The children apply their newly acquired skills when the family goes on an excursion to the woods.

————. *Weeds and Wildflowers*. 1981. This book provides an introduction to weeds that are always "weeds" and weeds that are considered wild flowers. Beautiful, clear photographs with helpful captions enhance the text.

Pohl, Kathleen. *Dandelions*. 1987. Simple read-aloud text describes the life cycle of the dandelion.

Polgreen, John and Polgreen, Cathleen. *Good Morning, Mr. Sun.* 1963. Jeff is up early and says, "Good morning, Mr. Sun." He follows the sun throughout the day as it goes on its journey through the sky. Jeff senses the effect of the sun on the earth.

Potter, Beatrix. *The Tale of Peter Rabbit*. Illus. Masha. 1902. Peter, a fiesty little rabbit, disobeys his mother and gets caught in Mr. McGregor's garden. Potter's charming, colorful illustrations along with her storytelling power make Peter's adventures an all-time favorite.

Potter, Marian. *The Little Red Caboose*. Illus. Tibor Gergely. 1953. The little red caboose saves the train from rolling down the mountain.

Poulet, Virginia. *Blue Bug's Beach Party*. Illus. Stan Fleming and Mary Maloney. 1975. Blue Bug and his friends clean up the beach before they have their party. This book teaches a good lesson about not being a litterbug.

Powell, Elsa. *Deserts*. 1982. This book provides a simple description of the climate, plant life, and animals of the desert. Colorful photographs with helpful captions accompany the text.

Powzyk, Joyce. *Animal Camouflage*. 1990. Large, beautiful pictures and unusual subjects introduce ways that animals camouflage themselves, including coloration, mimicry, and disguise.

Prokofiev, Sergei S. *Peter and the Wolf.* Retold by Ann King Herring; illus. Kozo Shimuzu; photographer Yasuji Yajima. 1969. This book tells the story of Prokofiev's programmatic music "Peter and the Wolf." It is cleverly illustrated with photographs of fabric illustrations.

Provensen, Alice, and Provensen, Martin. *Karen's Opposites.* 1963. This rhyming concept book teaches opposites.

Quackenbush, Robert M., ed. *Poems for Galloping.* Illus. by editor. 1963. This book is a compilation of poems about walking, galloping, running, swinging, hopping, sliding, marching, skipping, stretching, pushing, pulling, leaping, twisting, and turning. These poems may be read to motivate children in motor development and music activities.

————. *What Has Wild Tom Done Now?* 1981. This simple book describes humorous highlights from the life of Thomas Edison. Lively illustrations accompany the text.

Quigley, Lillian. *The Blind Men and the Elephant.* Illus. Janice Holland. 1959. Six blind men touch different parts of an elephant and disagree about what an elephant is. The story may be used to help students appreciate the value of good vision.

Radlawer, Ruth. *Mesa Verde National Park.* Photographer Rolf Zillmer. 1977. This book describes the ancient cliff dwellings at Mesa Verde National Park in Colorado. Large color photographs have helpful captions.

Rand, Joyce. *A Hippo with Feathers.* Illus. Kris Stein. Bob Jones University Press, 1992. Full-color, humorous illustrations and read-aloud text demonstrate the perfection of God's creation.

Raynor, Dorka. *Grandparents Around the World.* 1977. This intriguing picture book presents full-page photographs of grandparents and children taken in various countries around the world. Brief identifying text accompanies each photograph.

Repp, Gloria. *A Question of Yams.* Bob Jones University Press, 1992. Kuri's father dares to serve God, defying the traditions of the Head Men, and Kuri watches to see what will happen.

Rey, Hans A., and Rey, Margaret. *Curious George Goes to the Hospital*. 1966. George swallows a piece of puzzle and has to go to the hospital to have it removed. His experiences at the hospital will help children overcome fear of hospitals and doctors.

Rice, Eve. *City Night*. Illus. Peter Sis. 1987. Lyrical text depicts the beauty and diversity of a city at night. Beautiful full-page illustrations enhance the text.

―――. *Goodnight, Goodnight*. 1980. The simple text and striking black illustrations portray the concept of night coming to the city.

―――. *What Sadie Sang*. 1976. Sadie's mother takes her for a walk, and Sadie sings the whole way. Since she is so young, the only sounds that come out when she sings are "ghee, ghee, ghee!" She happily sings to everyone she sees as she rides along in her carriage.

Riley, Jane. *The Little Seal with Meal Appeal*. Illus. June Talarczyk. 1963. A brave little seal named Suki endangers his own life by leading Eskimo hunters away from the other seals.

Rinkoff, Barbara. *Guess What Grasses Do*. 1971. The book describes the importance of grasses to all people as food, transportation, clothing, and entertainment.

Ripper, Charles L. *Bats*. 1954. The detailed text and numerous illustrations help children understand some basic concepts about bats.

Robbins, Ken. *Building a House*. 1984. Black-and-white photographs show the building of a house from the design stage to the finishing details. The book also includes a description of the job of each worker as well as the materials he uses.

―――. *A Flower Grows*. 1990. Rhythmic text describes the life cycle of an amaryllis flower. Photographs are hand-tinted and especially appealing.

Rockwell, Anne. *I Like the Library*. 1977. A young child describes all the things that are available at the library.

Rockwell, Anne, and Rockwell, Harlow. *How My Garden Grew*. 1982. A little girl describes her pleasure and pride in growing a garden all by herself.

————. *The Toolbox.* 1971. This book identifies and describes all the tools in father's toolbox.

Romanek, Enid Warner. *Teddy.* 1978. Teddy, a little bear, tells about each step of a bear's day. The amusing etchings will captivate the young child.

Rose, Mary Catherine. *Clara Barton: Soldier of Mercy.* Illus. E. Harper Johnson. 1960. This easy-to-read biography reveals that Clara was so shy in her youth, it appeared she would have a hard time being successful in life. However, not only would Clara succeed, but she would become the most famous nurse of the Civil War. Her postwar efforts for the Red Cross greatly broadened her ability to touch lives.

Rosenthal, Bert. *Basketball.* 1983. This information book explains the fundamental aspects of basketball, including equipment, scoring, and game rules.

Rossetti, Christina G. *What is Pink?* Illus. Margaret A. Soucheck. 1963. The book contains lovely illustrations of a poem about colors.

Rudin, Ellen. *Talk About School.* Illus. Kelly Oechsli. 1988. The simple text and bright pictures in this book are designed to encourage discussion about what goes on in a modern school setting.

Runyon, Leilah E. *I Learn to Read About Jesus.* Illus. June Kallmeyer. 1962. This Bible primer tells about the life of Jesus as a baby and a child.

Rylant, Cynthia. *Night in the Country.* Illus. Mary Szilagyi. 1986. In a few well-chosen words, the author describes the mysterious, melodious sights and sounds of nighttime in the country. Full-page color illustrations enhance the text.

————. *When I Was Young in the Mountains.* Illus. Diane Goode. 1982. Lyrical text and beautiful photographs recount the pleasures of life in the mountains.

Saint-Saëns, Camille. *Carnival of the Animals.* Trans. Keisuke Tsutsui; adapt. and illus. Kozo Kakimoto. 1971. An old man with a shaggy beard gets up one morning, hoping for inspiration for a tune to play on the piano. As he thinks of various animals, he gets his inspiration and translates animal sounds into music. Then he shaves his beard, dresses, and goes to the concert.

Sapienza, Marilyn. *Stone Soup.* 1986. In this simple folktale, two hungry traveling pigs outsmart a selfish group of townspeople into giving them the ingredients for a pot of soup.

Sargent, Robert. *The Adventurous Moth.* 1968. A lonely little moth finally finds happiness in the forest with all the woodland animals—and a box of old hats.

Schaaf, Peter. *The Violin Close Up.* 1980. The author of this book gives the reader a close-up look at the violin. He names and illustrates the parts of a violin and describes how it makes music. The children will enjoy this book more if a violin is brought to class the day this story is read.

Schackburg, Richard. *Yankee Doodle.* Woodcuts by Ed Emberley. 1965. Interesting notes by Barbara Emberley about the writing of this song and the meaning of some of the words add to the attraction of this book. Its horizontal format, allowing space for armies to march from one page to the other with rows and rows of tents, enhances its military presentation.

Schlein, Miriam. *Billy, the Littlest One.* Illus. Lucy Hawkinson. 1966. A child tells what it is like to be the smallest one of his family and friends. He grows and grows and then finds a friend that is smaller than he.

———. *The Rabbits' World.* Illus. Peter Parnall. 1973. This is the story of a snowshoe rabbit as he grows up.

———. *Snow Time.* Illus. Joe Lasker. 1962. Snow causes many people to work, but children have fun. The book answers the question: what do you do with snow? It discusses the pleasure and difficulties caused by snow.

Schneider, Nina. *While Susie Sleeps.* Illus. Dagmar Wilson. 1948. This book describes all the community night sounds and activities that go on while Susie sleeps.

Schwartz, Alvin. *Ten Copycats in a Boat and Other Riddles*. 1980. This book features simple riddles and colorful drawings.

Schwartz, Elizabeth. *When Animals Are Babies*. 1964. These simple and beautiful illustrations depict the babyhood and habitat of more than twenty animals.

Selsam, Millicent E. *All Kinds of Babies*. Illus. Symeon Shimin. 1967. Some animal babies look like their parents, but others are different from their parents. When they grow up, they will look just like their parents.

———. *The Amazing Dandelion*. Photographer Jerome Wexler. 1977. Simple text, diagrams, and close-up photographs depict the life cycle of the dandelion.

———. *Night Animals*. 1979. This book describes nighttime activities of owls, foxes, fireflies, beavers, bats, and other nocturnal animals. Black-and-white illustrations make the night scenes realistic.

———. *Peanut*. Photographer Jerome Wexler. 1969. Simple text along with black-and-white photographs and clear drawings illustrate the development of the peanut.

———. *When an Animal Grows*. Illus. John Kaufmann. 1966. This book shows the development of the mountain gorilla, song sparrow, sheep, and the mallard duck for the first several months of their lives.

Serventy, Vincent. *Kangaroo*. 1985. Simple text and full-color photographs describe the life cycle and natural environment of the kangaroo.

Seuling, Barbara. *Stay Safe, Play Safe*. 1985. This simple book teaches children about safety rules and emphasizes the role they can play in helping others remember.

Seuss, Dr. *One Fish, Two Fish, Red Fish, Blue Fish*. 1960. This nonsense book contains many concepts about colors, numbers, and rhyming sounds which will amuse the beginning reader.

————. *Yertle the Turtle and Other Stories.* 1958. Yertle the Turtle exalts himself as the ruler over all he sees. His fall from power, however, comes even more quickly than his rise to power. Gertrude McFuzz likewise learns a humbling lesson. She discovers that the beautiful tail full of feathers that she wanted actually weighted her down so much that she could not fly. The third story has lowly Mr. Worm pointing out to Mr. Bear and Mr. Rabbit the foolishness of their empty boastings.

Shannon, Terry. *Come Summer, Come Winter.* Illus. Charles Payzant. 1956. A picture story of all the seasons of the year, this book gives the weather signs and animal behavior of each season.

Shaw, Evelyn. *Octopus.* Illus. Ralph Carpentier. 1971. An easy-to-read information book in story form. Illustrations are attractive and detailed.

Shivkumar, K. *The King's Choice.* Illus. Yoko Mitsuhashi. 1961. "To be a king is good. But to be kind is better." This folktale from India retells the story of the kindness of a camel to his lion king.

Shortall, Leonard. *Just-in-Time Joey.* 1973. Six-year-old Joey becomes interested in all the elm trees of the neighborhood when a crew of tree men work near his grandmother's house. His quick thinking saves a healthy tree from being cut down.

Showers, Paul. *Columbus Day.* Illus. Ed Emberley. 1965. This is the story of Christopher Columbus and his landing in the New World.

————. *A Drop of Blood.* Illus. Don Madden. 1967. Questions that children would have about blood are answered in simple language with cartoonlike illustrations. Some of the topics covered are why the blood supply does not run out, how red and white cells and platelets protect us from disease, how bleeding stops, and what blood is.

————. *Ears Are for Hearing.* 1990. This information book conveys useful facts about the ears, including detailed anatomical descriptions and colorful, simple illustrations.

————. *Find Out by Touching*. Illus. Robert Galster. 1961. This concept book is about our fingers and how we use them for our work and play.

————. *Hear Your Heart*. Illus. Joseph Low. 1968. The author explains in simple language the basic functions of the heart as it pumps blood in and out to the whole body. The various heart rates at different stages of life are explained. Simple experiments are suggested in order to hear the heart beat and to enhance understanding of how the heart beats.

————. *How Many Teeth?* Illus. Paul Galdone. 1962. All children experience losing a tooth; so they will enjoy finding out the facts about their teeth. A light approach to this subject makes it even more enjoyable.

————. *How You Talk*. Illus. Robert Galster. 1966. Some simple experiments and explanations allow the young reader to learn how sound is made. The role that the larynx, lungs, mouth, nose, tongue, lips, and teeth play in this process are all mentioned.

————. *In the Night*. Illus. Ezra Jack Keats. 1961. Mr. Showers explores through a child's eyes what things he can see in the night and what other creatures can see at night. A boy goes to bed and his mother turns the light out. As his eyes begin to adjust to the darkness, he can see more and more things. Soon he begins to drift off into sleep.

————. *No Measles, No Mumps for Me*. Illus. Harriett Barton. 1980. Lively text and simple illustrations explain how shots and medicines help to protect from certain diseases that children used to get.

————. *What Happens to a Hamburger*. Illus. Anne Rockwell. 1970. Description is given of how not only hamburger but also milk, bacon, carrots, peaches, scrambled eggs, and candy bars are turned into bones, muscles, and energy. Fun experiments and attractive illustrations help make understandable the whole process of digestion.

Shulevitz, Uri. *Rain Rain Rivers*. 1969. Simple, lyrical text describes a child's view of what happens during a heavy rainfall.

Silcott, Philip B. *Cowboys.* Photographer Martin Rogers. 1975. This book presents interesting details of a cowboy's life in story format. Beautiful color photographs accompany the text.

Simon, Norma. *See the First Star.* Illus. Joe Lasker. 1968. Johnny cannot see a squirrel, a robin in a tree, or the first star shining in the sky. Father decides to take him to the eye doctor. Johnny is very excited when he gets his new glasses and can see things far away. This book is excellent for helping children accept the peer who must wear glasses.

————. *Why Am I Different?* 1976. Easy-to-understand text and excellent drawings present the differences between children.

Simon, Seymour. *Hot and Cold.* Illus. Joel Snyder. 1972. The simple, appealing text presents questions for discussion and activities that investigate the concepts of heat and cold.

Sivulich, Sandra Stroner. *I'm Going on a Bear Hunt.* Illus. Glen Rounds. 1973. A little boy decides to hunt for a bear. When he finds one, he is so frightened he runs home. This is an illustrated adaptation of the traditional action story.

Slobodkin, Florence, and Slobodkin, Louis. *Sarah Somebody.* 1969. Sarah is a nine-year-old Jewish girl living in Poland around the 1900s. Girls were not traditionally educated then, but Sarah gets that chance. She brings joy to her grandmother who, for the first time in her life, sees her name written. Sarah also uses her beautiful handwriting to make money, not for herself, but to help one of her classmates.

Smith, Betsy. *A Day in the Life of a Firefighter.* 1981. Simple text and simple photographs convey the essence of a firefighter's life.

Smith, Robert Paul. *When I am Big.* Illus. Lillian Hoban. 1965. A small boy looks forward to the time when he will be able to do all the responsible and exciting jobs that an adult does.

Snow, Pegeen. *Eat Your Peas, Louise.* Illus. Mike Venezia. 1985. Very simple text tells a humorous story about Louise and her peas. Large, colorful pictures accompany the text.

Spier, Peter. *Noah's Ark.* Illus. Peter Spier. 1977. With the exception of a poem at the beginning, this is a wordless book giving a pictorial story of Noah and the ark. Readers of all ages will find the detailed illustrations appealing.

Standiford, Natalie. *The Bravest Dog Ever.* Illus. Donald Cook. 1989. This book recounts the true story of Balto, a sled dog who saved Nome, Alaska, from a diphtheria epidemic by delivering medicine through a raging snowstorm.

Stanek, Muriel. *One, Two, Three for Fun.* Illus. Seymour Fleishman. 1967. Numbers can be found in the everyday games of children.

The Star-Spangled Banner. Illus. Peter Spier. 1973. This is an illustrated book about our national anthem.

Steele, Mary Q. *Anna's Garden Song.* Illus. Lena Anderson. 1989. This is a book of whimsical poems about a young girl's experiences with growing garden plants. Amusing and instructive full-color illustrations accompany the text.

Steele, Philip. *Land Transport Around the World.* 1986. Brief text and lavish color illustrations introduce different means of transportation used in several other countries.

Steig, William. *Sylvester and the Magic Pebble.* 1969. Sylvester, a young donkey, finds a magic pebble that will grant all wishes. When Sylvester faces a hungry lion, he wishes he were a rock, and he magically turns into one. His parents happily turn him back into a donkey again, but quite by accident.

Stephen, R. J. *Fire Engines.* 1986. Captioned photographs, colorful diagrams, and simple text describe modern fire engines and fire-fighting equipment.

Stevenson, Robert Louis. *A Child's Garden of Verses.* Illus. Tasha Tudor. 1988. Still with a nineteenth-century England flavor, these verses are as fresh as ever.

Stewart, Elizabeth Laing. *Little Dog Tim.* 1959. Little dog Tim wants to be friends with the kittens, but he has a difficult time knowing how to get their attention.

Stobbs, William. *Henny-Penny.* 1970. Henny Penny thinks the sky is going to fall when an acorn falls on her. She gathers all the animals together to go tell the king.

Stokes, Bill. *You Can Catch Fish.* Illus. Nancy Mack. 1976. This amusing book explains the art of fishing for the young, aspiring fisherman.

Stover, Jo Ann. *If Everybody Did*. Bob Jones University Press, 1989. Hilarious pictures portray what would happen if everyone did as he pleased.

————. *They Didn't Use Their Heads*. Bob Jones University Press, 1990. This amusing tale makes an unforgettable case for good behavior.

Supraner, Robyn. *Giggly-Wiggly, Snickety-Snick*. Illus. Stan Tusan. 1978. This book introduces children to the adjectives hard, soft, smooth, bumpy, tickly, sharp, sticky, stretchy, cold, hot, crunchy, squishy, fluffy, curly, and straight.

Suteyev, V. *Three Kittens*. Trans. Mirra Ginsburg; Illus. Giulio Maestro. 1973. Three kittens—black, gray, and white—run after a mouse, jump into a can of flour, and become three white kittens. They run after a toad, climb into a pipe, and become three black kittens. They jump into a pond after fish and become three clean kittens—black, gray, and white.

Swift, Hildegarde H., and Ward, Lynd. *The Little Red Lighthouse and the Great Gray Bridge*. 1970. The Little Red Lighthouse is very proud of his position as master of the river until he is replaced by the Great Gray Bridge. He feels so small and unwanted until one night in a thick fog the Great Gray Bridge needs his help.

Swim, Robert C. *Paulossie, An Eskimo Boy*. 1964. This story about an Eskimo boy portrays the reality and hardships of life in Alaska.

Tafuri, Nancy. *Early Morning in the Barn*. 1983. Basic text and simple illustrations feature morning sounds in the barnyard.

————. *Have You Seen My Duckling?* 1984. This simple book about a missing duckling hiding somewhere on the page appeals especially to the young reader or listener.

Talbot, Winifred. *Denny's Friend Rags*. Illus. Ruth Brophy. 1965. Denny is given a small sailboat for his birthday. He sails it on the lake and tries to rescue it by using his dad's rowboat. He is rescued by Rags, his dog. This good book illustrates the principle that you cannot do wrong and get away with it.

Taylor, Mark. *Henry Explores the Mountains.* Illus. Graham Booth. 1975. Henry takes an outing in the woods to explore the mountains with his dog Angus. The day proves very exciting as they encounter a forest fire, an avalanche, and even a helicopter ride when they become heroes for reporting the fire.

Terry, Trevor and Linton, Margaret. *The Life Cycle of an Ant.* 1988. Simple text and large-scale illustrations describe the life cycle of an ant. The book also includes instructions for making an ants' nest.

Tester, Sylvia Root. *Over, Under, and All Around.* Illus. Rose-Mary Fudala. 1977. This concept book introduces various spatial relationships such as over, under, around, and behind.

Thomas, Patricia. *"There Are Rocks in My Socks," Said the Ox to the Fox.* Illus. Mordecai Gerstein. 1979. This book uses hilarious rhyming text replete with words describing tactile sensations. Children will also enjoy the details of the cartoon-type illustrations.

Thomas, Ulrich. *Applemouse.* 1972. Applemouse gnaws his way into an apple and makes it his home. One day he eats too far up through the apple. When it rains, he gets soaked, and the apple finally falls apart. Applemouse makes a new home in an empty shell.

Thompson, Brenda, and Giesen, Rosemary. *Flags.* Illus. David Brogan and Rosemary Giesen. 1977. This First Fact Book describes some national and other well-known flags.

The Three Billy Goats Gruff. Illus. Marcia Brown; trans. G. W. Dasent. 1957. This is the traditional tale about the three Billy Goats Gruff, in which Big Billy Goat kills the troll.

The Three Pigs. Illus. Barbara Pritzen. 1973. This is the traditional story of the three little pigs and their defeat of the wolf.

Tolstoy, Aleksey. *The Great Big Enormous Turnip.* Illus. Helen Oxenbury. 1968. The turnip grows so big that an old man, an old woman, a granddaughter, a dog, a cat, and a mouse have to work together to pull it out of the ground.

Tresselt, Alvin. *The Beaver Pond.* Illus. Roger Duvoisin. 1970. This book traces the life story of a pond. It discusses the way the pond came to be, how it is used by many animals for food and shelter, and how it eventually becomes just a stream again.

———. *The Dead Tree.* Illus. Charles Robinson. 1972. The old oak tree, home for many animals, eventually dies and adds richness to the land around it where other oak trees grow. Watercolor pictures are used to illustrate the life and death of the tree.

———. *Johnny Maple-Leaf.* Illus. Roger Duvoisin. 1948. This book discusses the cycle of seasons in the life of a maple leaf.

———. *The Mitten.* Illus. Yaroslava. 1964. This is an old Ukrainian folktale about a little boy who lost his mitten in the forest while gathering firewood for his grandmother on the coldest day of winter. In this fanciful tale, the mitten becomes a shelter for an amazing number of forest animals.

———. *Rain Drop Splash.* Illus. Leonard Weisgard. 1946. The brief, poetic text follows a raindrop until it reaches the sea. Appealing illustrations enhance the text.

———. *Sun Up.* 1949. This simple book evokes the mood of a hot summer day broken by a thunderstorm. Colorful, appropriate illustrations enhance the text.

———. *Wake Up, City!* Illus. Roger Duvoisin. 1957. This book illustrates sounds of a city waking up in the morning.

———. *Wake Up, Farm!* Illus. Roger Duvoisin. 1955. All of the animals and people on the farm wake up to the crowing of the big rooster.

Turkle, Brinton. *Deep in the Forest.* 1976. This beautifully illustrated story without words is about a curious bear who explores a cabin in the forest. It is a revised version of the plot of the traditional *Three Bears.*

———. *Thy Friend, Obadiah.* 1969. This is a charmingly illustrated story about Obadiah, a little boy of colonial America living on Nantucket island, and his friend, a sea gull.

Turner, Dorothy. *Potatoes*. 1989. The simple text describes the history of potatoes, how they are grown, and their nutritional value. Photographs are interspersed with simple, bright illustrations.

Udry, Janice May. *Alfred*. Illus. Judith S. Roth. 1960. Henry is afraid of dogs. One day he finds out that a dog wants to be his friend.

———. *Emily's Autumn*. Illus. Erik Blegvad. 1969. While staying with Grandmother, Emily takes her cornhusk doll for a walk through summer and autumn.

———. *A Tree is Nice*. Illus. Marc Simont. 1956. This informative book explores the many ways trees are used in our world.

Van Woerkem, Dorothy. *Hidden Messages*. Illus. Lynne Cherry. 1979. Easy-to-read text and engaging illustrations describe Ben Franklin's discoveries about ant communication and Jean Heri Fabre's experiments with moths.

———. *A Hundred Angels Singing*. Illus. Art Kirchhoff. 1976. A little girl thinks about the first Christmas and compares it to Christmas today.

Verleyen, Cyriel. *The First Train*. Illus. Henry Branton. 1968. Samuel Smith, a newspaper man, writes the story of Trevithick's invention of the first horseless steam wagon in England and a big steam wagon to run on wooden rails. Years pass and Samuel Smith writes about George Stephenson's invention of the steam locomotive, and, in 1830, Stephenson's first passenger train.

Verrier, Suzanne. *Titus Tidewater*. 1970. Titus Tidewater, a handsome lobster, attempts to rescue a pretty lobster named Daphne. Titus becomes entangled in a fisherman's net and soon finds himself in a lobster pond. Children will enjoy learning what becomes of Titus and his friend in this charming story.

Voight, Virginia. *Nathan Hale*. Illus. Frank Aliose. 1965. This is the story of an American soldier of the War of Independence who volunteered to become a spy for General Washington against the British. Nathan Hale was caught and forced to admit his role. He gave up his life for the cause of independence, with his last words being, "I only regret that I have but one life to lose for my country."

Voorhees, Carolyn. *Why So Sad, Little Rag Doll?* Illus. Georgetta Lucas. 1963. This fanciful story is about a little rag doll who is envious of all the other toys that stay on the shelf. The bride doll helps the rag doll to see that she really is the one to be envied because she is the most loved by her owner Betsy.

Waber, Bernard. *An Anteater Named Arthur.* 1967. These fanciful and amusing incidents in the life of an anteater named Arthur will appeal to the young reader.

————. *A Firefly Named Torchy.* 1970. Torchy has a problem. He cannot twinkle like other fireflies. His light is too bright for the woodland creatures. One night he finds himself in the city with all the bright neon blinking lights, and he flashes his light all night long. He is so worn out "that on his way home without even thinking, he begins to twinkle."

————. *Ira Sleeps Over.* 1972. Ira's anticipated overnight stay with his friend becomes a special kind of struggle when his sister brings up the subject of his favorite sleep-time toy.

Wackerbarth, Marjorie. *Bobby Learns About Woodland Babies.* Illus. Lawrence Spiegel. 1968. Bobby Strong visits his grandfather, who lives in a small town near the woods. Together Bobby and his grandfather roam the woods and observe seven different kinds of wild babies; a beaver, twin bears, a porcupine, a raccoon, a fox, a woodchuck, and a skunk.

Wake, Susan. *Citrus Fruits.* 1990. This book describes several citrus fruits, their importance, and their histories. Photographs, diagrams, and captions are instructive. Also included are recipes for a pomander ball, lemonade, and chutney.

————. *Vegetables.* 1990. Simple text describes different types of vegetables, their histories, and how they are grown. Helpful captions accompany full-color illustrations and diagrams.

Walker, Barbara. *Pigs and Pirates.* Illus. Harold Berson. 1969. Brightly illustrated with personalities in the faces of the pigs, this clever story of three swineherders charms us. After the boys teach the pigs tricks, including answering a flute, pirates invade the island and steal all the pigs. Sounding their flutes, the boys call to the seabound pigs. The ship capsizes as all the pigs and pirates rush to one side of the vessel.

Walter, Frances, and Pearson, Violet T. *Here's Benjie!* 1976. This animal story is a personification of a beaver family, with young Benjie as the main character. Children will enjoy the adventures Benjie participates in, while they learn many facts not only about beavers but also about some of the friends and enemies of the beaver. Several Christian principles that will apply directly to everyday life of children are presented through these animals.

Walters, Marguerite. *The City-Country ABC*. Illus. Ib Ohlsson. 1966. This clever turnabout book is a poem about the alphabet.

Wannamaker, Bruce. *God's Care is Everywhere*. 1982. Simple text affirms the evidences of God's love and care in nature and in human relationships.

Ward, Lynd. *The Biggest Bear*. 1952. Johnny Orchard sets out to bring back the biggest bear in the forest, but instead he comes home with a very little bear. His little bear eats everything, grows up very quickly, and becomes a general nuisance to everyone. How Johnny's problem is solved gives a charming surprise ending to this story.

Waters, John F. *Hungry Sharks*. Illus. Ann Dalton. 1974. Described for children is the shark's sense of smell, his "distance-touch" system, his sense of movement, and his special body construction enabling him to eat almost anything. The shark's ears, eyes, and nostrils are described to aid in developing an understanding of how these animals operate.

Watkins, Dawn. *The Cranky Blue Crab*. Illus. Tim Davis. Bob Jones University Press, 1990. Crusty the Crab, bored and unhappy, sets out to find adventure in Sea Meadow.

————. *A King for Brass Cobweb*. Illus. Holly Hannon. Bob Jones University Press, 1990. Chipmunk leaves the comforts of home to seek a king who is wise and brave and true.

————. *Pocket Change*. Illus. Tim Davis. Bob Jones University Press, 1992. Five illustrated fables tell of alligators, monkeys, cheetahs, and many other animals that do and say remarkable things.

————. *Pulling Together*. Bob Jones University Press, 1992. What can a boy do to help his family keep its horses? Matthew takes a risk and makes a sacrifice so Ben and Dolly can compete at the county fair.

————. *The Spelling Window.* Illus. John Roberts. Bob Jones University Press, 1993. Shelly has no time for the spelling window or for her deaf neighbor, Seth, who signs to her sister through it. Why should she?

————. *Very Like a Star.* Illus. Dana Thompson. Bob Jones University Press, 1990. Rigel of Buzzle Hive has to discover whether she is like the star for which she is named.

————. *Wait and See.* Photographer Suzanne Altizer. Bob Jones University Press, 1991. Full-color photographs and intriguing rhymes invite the reader to test his ability to observe and draw conclusions.

Watson, Jane Werner. *Wonders of Nature.* Illus. Eloise Wilkin. 1958. This book tells of the wonders of plants, animals, the sea, the sky, and the seasons. Teachers may follow up by pointing to God as the source of these wonders.

Watts, Barrie. *Apple Tree.* 1986. Simple text describes how an apple develops from a blossom in the spring to a ripe fruit in the autumn. Diagrams and colorful photographs are included.

————. *24 Hours in a Forest.* 1990. This informative book tells what happens to the plants and animals of the forest during a twenty-four-hour period. Beautiful full-color photographs accompany the text.

Weisgard, Leonard. *Mr. Peaceable Paints.* 1956. This interesting story about a sign painter in colonial America describes the customs and procedures for displaying signs in a time when most people could not read.

Wexler, Jerome. *Flowers, Fruits, Seeds.* 1987. Simple text is used to describe the cycle from flower to fruit to seed. The full-color photographs are especially appealing.

Whitney, Alma Marshak. *Just Awful.* Illus. Lillian Hoban. 1971. Just after lunch, James cuts his finger while playing on the playground. James feels bad, so his teacher, Mrs. Smith, sends him to the school nurse. James is scared, but the nurse helps him by giving him the three-part treatment: cleaning, bandaging, and then hugging. James feels much better and returns to his classroom wearing a big smile.

Whyman, Kathryn. *Wood*. 1987. This book follows the process of making paper, beginning with the tree in the forest.

Wiese, Kurt. *The Thief in the Attic*. 1965. Well-illustrated story about a noisy crow. The book also depicts several different kinds of animal homes.

Wiesner, David. *Hurricane*. 1990. This is the story of two boys who experience a hurricane. The morning after, they find an uprooted tree that becomes the basis for imaginary adventures.

Wiest, Robert, and Wiest, Claire. *Down the River Without a Paddle*. 1973. D. Plexippus, a caterpillar, takes a trip down the river on a leaf and then turns into a butterfly.

Wiewandt, Thomas A. *The Hidden Life of the Desert*. 1990. Photographs and text provide a guided tour of the animals, plants, and ecology of America's Southwest desert.

Wildsmith, Brian. *Brian Wildsmith's ABC*. 1963. This book includes one illustration for every letter of the alphabet with the name of the illustration written in lowercase and capital letters.

―――. *The Little Wood Duck*. 1973. The youngest wood duckling cannot swim like his brothers and sisters no matter how hard he tries. Instead he just swims in circles. All the other woodland animals make fun of him until one day his swimming round and round makes the hungry fox so dizzy that he faints while all the ducklings escape to safety.

―――. *The Owl and the Woodpecker*. 1971. The owl and the woodpecker cannot get along. They both live in the same tree, but the routines of their lives interfere with each other. The owl sleeps during the day and the woodpecker at night. One day the woodpecker saves the owl's life when their tree is being blown down. After that, the owl and the woodpecker become good friends.

————. *Brian Wildsmith's Wild Animals.* 1967. This book describes each type of wild animal and names a characteristic of its nature.

Williams, Garth. *The Chicken Book.* 1970. This rhyming book shows that chicks cannot just wish for food. They must learn how to scratch for it.

Wilson, Sarah. *Muskrat, Muskrat, Eat Your Peas!* 1989. A simple but engaging story about a muskrat family that plants a garden.

Wing, Henry. *What Is Big?* Illus. Ed Carini. 1963. As a child compares his size to that of various animals, he finds that he is bigger than some and also smaller than some.

Wolcott, Patty. *Beware of a Very Hungry Fox.* Illus. Lucinda McQueen. 1975. Little chipmunks meet a very hungry fox in the forest, but they do not become his dinner.

————. *The Cake Story.* Illus. Lucinda McQueen. 1974. The animals eat the bear's cake while the bear sleeps.

Wondriska, William. *Puff.* 1960. Puff is a little steam engine who helps the circus during a snowstorm.

Wong, Herbert H., and Vessel, Matthew F. *My Plant.* Illus. Richard Cuffari. 1976. A story format is used to describe the experiences of city children who grow some plants. Attractive illustrations accompany the text.

Wood, Audrey. *The Napping House.* 1984. A charming cumulative tale about a rainy night's events that end with the sunshine of morning. Superb full-color illustrations bring the story to life.

Woolley, Catherine. *I Like Trains.* Illus. George Fonseca. 1965. This informational book tells about freight trains, passenger trains, and express trains. It describes the facilities of the passenger train.

Wright, Betty Ren. *I Want to Read.* Illus. Aliki. 1970. Sue and her brother have learned to read, and everywhere they go, they read the signs and information. The book provides good motivation for beginning reading.

Wright, Ethel. *Saturday Walk.* Illus. Richard Rose. 1954. A little boy sees many workers and wheels when he goes for a walk on Saturday with his father.

Yashima, Taro. *Umbrella.* 1958. Momo, a little Japanese girl, can hardly wait for rain so that she can use her new umbrella. When it finally rains, she enjoys hearing the raindrops make music on her umbrella.

Yates, Elizabeth. *Carolina's Courage.* Bob Jones University Press, 1989. Carolina Putnam is a little girl, but she finds out what it means to have the true spirit of a pioneer.

———. *Sarah Whitcher's Story.* Illus. Nora S. Unwin. 1971. Sarah is lost in the woods during the pioneer days. Search parties are unable to locate her. However, Sarah is protected by a bear in the woods. She is eventually found by a man who has had a dream about her.

Yolen, Jane. *All in the Woodland Early.* Illus. Jane Breskin Zalben. 1979. A little boy and girl go on a woodland hunt and find animals whose names begin with all the letters from A to Z. This book also includes music for the text.

———. *Owl Moon.* 1987. This is a memorable account of a girl's first experience in owling, a family tradition. The beautiful, watercolor illustrations portray the events of the serene winter night beneath a glowing "owl moon."

Younger, Jesse. *The Fire Engine Book.* 1982. Many illustrations of firefighting scenes add to the appeal of this shape book.

Ziefert, Harriet. *A New Coat for Anna.* 1986. An engaging story with read-aloud text and lovely illustrations describe the progress of Anna's new wool coat from sheep to tailor.

Ziegler, Sandra. *A Visit to the Bakery.* 1987. Simple text and close-up color photographs portray the bread-baking process.

Zion, Gene. *Harry the Dirty Dog.* Illus. Margaret Bloy Graham. 1956. Harry, a white dog with black spots, dislikes baths so much that he hides the scrubbing brush. When he gets very dirty and no one recognizes him, he digs up the brush and begs his family to give him a bath.

———. *Hide and Seek Day.* Illus. Margaret Bloy Graham. 1954. Jimmy decides to play a game of hide and seek all day.

Zolotow, Charlotte. *Big Sister and Little Sister.* Illus. Martha Alexander. 1966. Big sister and little sister take care of each other.

————. *Flocks of Birds.* Illus. Joan Berg. 1965. Birds fly over different sections of the country in the fall.

————. *Hold My Hand.* Illus. Thomas di Grazia. 1972. Two children hold hands and watch snowflakes drop all around them until several inches have fallen and it stops snowing.

————. *The Storm Book.* Illus. Margaret Bloy Graham. 1952. A small boy is frightened and wants to know all about a summer storm and what people do when it storms.

Grade 3 - Grade 6

Alexander, Lloyd. *The Truthful Harp.* 1967. Fflewddur Flam is given a harp that sounds beautiful when played. However, he finds that some of the strings break on several occasions. He finally realizes that they break only when he tells a lie. This leads to Fflewddur Flam's trying to mend his ways. The illustrations effectively capture the personality of this amusing character.

Andersen, Hans Christian. *The Fir Tree.* 1970. The delicate and charming illustrations enhance the story about the little fir tree that gloriously serves as a Christmas tree but must later mourn its saddened condition.

————. *The Little Match Girl.* 1968. This is a moving story of a lonely, cold, little match girl who sees visions in the flames of the matches she cannot sell. The last vision is of the loving grandmother who is dead and comes to take the child. The illustrations are especially effective.

————. *The Nightingale.* 1965. The nightingale's lovely singing saves the life of the Chinese emperor. The text of this Andersen tale is highly enhanced by the rich detail of Oriental glamour.

Anderson, C. W. *The Blind Connemara.* 1971. As Rhonda works at a stable, she comes to love a beautiful white pony soon to be completely blind. She accepts the pony as a gift and compassionately trains it. Rhonda's story encourages many around her, especially some young handicapped children.

Bailey, Carolyn S. *Miss Hickory.* Illus. by Ruth Gannett. 1946, 1974, 1977. Miss Hickory appears to be a doll made of apple wood with a hickory nut head. When the family lives in Boston for the winter, Miss Hickory has all sorts of adventures with many animals in the New Hampshire home. The lithographic illustrations are delightful. The author won the Newbery Award for this book.

Bannon, Laura. *Hop-High, the Goat.* 1960. Singing Girl, a Navaho Indian, enjoys her bumbling, mischievous goat. The family considers making goat meat stew until the goat proves itself a hero by rescuing the lost sheep. The author's profuse illustrations enhance the appeal of the book.

Barr, Jene, and Chapin, Cynthia. *What Will the Weather Be?* 1965. This book summarizes the tools a weatherman uses, and how his predictions affect daily planning for vacations and other activities. The tools discussed include the thermometer, barometer, weather vane, and satellites.

Barrie, Sir James M. *Peter Pan.* 1904. Wendy, John, and Michael go with Peter Pan to Never-Never Land where children never grow up. Adventure abounds with the fairy Tinker Bell, pirates, and redskins. Adults can enjoy the mild satire while children appreciate the world of make-believe.

Baum, L. Frank. *The Wizard of Oz.* 1956. With the aid of a cyclone, Dorothy and her dog Toto are taken to the land of the Munchkins. In this dream world she finds Scarecrow, Tin Woodman, and Cowardly Lion. They follow the yellow brick road to visit Emerald City and see the Wizard of Oz, who is supposed to help Dorothy return to her family in Kansas.

Baylor, Byrd. *Coyote Cry.* 1972. Antonio and his grandfather hear coyotes crying in the distance. Antonio learns not to be so afraid of the coyotes when he finds one of his missing pups is being cared for by a coyote.

Bennet, Rowena. *Runner for the King.* 1944. Roca must get a message to the Emperor, but the hindrances are severe. A puma attacks him, a landslide blocks his path, and the rope bridge high above the gorge breaks. But in spite of these odds, Roca successfully reaches the King Emperor of the Inca Empire to warn him of the imminent danger.

Blades, Ann. *Mary of Mile 18.* 1971. In Mary's snow-covered, isolated village, a wolf pup becomes a tagalong. Mary's father reminds her that no pet is allowed in the family unless it will be a help. The pup appears at the right place and time to give warning of an encroaching coyote. The pup finds a new home with Mary by showing how helpful he could be.

Branley, Franklyn M. *Darkness in Daytime.* 1973. The book discusses some superstitions regarding an eclipse of the sun. Today this phenomenon can be predicted by watching the predictable movements of the earth and moon. The author explains how one may safely look at an eclipse.

————. *Oxygen Keeps You Alive*. 1971. The author discusses the importance of oxygen in plants, animals, and man. Clear, colorful drawings.

————. *Roots Are Food Finders*. 1975. The roots of some plants spread widely, others grow deep. However, all roots provide the food and nutrition needed by plants. Animals which get their food from plants are also ultimately dependent on roots. Some easy-to-do experiments for children are included in the book.

————. *Sunshine Makes the Seasons*. 1974. The author explains that the tilt of the earth and the revolution of the earth around the sun bring our change of seasons.

Brecht, Edith. *The Little Fox*. 1968. Benjy's elderly friend, Slim, trusts him enough to leave his baby fox, Goldie, in Benjy's care. Benjy thinks he is a failure when Goldie escapes. Benjy awaits Slim's return, hating to tell him the news. But on the same day that Slim returns, Goldie appears also—with three of her own young pups.

Brink, Carol R. *Andy Buckram's Tin Men*. 1966. Andy builds four robots, the last one able to row a boat. During a storm, the robots more or less came to life after being electrified by lightning. The robots end up with Andy, a baby cousin, and a friend on a deserted island. The author comfortably and skillfully moves from the plausible to the fantastic in this story.

————. *Caddie Woodlawn*. 1973. Caddie is an adventurous tomboy living in Wisconsin in 1864. This is the first in a series of stories about her pioneer life, based on the reminiscences of the author's grandmother.

Bronson, Wilfrid S. *Pinto's Journey*. 1948. Pinto Goodluck is an Indian boy who wants some turquoise for his father. He embarks on a dangerous journey near Santa Fe, New Mexico, in order to get the turquoise, and he encounters numerous exciting adventures on the trip.

Burnett, Frances H. *The Secret Garden.* 1911. Mary realizes how unruly she has been when she meets her pampered cousin Colin. Mary and Colin both begin to change when they discover an abandoned garden that once belonged to Colin's deceased mother. Besides the garden, a robin and a boy who loves nature are instrumental in causing a remarkable change in Mary and Colin.

Burton, Hester. *In Spite of All the Terror.* 1968. This war story set in 1939 brings Liz, an orphaned city dweller, to an upper-class family in the country. The war draws the family and Liz closer as they experience some of the tragedies of Dunkirk. Later the family takes in Liz's cousin Rose, bringing Liz to a greater point of maturity.

Canfield, Dorothy. *Understood Betsy.* 1917. Elizabeth Ann, a spoiled, sickly girl, goes to a Vermont farm and in this wholesome but rugged environment becomes a stronger young lady.

Carroll, Lewis, pseudonym. See Dodgson, Charles Lutwidge.

Chrisman, Arthur Bowie. *Shen of the Sea: Chinese Stories for Children.* Dutton, 1953. This collection of Chinese stories reveals much about the thought and philosophy of the Chinese people. The tales of Ah Mee, the Rain King's daughter, and Ah Teha will amuse children while teaching them much about the Chinese people.

Clark, Ann Nolan. *Blue Canyon Horse.* 1954. Longing to be free, a young mare flees her pasture in the canyon and joins a wild herd. However, when her colt is born, she returns to the secure home she had enjoyed with her young Indian master. The story is told in verse.

———. *In My Mother's House.* 1941. From a child's point of view the story reflects the day-to-day life of the Tewa Indians. Illustrations are by an Indian artist.

———. *Little Navajo Bluebird.* 1943. Little Bluebird determines she will never go away to school. She has seen school turn her brother against the old ways of her Navajo people. However, she reconsiders when she learns the school has much to offer that will eventually help her.

Cleary, Beverly. *The Mouse and the Motorcycle.* 1965. Ralph, the mischievous mouse, rides a mouse-sized motorcycle through the hotel corridors. Keith, the owner of the toy, becomes good friends with Ralph in this fantasy.

Coatsworth, Elizabeth. *Away Goes Sally.* 1934. Sally moves with her family to the wilderness of New England after the Revolutionary War. In order to keep a promise that the house would not be abandoned, they travel in the house on runners pulled by oxen.

———. *The Princess and the Lion.* 1963. Princess Mariam plans for her brother's escape from prison because she thinks he will not be chosen as heir to the throne. Surprisingly, the old King announces Michael's promotion, causing Mariam to have to take a dangerous journey to tell Michael. If Michael escapes, it will mean certain death.

———. *The Sod House.* 1954. Llse Trauble's family comes from Germany to find freedom in the New World. They join northern families who are settling in Kansas to keep a majority vote for their side. This pre-Civil War conflict finds the Trauble family standing firmly for their beliefs in spite of all difficulties.

Collodi, Carlo. *The Adventures of Pinocchio.* 1946. Pinocchio, a simple piece of wood carved by Geppetto, becomes a living marionette. His curiosity, adventuresome spirit, and quick mind get Pinocchio in and out of trouble. Finally, he gets his desire to become a real boy.

Dalgliesh, Alice. *Adam and the Golden Cock.* 1959. A young boy guards his sheep in Connecticut in 1781 when the French general Rochambeau comes through his hometown. The troops provide much excitement for Adam as they spend several days there before moving to aid General Washington's troops during the American Revolution.

DeAngeli, Marguerite. *The Door in the Wall.* 1949. In this medieval story Robin's plans to become a knight are foiled when he is permanently crippled. Robin is taken by a friar to a hospice where he is well cared for and regains his strength. He seeks new ways of service to his lord. His chance comes when the enemy thinks he is a harmless handicapped boy. He delivers a message that saves his lord from destruction.

————. *Yonie Wondernose.* 1944. Yonie got his nickname, Wondernose, because of his insatiable curiosity that often distracted him from his duties. On this occasion if Yonie can meet the challenge of getting all his work done, his father has a reward for him. Yonie not only gets his chores done, but he also saves the animals in a barn fire.

D'Aulaire, Ingri, and D'Aulaire, Edgar Parin. *Abraham Lincoln.* 1957. This biography focuses on Lincoln's early life.

DeJong, Meindert. *Far out the Long Canal.* 1964. Moonta is a nine-year-old Dutch boy who has never learned to skate. He is teased by his peers as he tries to skate but encouragement comes later.

————. *The House of Sixty Fathers.* 1956. This is a powerful story about a young Asian boy named Tien Poa who is separated from his family during wartime. During his journey through enemy territory, he saves the life of an American soldier who befriends and helps him.

————. *The Last Little Cat.* 1961. A little cat finds itself rejected by its mother and accidentally falls into the same kennel with an old, blind dog. The dog shares its food with the cat. Later, after separation, the cat finds its old friend, the dog, in the home of a kind man.

————. *Smoke Above the Lane.* 1951. A tramp becomes friends with a little skunk as they travel together in the boxcar of a freight train. Children will enjoy the humor of the skunk's appearance at a Labor Day parade, as well as the friendship formed by this unlikely pair.

————. *The Wheel on the School.* Illus. Maurice Sendak. 1954. Children from the Dutch village of Shora learn that storks once perched on the roofs of the people's houses. The children begin a campaign to get the storks back. They influence the whole village with their efforts and exhibit great courage against storms that threaten their goal. The illustrations are an integral part of this book and others by DeJong.

Dodge, Mary Mapes. *Hans Brinker and the Silver Skates.* 1954. Hans wishes to win the silver skates by winning a racing contest. He realizes that his chances are slim, however, with only wooden skates for the contest. Hans and his sister are fine examples as they care for their sick father while facing scorn and poverty.

Dodgson, Charles Lutwidge [Lewis Carroll, pseudonym]. 1865. *Alice's Adventures in Wonderland* and *Through the Looking Glass.* Grosset and Dunlap, 1988. Alice has some strange adventures in a dream where she escapes to an underground world. There she talks with animals including the Cheshire Cat, March Hare, Mad Hatter, and Mock Turtle. In the second story, Alice embarks on a world behind a looking glass where everything is backwards. She meets some other fascinating characters, including Tweedledum and Tweedledee, Humpty Dumpty, and the Lion and the Unicorn.

DuBois, William Pène. *The Giant.* 1954. The story tells of a young, giant-sized boy who is trying to find a place where he can be accepted without fear or ridicule. The author finds the boy and helps him meet his objective. Behind the story is a message of tolerance and kindness toward others.

————. *Twenty-one Balloons.* 1947. Professor Sherman, ready for a change after forty years of teaching math, sets off in a balloon across the Pacific Ocean, only to find himself being rescued three weeks later in the Atlantic. This Newbery winner will provide a touch of unbelievable and delightful humor.

Edmonds, Walter D. *The Matchlock Gun.* 1941. Edward's mother, being left with the children, is uncertain of what might happen if the encroaching Indians get past the militiamen. Edward admires the matchlock gun hanging over the fireplace; he wishes his father would use it instead of his musket. Instead, Edward himself uses it against three Indians who would have destroyed the family and the house.

————. *Two Logs Crossing.* 1943. Young John Haskell wants to pay off his dead father's debts and support his mother, brothers, and sisters. He does so by going fur trapping with an Indian friend. By trapping each winter, he pays the debt and improves his family's condition.

Edwards, Julie. *Mandy.* 1971. This melodrama finds Mandy, a lonely orphan, discovering her own secret cottage. After a good cleaning, this place meets some of Mandy's needs.

Elgin, Kathleen. *The Human Body: The Ear.* 1967. The ear is described and illustrated so that children can understand its role in the hearing process and in the body's sense of equilibrium.

Enright, Elizabeth. *The Four-Story Mistake.* 1942. The Melendy family moves from their New York house to a four-story monstrosity in the country. But they find some intriguing adventures in the "four-story mistake."

———. *Gone-Away Lake.* 1957. Two children go on an excursion for their summer holiday. They find a swamp as they pursue a rare butterfly. Beyond the swamp are some dilapidated but elegant homes full of mystery. This delightful book is full of excitement, day dreaming, and pleasant summer breezes.

———. *The Saturdays.* 1941. Four children decide that they could have more fun than usual if they would pool their allowances with each one having his own special Saturday.

———. *Spiderweb for Two.* 1951. While their brothers and sisters are away, Randy and Oliver Melendy search out the clues of a mysterious treasure hunt.

———. *Thimble Summer.* 1938. Girls will enjoy reading about Garnet's experiences on a Wisconsin farm. Her summer days of happiness begin as soon as she finds a silver thimble in the dried creek bed. Thus, Garnet becomes convinced that the thimble is the cause of these good days.

Estes, Eleanor. *Ginger Pye.* 1951. Ginger, the dog in the Pye family, is lost just about the time a man in a mustard-colored hat appears. A clever three-year-old named Uncle Bennie helps the family find the dog and dispels suspicion of the man.

———. *The Hundred Dresses.* 1944. This is a sensitive story about a young Polish immigrant and her struggle to "fit in" at school. The story has a strong, positive message about the pain caused by senseless teasing.

————. *The Moffats*. 1941. The Moffat family lives in Connecticut around the time of World War I. Janey is the Moffat through whom the reader sees all the adventures of this lively but poor family. The story is sensitive but not sentimental. The pen and ink sketches allow the child to visualize the time period and give an enjoyable lift to almost every other page.

Faulkner, Georgene, and Becker, John. *Melindy's Medal*. 1945. Melinda is overjoyed when her family moves to a new housing project. However, she is not satisfied with herself because all the men in her family have won medals for brave war actions. She gets her chance to display courage when a fire breaks out at school, and she saves the lives of all the children. She, too, receives a medal of honor.

Fenner, Phyllis. *Horses, Horses, Horses*. 1949. This book contains a wide selection of excellent horse stories that anyone will enjoy. The selections include stories about palominos, pintos, polo ponies, as well as plow horses.

Field, Rachel. *Calico Bush*. 1931. This pioneer adventure story finds Maggie saving the lives of the England family to whom she had been "bound out." She does this by making a Maypole dance arrangement for some attacking Indians. The story imparts knowledge of the hardships of the colonial period in one of the first settlements of Maine.

————. *Hitty—Her First Hundred Years*. 1929. Children and adults will learn about nineteenth-century life from Hitty, the doll made from mountain ash. She begins her life in a window shop of a quiet Maine village. Then she travels for the next one hundred years.

Fife, Dale. *North of Danger*. 1978. In order to warn his father, a scientist being sought by the Nazis, Arne manages to stay in Norway when the town is being evacuated. Arne braves a two-hundred-mile trip with winter approaching. One of his concerns is a trapper, whom he mistrusts at first but later the trapper proves helpful in getting to Arne's father. This exciting account will attract even reluctant readers.

Froman, Robert. *Mushrooms and Molds*. 1972. Readers will learn that mushrooms and molds are different from most other plants. These plants reproduce by spores and do not produce their own food as other plants do. Suggested activities and demonstrations are given to help children understand these plants with which they have probably had little contact.

Gannett, Ruth S. *My Father's Dragon*. 1948. This nonsensical fantasy describes Elmer Elevator's trip to Wild Island to free the captive baby dragon. He succeeds by using such devices as chewing gum, toothpaste, and lollipops, but not before he encounters dangers from other wild animals.

Gans, Roma. *Bird Talk*. 1971. Birds "say" things that children are often curious about. This book reveals much about bird songs. There are mating calls, warning calls, songs of happiness, and songs of sadness.

Gardiner, John Reynolds. *Stone Fox*. 1983. This is a superb, heart-warming story about a courageous young boy and his love for his aging grandfather.

Gates, Doris. *Blue Willow*. 1940. This is a powerful story about a young girl named Janey and her migrant family during the depression years.

————. *The Cat and Mrs. Cory*. 1962. Mrs. Cory becomes the owner of a cat about the same time her convalescing nephew comes to live with her. From her newly purchased house, Mrs. Cory, her nephew, and the cat attempt to solve a mystery of several parakeet disappearances. The delightful cat has the uncanny ability to talk—but only to Mrs. Cory.

Goldin, Augusta. *The Bottom of the Sea*. 1967. Children seldom realize that the geography below the sea is similar to that above sea level. There are mountain ranges, cliffs, mudflats, and volcanoes below the sea. This book introduces children to an exciting new world.

————. *Salt*. 1965. Interesting information including the location of and the mining of salt. Also introduces the child to a simple experiment in which he sees salt crystals growing.

————. *Straight Hair, Curly Hair.* 1966. Hair texture, length, and fullness are discussed so that children understand some of the principles of heredity. Colorful and numerous illustrations help explain some simple experiments.

————. *The Sunlit Sea.* 1968. There is a busy world of plants and animals that live within the sunlit portion of the sea. Some creatures make noises, and others quietly wait for their food. The appealing illustrations teach about marine life.

Grahame, Kenneth. *The Reluctant Dragon.* 1953. This story tells of a young boy who makes friends with a dragon found in a cave. The dragon has slept there while the rest of his species has gone. The humor and delightful illustrations make this an attractive book.

————. *The Wind in the Willows.* 1933. This is a classic work about four rodent friends whose charming personalities and myriad adventures are made irresistible through Grahame's elegant style.

Hale, Lucretia. *The Complete Peterkin Papers.* 1960. The Peterkin family always seems to be in trouble, but the Lady from Philadelphia rescues them just in time. These humorous anecdotes are probably most effectively used with young people when read aloud.

Harris, Beth Coombe. *The Little Green Frog.* n.d. Biddy, a missionary's eight-year-old daughter, is forced by ill health to come to America temporarily. Her testimony and spirit endear her to the hearts of many who help supply money to build a hospital for Biddy's parents in China. Biddy herself faces a difficult decision in her efforts to raise the money when she finds out that her treasured frog is worth several thousand dollars.

Hawes, Judy. *Bees and Beelines.* 1964. Children will learn much fascinating information about bees from this book. They will learn how bees communicate with each other, not by talking but by touching other bees and by movements which signify certain messages. This book is written to make the scientific explanations understandable for children.

Hays, Wilma Pitchford. *Christmas on the Mayflower*. 1956. Giles, having been on the *Mayflower* for months, finally gets to go ashore. In this vivid but fictionalized story of the first Christmas in the New World, Giles helps the women decorate and tries to discover ways to make toys for the younger children. Great appreciation for these early settlers is a natural response from the reader.

————. *Fourth of July Raid*. 1959. With a warning that the British will soon attack, Tom and his family hide as many of their belongings as possible. Tom is anxious to go with his father to fight, but instead he displays his bravery at home. He helps a neighbor retrieve important papers, and he helps a group of men drive the British away against incredible odds.

Henry, Marguerite. *Brighty of the Grand Canyon*. 1953. Taken from a true story. Brighty is a little burro that lives in the Grand Canyon. He vindicates his friend, the old prospector, by helping to find his murderer. No one can read this book without gaining an enhanced picture of the canyon.

————. *Justin Morgan Had a Horse*. 1954. Justin Morgan, a plain workhorse, rises to fame as President James Monroe's horse. This is accomplished because a young boy loves the horse and rescues him from a cruel master. From this horse comes the famous American breed of Morgan horses.

————. *Misty of Chincoteague*. 1947. Each year ponies from the island of Chincoteague in the Chesapeake Bay are sold for children's use. This is the story of Phantom, one of these wild freedom-loving ponies, and her foal, Misty. Both are tamed by Paul and Maureen.

————. *Sea Star*. 1949. Misty, a tamed wild horse, becomes involved in saving the life of a little, wild orphan horse. The orphan horse is discovered by the same two children who had found Misty earlier.

————. *Stormy, Misty's Foal*. 1963. This story is based on true accounts of a foal being born in the aftermath of a storm that virtually ruined Chincoteague Island.

Hess, Donna. *A Father's Promise*. Bob Jones University Press, 1987. When Nazi forces invade Poland and bomb his home city of Warsaw, Rudi finds out that because he is a Jew—and a Christian—he is Hitler's enemy. In the next few years, he learns how to survive in hiding, how to be truly brave, and how to overcome the hatred of his enemies.

Holling, Holling Clancy. *Paddle-to-the-Sea*. 1941. A boy puts his hand-carved Indian in a canoe in the water above Lake Superior. It takes four years for it to go through the Great Lakes, the St. Lawrence River, and then out to sea. The book serves as a colorful geography lesson.

Howard, Milly. *These Are My People*. 1984. Set against the back-drop of war between Japan and China during the 1930s, this is the story of Gladys Aylward and her courageous mission work with the Chinese people.

———. *Brave the Wild Trail*. Bob Jones University Press, 1987. Josh goes along on a cattle drive through Florida's dangerous wilderness.

Hyde, Dayton O. *Cranes in My Corral*. 1971. Mr. Hyde raises Eeeny, Meeny, Miney, and Mo on his ranch in Oregon. These sandhill cranes follow Mr. Hyde, and he learns to imitate the whooping dance with the birds. Migratory season causes the birds to leave Oregon, but Mr. Hyde finds them and returns them to his ranch.

Kaufmann, John. *Streamlined*. 1974. Children will learn from this account why certain-shaped bodies have the most effective mobility in water. Simple experiments are designed to help develop this understanding and to apply it to other things.

Kipling, Rudyard. *The Elephant's Child*. 1970. This is one of the stories from *Just So Stories*. The stubborn elephant's child goes to the "great, green, greasy Limpopo River" in order to find knowledge. Crocodile helps him find it, and as a reminder of his lesson, the elephant gets a trunk.

———. *Just So Stories*. 1952. Children will love these humorous, nonsensical animal stories, especially the explanation about how the elephant got his trunk and how the camel got his hump.

Kjelgaard, Jim [James Arthur]. *Haunt-Fox*. 1981. In this realistic animal story, a young boy and his dog hunt the fox and finally trap it. Because he did not catch it fairly, however, the boy sets the fox free. One will learn much through this story about the fox's care of his mate and cubs.

———. *Snow Dog*. 1980. This story of a wild pup living in the wilderness will attract dog lovers. This dog's stamina and intelligence help it to survive many difficulties. The pup is finally befriended by a trapper.

Knight, Eric M. *Lassie Come-Home*. 1978. Lassie finds her way back across miles of rough mountain country to her beloved young master. The boy's family has to sell Lassie because of a financial crisis, but Lassie's determination helps her escape from the Scottish kennels and get back to England.

Konigsburg, E. L. *Altogether, One at a Time*. 1971. Four short stories make the point that some things can be both bad and good at the same time.

———. *Father's Arcane Daughter*. 1976. Caroline, an older half-sister of Winston and Heidi, had been kidnapped and presumed dead seventeen years earlier. Therefore Winston and Heidi are guarded every waking moment. Not until Caroline reappears do the other two children enjoy any freedom and happiness.

———. *From the Mixed-Up Files of Mrs. Basil E. Frankweiler*. 1967. This is a humorous tale about eleven-year-old Claudia and her younger brother who decide to run away from home and hide out in the Metropolitan Museum of Art. The mystery they "uncover" on this excursion brings them to the home of the eccentric Mrs. Basil E. Frankweiler.

Lamb, Charles and Lamb, Mary. *Tales from Shakespeare*. 1906. Written in prose, twenty of Shakespeare's plays reflect the vocabulary and style of the original works, yet older elementary children will be delighted by them.

Landin, Les. *About Policemen Around the World*. 1964. This informational book describes the duties, uniforms, and other distinctions of policemen from France, England, Italy, Japan, Chile Australia, Canada, and America (past and present).

Lang, Andrew. *Blue Fairy Book*. 1948. Many old favorite fairy tales are included in this collection of thirty-seven.

————. *Green Fairy Book*. 1948. These forty-two fairy tales come from such sources as the Grimm brothers, Madame D'Aulnoy, Paul Sebillot, and the Comte de Caylus.

————. *Red Fairy Book*. 1948. This is a collection of fairy tales with over a hundred line drawings. The folklore comes from French, Scandinavian, German, and Rumanian sources.

————. *Yellow Fairy Book*. 1948. These forty-eight folktales are derived from such countries as Germany, France, Iceland, Russia, and Eastern European countries. Also included are tales from the North American Indians.

Langton, Jane. *Her Majesty Grace Jones*. 1974. This story is set in the Great Depression years when Pop is without a job, and the car must be turned in for cash. Grace escapes to her world of fantasy where she is the heir to the British throne. She writes to King George for help but finally realizes that she was being foolish and selfish.

Lawson, Robert. *Ben and Me*. 1939. In this fanciful tale, Amos the mouse finds his way into Ben Franklin's cap and from this new dwelling serves as Ben's advisor. Of course, Amos's advice serves Ben so successfully that it makes Ben a famous man in history.

————. *Mr. Revere and I*. 1953. The accounts of Paul Revere's life and the American Revolution are told by Scheherazade, Paul Revere's horse, who advises and leads the American Revolutionary War hero to his glory. Children will love having this book read to them.

————. *Rabbit Hill*. 1944. The animal kingdom living around Rabbit Hill, especially Father, Mother, and Little Georgie Rabbit, are concerned about the new human inhabitants. With a hard winter coming, the animals are worried about whether these folks would be good providers for the animals. The animals find out all too soon that the winter will be tough.

Note: Readers can enjoy each of the following books in Lewis's Chronicles of Narnia *as a fantasy story that stands by itself. These books are listed in series order, not in alphabetical order.*

Lewis, C. S. *The Lion, the Witch, and the Wardrobe.* 1950. In this, the first of Lewis's seven Narnia stories, Lucy, Susan, Peter, and Edmund discover the world of Narnia, and Aslan dies to save the traitorous Edmund from death.

———. *Prince Caspian: The Return to Narnia.* 1951. In this second book of the series, the children help Prince Caspian and his talking beasts conquer the evil Telmarines.

———. *The Voyage of the Dawn Treader.* 1952. This intriguing tale tells how Prince Caspian and the children make their way eastward through the magic waters to the End of the World.

———. *The Silver Chair.* 1953. In this adventure the children and a marshwiggle named Puddleglum help the captive Prince Rilian escape from an underground kingdom ruled by the wicked Emerald Witch.

———. *The Horse and His Boy.* 1954. This story tells how a talking horse and a boy prince are directed by Aslan to travel from Calormen to save Narnia from invasion.

———. *The Magician's Nephew.* 1955. This book in the series explains how the four children were brought to Narnia, how the world of Narnia was created, and how Aslan gave the gift of speech to the animals who live there.

———. *The Last Battle.* 1956. In this last book of the series, the world of Narnia comes to an end, and the children are taken into a new paradise to live forever with Aslan.

Lindgren, Astrid. *Mio, My Son.* 1956. This book relates a magical story of a lonely boy who becomes a prince. He is carried away by a genie to a faraway land.

Little, Jean. *From Anna.* 1972. Things begin to change for Anna when she has to move with her family from Germany to Canada during World War II. She had been an awkward girl, sensitive, lonely, and unattractive. In Canada she realizes that she can make friends on her own, and a doctor finds that her eyesight is very poor. These events help Anna to have a new outlook on her life.

————. *Kate*. 1971. Kate, a half-Jewish friend to Emily, learns about her Jewish heritage and gains insight into relationships with her family and friends.

————. *Look Through My Window*. 1970. Emily, an only child, moves with her family to an eighteen-room house so that they can take in four of her "wild" cousins. Emily discovers that living in a large family is both fun and rewarding, especially after she meets Kate, who becomes a good friend.

————. *Spring Begins in March*. 1966. Meg, the youngest in the family, feels immense pressure from home and school burdens. With the discovery of her grandmother's diary comes greater understanding of Grandma and of Meg herself. Girls will enjoy reading about a character with similar struggles that they face.

Lofting, Hugh. *The Story of Dr. Dolittle*. 1920. Doctor Dolittle has so many pets in his house that his patients will not come to him; therefore, he treats only his pets. He sails to Africa upon hearing that an epidemic is breaking out among the monkeys there. These stories were actually written to the author's children while he served in the Irish Guards.

————. *The Voyages of Dr. Dolittle*. 1922. A Newbery winner, this story relates Tommy Stubbins's friendship with Doctor Dolittle. The two of them go on a voyage of discovery on which a series of unusual events occur. Doctor Dolittle discovers the key to the language of shellfish, he creates a scene as matador, and he is crowned king by some natives on an island.

Low, Elizabeth. *Snug in the Snow*. 1963. Jamie and his aunt are waiting to leave tomorrow after closing up their New England cottage for the winter. But a snowstorm is moving in. Jamie hopes that it snows enough to keep his aunt and him from being able to leave so that he can see the snow, feel it, and watch his animal friends find their food in it.

Lowry, Lois. *Number the Stars*. 1989. Annemarie Johansen, a ten-year-old girl, learns what true bravery is as she and her family struggle to survive the German occupation of Copenhagen, Denmark, in 1943.

McCloskey, Robert. *Homer Price*. 1943. In this episodic tale the charming character Homer Price uses his intelligence and common sense to unravel mysteries.

McClung, Robert M. *Black Jack: Last of the Big Alligators.* 1967. Young readers will learn about alligators by personally getting to know Black Jack. Included are the accounts of Black Jack's birth and the dangers he faces from other animals, hunters, and the weather. Children will enjoy reading about this fearsome reptile.

―――. *Buzztail: The Story of a Rattlesnake.* 1958. Buzztail lets the reader personally get to know the timber rattlesnakes. Its multicolored diamond-shaped scales, its rattles, and its three-quarter-inch fangs mark it distinctly. A young farm boy is bitten by Buzztail in this account, and the emergency steps of action are outlined.

―――. *Honker: The Story of a Wild Goose.* 1965. Honker, a Canadian goose, travels along the Mississippi flyway during migration. This account of Honker and his flock reveals how dangerous the flight to a wintering area in the southern United States can be.

―――. *Ladybug.* 1966. The life cycle of the ladybug is explained in this colorful, easy text. The reader will learn to appreciate the fact that this beetle eats insects which are harmful to plants.

―――. *Luna: The Story of a Moth.* 1957. This story will interest youngsters as they learn of the luna moth's short life cycle. In only a few days, a female luna moth lays several hundred eggs. Only one of them survives from a cocoon to a caterpillar to a pupa and finally becomes a moth.

―――. *Redbird: The Story of a Cardinal.* 1968. The many stages of a cardinal's life are depicted: hatching, learning to fly, mating, nest building, and egg laying. Students learn about the danger facing baby birds; one of the birds is seized by an enemy and destroyed.

―――. *Tiger: The Story of a Swallowtail Butterfly.* 1953. This simple text tells the story of Swallowtail's first year. As he sheds his skin several times, each new skin shows a new design. After a long winter as a chrysalis, the skin splits open and the disheveled creature becomes a perfect tiger swallowtail butterfly.

————. *Vulcan: The Story of a Bald Eagle.* 1955. Vulcan is born in the crown of an old tree. At four months his wings expand to seven feet. After the eagle finds his mate, they build their nest and return each year until the nest is destroyed by lumbermen. This informational book, which reads like a story, will interest many children.

MacDonald, George. *The Golden Key.* 1976. This fairy-tale adventure takes Tangle and Mossy into a mysterious land. They separate where Tangle meets three old men and where Mossy begins to grow wiser and more beautiful. When they are reunited, they reach the rainbow and finally the "country whence the shadows fall."

————. *The Light Princess.* 1977. A spiteful aunt curses her infant niece in this fantasy. As a result, the child weighs nothing. The one thing she can enjoy is swimming, since her lack of gravity is no handicap in water. This ability allows her to meet a prince who brings her happiness ever after.

————. *The Princess and Curdie.* 1978. In this sequel to *The Princess and the Goblin,* Princess Irene lives with her father in the capital city of Gwynstorm. But danger follows her there, and Curdie must set out to rescue her.

————. *The Princess and the Goblin.* 1951. Curdie and Princess Irene, who live on the side of a mountain, encounter some bewildering experiences. The goblins who live in the caverns below the mines draw the two of them into danger. The children are led successfully out of danger with a magic ball of thread.

McGinley, Phylis. *The Plain Princess.* 1945. Spoiled Princess Esmeralda has a plain outward appearance, stemming from her sour disposition. An unfashionable woman answers the challenge of transforming this girl into a beautiful young lady. The woman kindly insists on Esmeralda's accepting responsibility and overcoming her selfishness. As a result, Esmeralda's countenance "magically" becomes appealing in this modern fairy tale.

MacGregor, Ellen. *Miss Pickerell Goes to Mars*. 1951. This science fiction tale combines fantasy and fact that enliven children's curiosity. Miss Pickerell returns from vacation to find that a rocket ship is on her property. Before long she is aboard the rocket and finds herself on Mars. Humorous illustrations enhance the book's appeal.

Mason, Miriam E. *Katie Kittenheart*. 1957. During the year she spends with Grandma on her farm, Katie has special fun with a stray cat and a family of mice. These animals help her prove her courage and responsibility.

Note: Readers can enjoy each of the following three books in the Bracken series as a fanciful story that stands by itself. These books are listed in series order, not in alphabetical order.

Massi, Jeri. *The Bridge*. Bob Jones University Press, 1986. In book one of the Bracken series, Princess Rosalynn helps to save the kingdom of Bracken.

————. *Crown and Jewel*. Bob Jones University Press, 1987. In book two of the Bracken series, Young Princess Rosewyn stumbles onto a secret plot against her father's crown.

————. *The Two Collars*. Bob Jones University Press, 1988. In this final book of the Bracken Trilogy, Krea, a seven-year-old slave, finds friendship, excitement, and danger.

Note: Readers can enjoy each of the following Massi books in the Peabody series as an adventure story that stands by itself. These books are listed in series order, not in alphabetical order.

————. *Derwood, Inc*. Bob Jones University Press, 1986. In this humorous story, the first of the Peabody series, a brother and sister detective team find adventure as close as the local mattress store.

————. *A Dangerous Game*. Bob Jones University Press, 1986. In this second Peabody book, Scruggs Grady gets caught up in an international spy ring.

————. *Treasure in the Yukon.* Bob Jones University Press, 1986. In the third Peabody book, Jack Derwood and Scruggs Grady search for lost gold.

————. *Courage by Darkness.* Bob Jones University Press, 1987. Jean Derwood is the focus of the fourth Peabody story. Her dreams of doing something heroic when the family goes to Alabama actually come true.

————. *Llamas on the Loose.* Bob Jones University Press, 1988. In the fifth Peabody book, Penny, Jack, and Scruggs find plenty of adventure while helping Doc Ericson on his new llama farm.

————. *Abandoned.* Bob Jones University Press, 1989. The last book in the series finds the Peabody gang stranded in the wilderness of New England.

Meadowcroft, Enid L. *By Secret Railway.* 1948. David Morgan befriends a freed slave boy in Chicago. A boarder with the Morgan family kidnaps the boy so that he can get the reward money. David proves his friendship by making a connection for the boy with the Underground Railroad. This story provides good historical information concerning Chicago in the latter half of the nineteenth century.

Means, Florence Crannell. *The Rains Will Come.* 1954. Lohmay, a Hopi Indian boy, is destined to become his people's religious leader in succession to his uncle. Drought and despair lead Lohmay into an ordeal with his gods. This paganism can be used to show the need of all to hear the gospel of the one true, living God.

Miles, Miska. *Uncle Fonzo's Ford.* 1968. Uncle Fonzo always manages to bungle things. If he picks Effie up at school, he is unable to get the top up on his 1910 model car. If he tries to fix a clock, it chimes fifteen times. But when he spills paint on Effie's new hat, he thinks of a solution that makes Effie accept and love Uncle Fonzo much more easily.

Morey, Walt. *Gloomy Gus.* 1970. Eric finds a bear cub in some woods near his house. Eric wants to keep the cub, but his father will not let him. With the help of his prospector friend, Ten-Day Watson, Eric and his beloved pet Gus are eventually reunited.

————. *Kavik, the Wolf Dog.* 1968. Kavik, a dog of one-quarter wolf lineage, wins the North American Sled Dog Derby. Numerous hardships overcome Kavik, including the loss of his mate. But Kavik is able finally to return to the one master who truly loved him.

————. *Runaway Stallion.* 1973. Known as Fly-by, this famous racehorse escapes and goes to the High Cascade Mountains in Oregon. He is found by Jeff Hunter, who has to rescue the horse from a bog. Jeff renames the horse Goblin, and together they face many adventures, tragedies, and victories.

Mowat, Farley, *Owls in the Family.* 1961. When Billy and his friends set out to have an owl as a pet, their adventures begin. They find Wol, a baby great horned owl whose nest has been destroyed by a storm. Within a few weeks, Wol is joined by Weeps, also an orphan whom Billy saves from certain death. The two owls become part of the family, pulling practical jokes on the family dog and generally getting into trouble.

Nye, Julie. *In My Uncle's House.* Bob Jones University Press, 1986. God uses a new friend and a magnificent horse to ease Travis McLarren's bitterness.

————. *Scout.* Bob Jones University Press, 1987. An injured dog, Scout, brings mystery and friendship into Jeff Wingate's life.

O'Brien, Robert C. *Mrs. Frisby and the Rats of NIMH.* 1971. This Newbery winner is seen by some as a commentary on life today, but children will simply enjoy the science fiction. Mrs. Frisby seeks advice from the rats concerning her mouse son, Timothy, who is sick. She learns that the rats had been part of an experiment at NIMH, and now they can read and write. Their advice helps her and she is able, in turn, to help them escape.

Orton, Helen Fuller. *The Treasure in the Little Trunk.* 1932. Set in New York State in 1832, this story is a fascinating mystery. Patty Armstrong's gold beads belonged to her grandmother. What happens to these beads and an adventuresome journey into the wilderness provide excitement for the reader.

Ransome, Arthur. *Swallows and Amazons*. 1931. This imaginative story has Roger, John, Titty, and Susan on numerous adventures finding buried treasure and finding Robinson Crusoe, Friday, and Captain Flint. These discoveries are made as they spend a summer on an island, sailing whenever and wherever they like.

Reid, J. Calvin. *Bird Life in Wington*. 1948. These simple stories that can be enjoyed by young and old provide principles for Christian living. The characters are familiar birds which illustrate human faults in humorous and skillful ways.

Repp, Gloria. *The Secret of the Golden Cowrie*. Bob Jones University Press, 1988. Connie Lawrence listens eagerly when Aunt Laura shares a puzzling secret with her.

Rich, Louise Dickinson. *Star Island Boy*. 1968. Larry is an eleven-year-old orphan who is sent with seven other wards of the state to live with a family off the coast of Maine. At last he finds a real home.

Rounds, Glen. *The Blind Colt*. 1960. A wild colt is born blind and grows up with a band of mustangs. A ten-year-old boy adopts and trains the colt. The story is a good example of perseverance in spite of a handicap and of compassion for an animal.

St. John, Patricia. *Star of Light*. 1953. Kinza, a rejected blind girl in Morocco, is kindly received as a daughter by a missionary woman. Hamid, Kinza's brother, also receives food and hears Bible stories from the missionary. Hamid is saved through this ministry, and Kinza is given hope as she attends an English school for blind children.

———. *Treasures of the Snow*. 1951. Annette bravely and lovingly assumes the responsibility of rearing her newborn brother Dani. Later Lucien teases young Dani and causes Dani to hurt his leg. Annette becomes Lucien's bitter enemy until Lucien fights a blizzard to get help from a doctor for Dani. Both Lucien and Annette find true peace when they accept Christ as their Savior.

Salten, Felix. *Bambi*. 1970. Bambi is a young fawn enjoying the forest and curious elements around him. Avoiding sentimentality, the author paints a realistic picture of the struggles Bambi faces with his enemy—man.

Sandburg, Carl. *Rootabaga Stories.* 1922. These humorous nonsensical stories can be effectively read aloud. They reveal a picture of America's Midwest, but not without whim and symbolism.

Sawyer, Ruth. *Roller Skates.* 1964. Lucinda, a ten-year-old girl, explores New York on roller skates in the 1890s. She makes several friends as she passes by. This story is based on true accounts in the author's life.

Selden, George. *The Cricket in Times Square.* 1960. Chester is a musical cricket that comes to New York's Times Square. He makes three new friends—Mario, a newsstand operator; Tucker, a Broadway mouse; and Harry, a wise cat—with whom he experiences the joy of special friendships.

———. *A Tree for Peter.* 1941. Children enjoy this story about a shantytown's reformation at Christmas time. A hobo brings happiness to Peter, who is handicapped and lonely. The man also helps Peter overcome his timidity and fears.

Seredy, Kate. *The Singing Tree.* 1940. Written as a sequel to *The Good Master,* the story for this Newbery honor book is set on a Hungarian farm during World War I. The Good Master's son turns the farm into a place of refuge for many needy people, including German orphans.

———. *The White Stag.* 1938. This Newbery winner is the legendary account of the founding of Hungary. Both a red eagle and a white stag lead the people into their promised land.

Shannon, Monica. *Dobry.* 1962. Dobry, a young Bulgarian boy who wants to become a sculptor, is encouraged by his grandfather to continue to fulfill his goal.

Sorensen, Virginia. *Miracles on Maple Hill.* 1972. Marly and her family move to the country in hopes of improving her father's health. Many miracles occur in the Pennsylvania maple sugar country, including miracles that are wrought by love in this family setting.

Spyri, Johanna. *Heidi.* 1945. This famous story of a Swiss girl and her love for the goats she attends in the beautiful highlands of the Swiss Alps has been enjoyed by children everywhere.

Sterling, Dorothy. *Freedom Train: The Story of Harriet Tubman.* 1954. This is a biography of a slave, Harriet Tubman, her escape, and the phenomenal feat of transporting groups of slaves to freedom. Also detailed are Harriet's efforts as a spy, scout, and nurse during the Civil War.

Taylor, Sydney. *All-of-a-Kind Family.* 1951. A Jewish family is depicted in this story of five girls. Although poor, the family shares a wealth of love and understanding. They explore the library, enjoy midnight snacks, play in their father's shop, and participate in Jewish holidays.

————. *More All-of-a-Kind Family.* 1954. A sequel to *All-of-a-kind Family,* this book can stand alone, but it is greatly enhanced if one has read the first one. With interest, the reader follows the celebration of Jewish holidays and other activities by believable characters.

————. *A Papa Like Everyone Else.* 1966. Gisella, separated from her father for five years, hopes to be reunited with him, but World War I prevents it.

Terhune, Albert Payson. *Lad: A Dog.* 1919. Dog lovers will enjoy this account of a collie that lived on the author's estate. This is considered one of the best-loved dog stories of all time.

Thomson, Andy. *Renegade in the Hills.* Bob Jones University Press, 1989. Josiah Eagle tries to keep a greedy rancher from capturing him.

————. *Sheriff at Waterstop.* Bob Jones University Press, 1986. Waterstop needs cleaning up, and Bret knows that Pa is the man to do it.

Thurber, James. *Many Moons.* 1943. A young princess falls ill and thinks she will get well only if she can obtain the moon. As she sees the moon, she thinks it is small and is made of gold. The court jester solves her problems. This picture storybook won the 1944 Caldecott Medal.

Travers, P[amela] L. *Mary Poppins.* 1981. Mary Poppins becomes the British nursemaid for the Banks family. However, there are clues that things are a bit unusual when she arrives via an east wind. She brings much adventure to Jane and Michael Banks with excursions to magical places.

Vandevenne, Jean. *Some Summer!* Bob Jones University Press, 1987. Charlie Scott has a great idea for the summer, but then Aunt Essie comes for a visit.

Voelker, Joyce. *Dear Terry.* Bob Jones University Press, 1990. Joyce doesn't know what to expect when Granny finds her a pen pal who lives in Vermont.

Walley, Susan. *Best of Friends.* Bob Jones University Press, 1989. Katie Crawford wants to be friends with Renee, the talented new girl in town.

Watkins, Dawn. *Jenny Wren.* Bob Jones University Press, 1986. A shy young girl comes to her new foster home with misgivings.

————. *Medallion.* Bob Jones University Press, 1985. Who shall be worthy to rule Gadalla? He must prove himself by winning the gold medallion. In this intriguing fantasy, Prince Trave, sure of his rights and disgusted with the selfish uncle who reigns in his stead, vows to get the medallion back. The only problem, he thinks, is to find it.

White, E. B. *Charlotte's Web.* 1952. In this barnyard setting with Charlotte, the spider, and Wilbur, the pig, Charlotte is able to save the pig's life by spinning messages in her web. Young children love this story of Fern's barnyard.

————. *The Trumpet of the Swans.* 1973. Louis is a trumpeter swan, but he is born without a voice. Even though he learns to read and write, without his voice he cannot court Serena, the lovely lady of his choice. Louis's father tries to help by stealing a trumpet for him. He travels about the country as a professional musician, earning enough to pay for the trumpet. He does win Serena's heart.

Wiggin, Kate Douglas. *Rebecca of Sunnybrook Farm.* 1925. Undaunted by the somber home of her two maiden aunts, Rebecca wins everyone's affection. Her friendliness and imagination make her appealing in this humorous New England setting.

Note: Readers can enjoy each of the following books in the Little House series as a story that stands by itself. These books are listed in series order, not in alphabetical order.

Wilder, Laura Ingalls. *Little House in the Big Woods.* 1953. This first book in a series relates the life of Laura and Mary and their parents in the Big Woods of Wisconsin. Their log cabin was miles away from any neighbors. Struggles with blizzards, wolves, and loneliness were certain, but Laura finds plenty of adventure in this western way of life.

———. *Little House on the Prairie.* 1953. In this second "Little House" book, Laura goes with her family into Indian country.

———. *Farmer Boy.* 1953. Almanzo Wilder's boyhood is described in this "Little House" segment. His experiences on his father's farm in upper New York State almost a hundred years ago describe rural life.

———. *On the Banks of Plum Creek.* 1953. After a move to Minnesota, the Ingalls family contends with tough battles from nature. A blizzard and a grasshopper plague are the enemies in this book.

———. *By the Shores of Silver Lake.* 1953. This segment of Laura's life finds her with her family on a Dakota homestead, miles from any other people.

———. *These Happy Golden Years.* 1953. This last "Little House" book describes Laura's school teaching and her marriage.

———. *The First Four Years.* 1971. This segment of Laura Wilder's life relates the events in the early years of her marriage to Almanzo. As they fight to keep their homestead claim in South Dakota, they find joy in their new daughter Rose, and in the little delights of nature around them.

Williams, Connie. *Right-Hand Man.* Bob Jones University Press, 1992. Sam Rogers is Mom-Jo's right-hand man, and he has to take a careful look at her prospects for a husband. But what happens when the wrong man shows up?

Yates, Elizabeth. *Mountain Born.* Bob Jones University Press, 1943, 1993. Wolves, weather, a black lamb, a trusty dog—all are part of young Peter's life on a mountain farm. His best friend is Benj, a wise old shepherd, who teaches him to care for the sprightly lamb that becomes his own special pet, his cosset. As Biddy grows into her place as leader of the flock, Peter grows too, learning the skills and joys of a shepherd's life.

Grade 6 - Grade 8

Alcott, Louisa May. *Eight Cousins*. 1875. In this engaging Alcott story, one girl and seven boy cousins find plenty of adventure and a good deal of mischief to keep them—and the reader—occupied.

———. *Jo's Boys*. 1886. In this, the last of Alcott's family books, the "little men" are in their twenties. The boys' school has now become a fine college, and Mr. March, Laurie, Amy, and the widowed Meg have all been drawn to Plumfield, reuniting the family once again.

———. *Little Men*. 1871. In this Alcott classic, Jo and her German husband have established a boys' school called Plumfield. Along with the boys, Meg's twins, Demi and Daisy, and a tomboy named Nan keep Plumfield in an uproar.

———. *Little Women*. 1862. In this the most famous of Alcott's classics, Victorian family life is portrayed with poignance and humor. The four March girls are vivid, compelling characters whose "growing up" experiences still have universal appeal.

———. *Rose in Bloom*. 1876. This sequel to *Eight Cousins* centers on Rose's homecoming. The cousins are now all "grown up," though some of the antics reveal that there is still a good deal of childhood in them yet.

Aldrich, Thomas B. *The Story of a Bad Boy*. 1951. This is an adventurous, funny, and sometimes moving account of a young boy growing up in Portsmouth, New Hampshire, in the 1800s.

Arnold, Elliott. *A Kind of Secret Weapon*. 1969. This story is about a young boy named Peter Andersen who must learn the meaning of loyalty, patriotism, and sacrifice as he works with his parents in the Danish Resistance against the Nazi occupation.

Burnford, Sheila. *The Incredible Journey.* 1961. This is a classic animal realism story about the journey of two dogs and a cat through the northwestern part of Ontario, Canada. When the animals' new owner, John Longridge, leaves for vacation, the animals set out to find their former owners. Their 250-mile journey is filled with adventure, and their story is one that animal lovers will thoroughly enjoy.

Byars, Betsy. *The Summer of the Swans.* 1970. In this Newbery award winning story, Sara longs to be as beautiful as her older sister Wanda. This longing makes her dissatisfied with just about everything until her younger brother Charlie, who is brain-damaged, disappears. Only then is she reminded of what is truly important and of the unique value of every individual.

Davis, Rebecca. *With Daring Faith.* Bob Jones University Press, 1987. This biography of Amy Carmichael shows how her strong faith and indomitable courage aided her in her mission work and in her attempts to rescue Indian children from Hindu temples.

Dickens, Charles. *A Christmas Carol.* 1843. In this classic Dickens tale, the miser Scrooge receives a visit from his former partner Marley—who has been "dead as a doornail" for several years. The fettered Marley informs Scrooge that he will be receiving three more "visitors." These visitors take the old miser on myriad adventures, the result of which brings the "squeezing, grasping, clutching, covetous old Scrooge" back to his senses.

Eggleston, Edward. *The Hoosier Schoolmaster.* 1959. In this intriguing story, Eggleston draws on his personal experiences as a Methodist circuit riding preacher for his detailed, realistic portrayal of Indian backwoods life in the 1800s.

Fleischman, Paul. *Joyful Noise: Poems for Two Voices.* 1988. In this wonderful book of poetry, Fleischman uses vivid imagery and wonderful imaginative comparisons to recreate the "joyful noise" of a myriad of insects from bookworms to butterflies.

George, Jean Craighead. *My Side of the Mountain.* 1988. This is an exciting survival story about a young boy named Sam Gribley who decides to go out on his own. Having learned from his father about his great-grandfather Gribley's land in the Catskill Mountains, Sam sets out. After a fairly uneventful journey, he finds himself deep in the forest—lost, hungry, and exhausted. As time passes, however, Sam succeeds in creating a life for himself. The only problem he cannot solve is loneliness. But the coming of spring brings a surprise that solves this problem as well.

Gray, Elizabeth Janet. *Adam of the Road.* 1942. This is an intriguing tale set in thirteenth-century England about a young boy, Adam Quartermayne, who travels across England with his minstrel father. During these travels, Adam makes many friends and experiences many difficulties, all of which help him to mature.

James, Will. *Smoky.* 1926. This award-winning classic shows how a cow pony relates to western life.

Juster, Norton. *The Phantom Tollbooth.* 1961. In this whimsical tale, Milo, a young boy who has a hard time figuring out what to do with himself, discovers a phantom tollbooth and sets out on an adventure that he—and the reader—will long remember.

Keith, Harold. *Rifles for Watie.* 1957. In this Civil War story, Jefferson Davis Bussey, a farm boy, joins the Union army. While a scout, he is captured by and forced to fight for Stand Watie's rebels. He also falls in love with Lucie, a rebel girl.

Kipling, Rudyard. *The Jungle Book.* 1894-95. The British novelist Somerset Maugham said that in *The Jungle Book* Kipling's "great and varied gifts find their most brilliant expression." This classic work captures the imagination on the first encounter and grows in richness and meaning with every reading.

Kjelgaard, Jim [James Arthur]. *Big Red.* 1973. This is a moving story about a champion Irish setter named Big Red and the part he plays in helping his young trainer, Danny, in his struggle toward maturity.

Latham, Jean Lee. *Carry On, Mr. Bowditch.* 1955. This fictionalized biography of Nathaniel Bowditch is a sea story to be remembered. Bowditch is known for his pioneering in scientific navigation procedures. His story is full of adventure and provides a vivid impression of how life was in the late 1700s and early 1800s.

McCauley, David. *Cathedral.* 1973. This is a highly detailed, interesting picture book which not only tells but also shows how a cathedral was constructed.

MacDonald, George. *The Boyhood of Ranald Bannerman.* 1869. Edited for young readers by Dan Hamilton, 1897. This is a rollicking adventure story about a young boy growing up in the heather hills of Scotland.

Meader, Stephen W. *Boy with a Pack.* 1939. Seventeen-year-old Bill Crawford peddles "Yankee notions" in Vermont, New York, Pennsylvania, and Ohio in 1837. His journeys also bring him into contact with horse thieves, canal boats, and the Underground Railroad.

———. *Clear for Action.* 1940. In the War of 1812, a Maine boy, Jeff Robbins, ships out on a cargo schooner bound for Cuba. But he and others are soon captured and impressed on a British frigate.

———. *Whaler 'Round the Horn.* 1950. This is an interesting story about a New Hampshire farm boy whose whaling career is brought to an unexpected end. After several adventures, he eventually finds a new life in Hawaii.

Meigs, Cornelia. *Invincible Louisa.* 1933. This is interesting biographical fiction about the life of the famous author Louisa May Alcott. The revelation of Alcott's family life will provide fascinating insights into her fiction.

Montgomery, L. M. *Anne of Green Gables.* 1908. This is the heart-warming story of the orphan, Anne, who finds a home with an elderly brother and sister. Anne, a redheaded tomboy who loves to dream, is a winsome girl who is at times hilariously funny. Her story is a classic that is full of adventure and memorable characters.

————. *Anne of Avonlea.* 1909. Anne, the tomboy, has come of age and is now a teacher. But maturity has in no way diminished Anne's indomitable spirit, her penchant for the dramatic, nor her heart-warming personality.

Morey, Walt. *Gentle Ben.* 1965. This is a classic tale for animal lovers. The story is set in Alaska and tells of a young man named Mark Anderson who befriends a huge brown bear.

O'Dell, Scott. *The Hawk That Dare Not Hunt by Day.* Bob Jones University Press, 1987. This fictional biography on the life of William Tyndale is told from young Tom Barton's viewpoint. Tom and his Uncle Jack smuggle Tyndale's newly translated Bibles into England. Their adventures keep the reader turning the page, and the lessons Tom learns prove equally engaging.

————. *Island of the Blue Dolphins.* 1960. Karana, the heroine of this nature story, is a young girl who has been left alone on her island. Her careful resourcefulness enables her to survive despite the dangers that surround her.

————. *The King's Fifth.* 1966. During the Spanish exploration of the Americas, fifteen-year-old Esteban is employed as a cartographer. In this adventurous historical tale, Esteban's work takes him on an exciting and dangerous journey in search of the fabled gold of Cibola.

Pyle, Howard. *Men of Iron.* Bob Jones University Press, 1993. This classic historical novel set in medieval England is about a young teen-age boy who, despite grave obstacles, rises from menial service to become a knight.

Rawlings, Marjorie Kinnan. *The Yearling.* 1938. This is a moving "coming of age" story about a boy named Jody Baxter and his pet fawn and their experiences in the scrub pine area of Florida.

Seredy, Kate. *The Good Master.* 1935. This is a moving epiphany story about a Hungarian girl, Kate, who comes to live with her uncle (the Good Master) on his farm.

Serraillier, Ian. *The Silver Sword.* 1959. This is a fascinating, compelling story about three Polish children who are searching for their lost father. Their search is a dangerous one and one which takes them across Europe during World War II.

Speare, Elizabeth George. *The Bronze Bow.* 1961. In this story, Daniel, desiring revenge for the murder of his parents by the Romans, decides to join Rosh's outlaw band in the hills. But a meeting with Christ changes his life.

————. *The Witch of Blackbird Pond.* 1958. Katherine "Kit" Tyler, an English girl from Barbados, comes to Connecticut unannounced to live with her Puritan uncle and aunt. Her different ways not only make her feel like an outcast but also place her in grave danger.

Sperry, Armstrong. *Call It Courage.* 1968. In this Newbery Medal winner of 1941, a Polynesian boy who fears the water and gains the scorn of his people must redeem himself by an act of courage.

Stevenson, Robert Louis. *Treasure Island.* 1883. In this classic a young boy, Jim, narrates his many adventures with pirates and their quest for booty.

Street, James. *Goodbye, My Lady.* 1941. Skeeter lives with his Uncle Jess in the Mississippi swamps and finds a rare breed of hunting dog. Skeeter patiently trains the dog whom he has named Lady, and the two become close. The day comes, however, when Skeeter must choose between his love for Lady and doing what is right.

Sutcliff, Rosemary. *Dawn Wind.* 1961. An intriguing story of a Britisher, Owain, who survives the battle with the Saxons at Aquae Sulis and helps a young girl, Regina, regain her health.

————. *Eagle of the Ninth.* 1954. In this Sutcliff story, a young centurion embarks on a difficult and dangerous quest in Roman Britain.

————. *Knight's Fee.* 1960. This story takes place in England after the Battle of Hastings. The action revolves around Randal, a kennel boy who was won in a chess game and given to a knight to raise.

————. *Lantern Bearers.* 1950. Aquila, one of the Roman soldiers to leave Britain with the Roman auxiliaries, finds that he has grown accustomed to and longs for Britain.

————. *The Mark of the Horse Lord.* 1965. In this adventure story, Phaedrus, a former slave and Roman gladiator, becomes a prince of the Dalriadain.

————. *The Silver Branch.* 1957. In Roman Britain, a young centurion and a young surgeon bring back the lost standard, the Eagle of the Ninth, into a battle.

————. *Simon.* 1980. The scene is the English Civil War in Oliver Cromwell's time. Simon Carey and his best friend, Amias Hannaford, fight on opposite sides.

————. *Warrior Scarlet.* 1958. Set during the Bronze Age, this is the story of young Drem who must prove his manhood.

Trease, Geoffrey. *Cue for Treason.* 1941. In this mystery, set in Elizabethan England, Peter Brownrigg, a beginning actor, befriends Kit Kirkstone, a girl playing boy's parts in English plays. Together they help to uncover a plot against the queen.

————. *Message to Hadrian.* 1955. This historical story takes place when the Roman Empire was at its height. Young Paul from the wild island of Britain travels to Rome in the excitement and urgency of outwitting the Roman "Mafia."

————. *Web of Traitors.* 1953. This story, set in ancient Athens, tells of Alex who discovers a plot by the Spartans to overthrow the state.

Tunis, John R. *Duke Decides.* 1941. Duke Wellington, the "Iron Duke," is captain of the track team at Harvard and goes on to the Olympics in Berlin.

————. *Go, Team, Go.* 1954. A championship basketball team from an Indiana high school has a star player expelled for gambling. After an unexpected loss and resignation of the first string, the substitutes take the floor.

————. *Silence over Dunkerque.* 1962. Sergeant Williams and one of his men are left behind in the evacuation of British troops from Dunkirk in 1940. Rescued by a young French girl, Williams is eventually reunited with his family.

Ullman, James Ramsey. *Banner in the Sky.* 1954. This is a compelling adventure story about a sixteen-year-old named Rudi who attempts to climb the highest mountain in Switzerland.

Verne, Jules. *Around the World in Eighty Days.* 1873. In this delightful classic, Phineas Fogg and his valet make their famous journey around the world.

————. *Journey to the Center of the Earth.* 1864. In this science fiction tale, Axel, his uncle, and a guide travel to the earth's center through an extinct volcano in Iceland.

————. *Twenty Thousand Leagues Under the Sea.* 1870. In this, another of Verne's science fiction classics, the brilliant scientist, Captain Nemo, explores undersea life in his submarine, *The Nautilus.*

Wyss, Johann David. *The Swiss Family Robinson.* 1813. This enduring tale vividly recounts the ingenuity, adventures, and antics of a Swiss family forced to survive on a desert island after being shipwrecked.

Yates, Elizabeth. *Amos Fortune, Free Man.* 1950. At-Mun, a young African prince, is captured by slave traders and brought to Massachusetts in 1710. As a slave, he wins others' respect by his honesty and competence. After buying his freedom, he touches many lives.

————. *Sound Friendships.* Bob Jones University Press, 1992. Willa Macy, who cannot hear, meets Honey, a Hearing Dog. Together they find a new world of independence and security.

Grade 6 - Grade 8:
Books for Analysis and Discussion

Note: *The following books might be used on the junior high level for the purpose of developing discernment in reading. Before being recommended, however, each book should be previewed by a parent or a teacher to determine its value for the individual student. The student's reading should be followed by a guided discussion that addresses the issues mentioned in the annotation and any other issues of concern to the parent or teacher. (For additional information on evaluating books with these purposes in mind, see pp. 157-66.)*

Armstrong, William H. *Sounder.* 1969. This is a compelling story about a black sharecropping family during the 1930s. The story provides an accurate, vivid portrayal of the circumstances faced by pre-civil-rights black families. The overall tone of the story is positive but the seriousness of the themes needs to be discussed.

Clifford, Eth. *The Remembering Box.* 1985. A well-written book about the relationship between a Jewish boy and his aging grandmother. The relationship between the grandmother and grandson is very positive, and the death of the grandmother is dealt with in a realistic but nonsentimental way. The story avoids the sensationalism that is prevalent in much of children's literature today. However, the concept of death apart from a Christian context should be addressed.

Forbes, Esther. *Johnny Tremain.* 1944. This classic revolutionary war story centers on a young silversmith apprentice named Johnny Tremain. Through a tragic accident Johnny changes from a cocky, immature boy to a humble, courageous young man. Although the moral tone of the story is positive, there are a few objectionable elements (e.g., profanity) which should be addressed in their context.

Henry, Marguerite. *King of the Wind.* 1948. This moving story won the 1949 Newbery Medal. It is the story of Sham, a beautiful red stallion born in the Sultan of Morocco's stable, and of a stable boy named Agba. Their adventures take them from the Sahara to France and finally to England. This is a beautifully written book, and although racing and racehorses are included in the plot, these elements play a minor role. The primary action focuses on the relationship between Agba and Sham. However, such issues as horse racing would need to be addressed in the context of the story.

Kelly, Eric. *The Trumpeter of Kracow.* 1928. This 1929 Newbery Award winning fiction is set in Poland during the middle ages. The story opens with action and continues to hold interest to the last page. The Tartar invasion of Kracow and other historical moments are recorded with vivid, exciting detail. There are, however, some objectionable elements (e.g., magic and superstition) which should be discussed in the historical context of the story.

Lisle, Janet Taylor. *Afternoon of the Elves.* 1989. This story, though powerful, should be used only if the maturity level of the reader will allow him to glean positive lessons from a guided discussion of the story. The novel shows the vivid contrast between a child who has a secure, nurturing home environment and one who must face life without these advantages. The major drawback to the story is its resolution. Without a Christian context, there was no way to end the book without a lingering note of despair. This point must be discussed if the story is to be of value. The primary benefit of reading such a book is that it may broaden a child's perspective, helping him see what some children must face in a fallen world. Such a perspective can be used to develop a greater compassion and sensitivity toward those who need Christ.

MacLachlan, Patricia. *The Facts and Fictions of Minna Pratt.* 1988. An intriguing, winsome story about a young girl growing up. The overall tone of the story is positive. There are, however, some objectionable elements which should be addressed (e.g., the erroneous concept of prayer presented in the story).

Naylor, Phyllis Reynolds. *Shiloh.* This is a moving story about a young boy who tries to reconcile his love for a dog with his responsibility to do what is right. The resolution of the story has merit, but there are also some ethical questions that need to be addressed (e.g.,profanity, lying, the mistreatment of animals, the rights that come with personal property,and the concept of God). A good companion book to study with this one is James Street's *Goodbye, My Lady.* Street's book deals with some of the same issues, but reconciles them in a more clear-cut, ethical manner. The concept of God presented in this story should also be discussed.

Paterson, Katherine. *The Great Gilly Hopkins.* 1978. This is a realistic look at a foster child's life and the problems such a child faces. The overall tone of the story is positive, and Bible reading and other religious activities are, for the most part, dealt with in a satisfactory manner. Also, the issue of understanding people who may at first seem unappealing is handled admirably. The ending, though not "happily ever after," is hopeful. Besides the serious subject matter of the book, there are also a few objectionable elements that should be discussed in the context of the story (e.g., profanity).

Taylor, Mildred D. *Roll of Thunder, Hear My Cry.* 1976. This is a 1977 Newbery Medal winner which provides a compelling portrayal of a black sharecropping family in Mississippi during the '50s. Some disturbing elements (e.g., burnings) which are historically accurate need discussion. Much, however, can be learned from the book. It is especially valuable for generating discussion on various historical and ethical issues.

Twain, Mark. *The Adventures of Tom Sawyer.* Although not regarded as highly as *Huckleberry Finn, Tom Sawyer* is enjoyed more by children. The adventures of Tom and Huck are exciting and often amusing. There are, however, several issues involving the behavior of the characters which should be addressed after the stories are read.

Grade 8 - Grade 12

Aldrich, Bess Streeter. *A Lantern in Her Hand*. 1928. The American prairie settler's life is seen in the life of Abbie Deal, a devoted wife and mother, who helps to bring a large family through hardships.

Austen, Jane. *Emma*. 1816. This is the story of a girl whose matchmaking attempts meet with little success and yet who becomes endeared to the reader.

————. *Mansfield Park*. 1814. This is an intriguing story about Fanny Price who, although materially poor, is morally superior to the more wealthy owners of Mansfield Park.

————. *Persuasion*. 1818. This is Austen's last completed novel. The heroine, Anne Elliott, and the hero, Captain Wentworth, must overcome myriad social obstacles before their eventual marriage.

————. *Pride and Prejudice*. 1813. The gradual union of two people comes about after pride and prejudice are no longer paramount obstacles.

————. *Sense and Sensibility*. 1811. The two heroines of this story, Elinor and Marriane Dashwood, find themselves fatherless and penniless and defrauded of a more substantial income by their stepbrother John Dashwood. Their circumstances change, however, when the two fall in love with two handsome and dashing young men.

Bjorn, Thyra Ferre. *Papa's Wife*. 1976. A Swedish pastor marries a Swedish girl and eventually they move to America. This is the amusing story of their family life.

Blackmore, Richard D. *Lorna Doone*. 1896. The romance between John Ridd and Lorna of the outlaw Doones is set in seventeenth-century England.

Brontë, Charlotte. *Jane Eyre*. 1847. The orphan Jane Eyre works as a governess to Mr. Rochester's ward and lives through some unusual circumstances and heartaches.

Brown, Liane I. *Refuge*. Bob Jones University Press, 1987. This is a true story of steadfast faith amidst the horror of the Russian occupation of Germany during the close of the Second World War.

Browning, Elizabeth Barrett. *Sonnets from the Portuguese*. 1850. These poems were written over a period of seven years. They were likely inspired by the author's love for her husband, Robert Browning.

Catton, Bruce. *Banners at Shenandoah*. 1976. This is the story of a young boy's adventures as he rides in the Union cavalry.

Cervantes, Miguel de. *Don Quixote*. 1605. This humorous story about a bumbling Spanish knight is a classic satire on chivalry.

Collins, David R. *Abraham Lincoln*. 1976. A simple biography of Abraham Lincoln, 1809-65.

Note: Readers can enjoy each of the following five books in the Leatherstocking tales as a story that stands by itself. These books are listed in series order as well as in alphabetical order.

Cooper, James Fenimore. *The Deerslayer*. 1841. Natty Bumppo, brought up by Delaware Indians, fights against the Hurons and defends settler Tom Hutter's family from attack. This is the first of the Leatherstocking Tales.

———. *The Last of the Mohicans*. 1826. Second in the series of five Leatherstocking Tales, this book deals with Natty Bumppo and the last of the Iroquois aristocracy.

———. *The Pathfinder*. 1840. Natty Bumppo is forty years old in this, the third of the Leatherstocking Tales. Pathfinder and others defeat the Iroquois.

———. *The Pioneers*. 1823. Natty Bumppo, in this sequel to *The Pathfinder*, is an older man who lives by the laws of nature and clashes with the new laws of civilization.

———. *The Prairie*. 1827. This last Leatherstocking Tale relates the last days of Natty Bumppo. He spends the end of his life as a trapper, constantly helping people.

Defoe, Daniel. *The Adventures of Robinson Crusoe*. 1719. Robinson Crusoe, the sole survivor of a shipwreck, lives on a deserted island many years before being rescued.

Dick, Lois Hoadley. *False Coin, True Coin*. Bob Jones University Press, 1993. Whom should Cissy believe? Her father, maker of counterfeit coins? Or John Bunyan, the prisoner who dares to speak of a loving God?

Dickens, Charles. *David Copperfield*. 1849-50. In this largely autobiographical work, David is sent by his harsh stepfather to London to work.

———. *Great Expectations*. 1860-61. Pip finds that he is to be related to a gentleman of "great expectations" due to an unknown benefactor.

———. *Nicholas Nickleby*. 1838-39. Nicholas Nickleby and his sister Kate are left penniless upon their father's death. Their only option is to seek the aid of their uncle, Ralph Nickleby, a shrewd and evil man.

———. *Oliver Twist*. 1837-38. Oliver falls into the hands of ruffians who train him to be a pickpocket. He attempts to escape from this way of life.

———. *A Tale of Two Cities*. 1859. The story, set in London and Paris during the time of the French Revolution, centers on the physical likeness of Charles Darnay and Sydney Carton and their love for the beautiful Lucie Manetta.

Dumas, Alexandre. *The Count of Monte Cristo*. 1845. Translated in 1846. Edmond Dantes gains a fortune and becomes the Count of Monte Cristo, but this change of circumstances is only the beginning of his adventures.

———. *The Three Musketeers*. 1844. Translated in 1846. The exploits of these young heroes are presented in a world of political intrigue, court life, and dueling.

Eliot, George. *Silas Marner*. 1861. Silas, despairing after being falsely accused of theft, raises a baby girl and through her love becomes a kind man again.

Goldsmith, Oliver. *The Vicar of Wakefield.* 1768. The novel, a romance of rural England in the thirteenth century, recounts the tribulations of a gentle but gullible vicar.

Hale, Edward Everett. *The Man Without a Country.* 1976. Officer Philip Nolan, tried for his part in the Aaron Burr conspiracy, declares that he wishes he had never heard of the United States. The court sentence grants his request.

Hautiz, Esther. *The Endless Steppe.* 1968. This is the moving story of a Polish deportee's imprisonment in a Siberian camp.

Hawthorne, Nathaniel. *The Great Stone Face and Other Tales of the White Mountains.* 1889. These tales and sketches of the White Mountains are among the most widely read of Hawthorne's works.

————. *The House of the Seven Gables.* 1851. A troubled family of Puritan New England deals with an inherited curse. Hawthorne deals with the consequences of past sins.

————. *The Marble Faun.* 1860. The fall of Adam is portrayed amidst the ruins and art treasures of Rome.

Hess, Donna. *In Search of Honor.* Bob Jones University Press, 1991. Jacques Chenier struggles to free himself from the prison of his own bitterness as the French Revolution sweeps Paris toward anarchy.

Hilton, James. *Good-bye, Mr. Chips.* 1935. This involves a character study of a teacher who was devoted to his students as he served three generations.

Hole, Dorothy. *Margaret Thatcher: Britain's Prime Minister.* 1990. An interesting biography that also provides an intriguing glimpse into Britain's system of government and its whirlwind political life.

Hunt, Irene. *Across Five Aprils.* 1964. This story, set during the Civil War, centers on nine-year-old Jethro Creighton and the many decisions that are forced on him during this time of political and social upheaval.

————.*Up a Road Slowly.* 1966. A touching story about a young girl's farm life from seven to seventeen. She has many problems, starting with her mother's death. The book ends as the girl successfully graduates from high school.

Irving, Washington. *The Legend of Sleepy Hollow.* 1820. Ichabod Crane vies with Brom Bones for the hand of Katrina Van Tassel and encounters the headless horseman.

Jones, Bob. *Daniel of Babylon.* Bob Jones University Press, 1984. The Old Testament contains no more thrilling history than that of Daniel, the statesman and prophet. In this novel the stories of the faithful, courageous Daniel come to life in the form of an imaginary journal, as Daniel might have written it.

Kingsley, Charles. *Westward, Ho!* 1982. This romance of sixteenth-century England and South America shows the Great Armada in battle and tells of Drake and Raleigh as they sail the seas in search of treasure for Queen Elizabeth.

Kipling, Rudyard. *Captains Courageous.* 1897. A series of unexpected events forces a pampered American youth to work for his living. The experience, though difficult, proves to be invaluable in helping the boy mature into manhood.

Ludwig, Charles. *Champion of Freedom.* 1987. A compelling biographical novel of Harriet Beecher Stowe and the influence of her most noted work *Uncle Tom's Cabin.*

————. *Defender of the Faith.* 1988. A fascinating biography of the memorable Queen Victoria of England.

Nordhoff, Charles, and Hall, James N. *Mutiny on the Bounty; Men Against the Sea; Pitcairn's Island.* 1946. The Bounty trilogy, a tale of dramatic and sometimes violent action, deals with the voyage of the *Bounty* to the South Pacific and the mutiny of its crew against Captain Bligh.

Nye, Julie. *Every Perfect Gift.* Bob Jones University, 1990. An unwanted stepmother helps Sheri James realize that gifts from God take many forms.

Orczy, Baroness Emmuska. *The Scarlet Pimpernel.* The Scarlet Pimpernel heads a band of Englishmen who assist French aristocrats trying to flee France during the Reign of Terror.

Repp, Gloria. *Night Flight.* Bob Jones University Press, 1991. In this sequel to *The Stolen Years,* Kelly Johnson puzzles over mysterious happenings in the Pine Barrens of New Jersey.

————. *The Stolen Years.* Bob Jones University Press, 1989. David must find his family's silver pistols and overcome the bitterness of his grandfather.

Scott, Sir Walter. *Ivanhoe.* 1819. The Norman Conquest is only the beginning of adventures for Wilfred, the Knight of Ivanhoe.

Stevenson, Robert Louis. *The Black Arrow.* 1888. Dick Shelton overcomes the schemes of many to win the hand of an orphaned heiress, Joanna Smedley, during the times of the English War of the Roses in the fifteenth century.

————. *Kidnapped.* n.d. David Balfour, a Whig and Lowlander, becomes involved in the uprising in favor of Prince Charles and the Stuarts in 1745.

Thomson, Andy. *Morning Star of the Reformation.* Bob Jones University Press, 1988. A fictionalized biography of John Wycliffe, set in medieval England. Readers will share in Wycliffe's student days at Oxford University and see him work toward his goal of translating the Bible into English for all Englishmen to read.

Tolkien, J.R.R. *The Hobbit.* 1966. Tolkien's elegant style and charming characterizations make this fantasy a classic. The unassuming Bilbo Baggins finds himself the unwilling warrior in the fight between good and evil.

Tunis, John R. *Iron Duke.* 1938. Jim Wellington, a high school graduate from the Midwest, goes to Harvard and experiences difficulties and disappointments. Then as a junior, he breaks the intercollegiate record for the two-mile run, and his values are strengthened.

Wallace, Lew. *Ben-Hur.* 1901. A historical romance during the time of Christ, this work describes in detail Roman and Jewish history.

Watkins, Dawn. *Zoli's Legacy I: Inheritance*. Bob Jones University Press, 1991. Zoli battles poverty, his father's displeasure, and his own pride in order to get an education.

————. *Zoli's Legacy II: Bequest*. Bob Jones University Press, 1991. Zoli takes over an orphanage of thirty boys as Hungary is drawn into World War II.

Yates, Elizabeth. *Hue & Cry*. Bob Jones University Press, 1991. Jared Austin's deaf daughter, Melody, befriends a young Irish immigrant who has stolen a horse.

————. *The Journeyman*. Bob Jones University Press, 1990. Jared Austin's quiet life is changed forever when a journeyman painter comes to visit.

Grade 8 - Grade 12: Books for Analysis and Discussion

Note: *The following books could be used on the high school level for developing literary skills and spiritual discernment. Before being recommended, however, each book should be previewed by a parent or teacher to determine its value for the individual student. The student's reading should be followed by a guided discussion in which the story is interpreted and evaluated using sound literary and biblical principles. (For additional information on evaluating books with these purposes in mind, see pp. 157-66.)*

Brontë, Emily. *Wuthering Heights.* 1847. This compelling classic well illustrates the essential selfishness of unbridled human passions and the ultimate destructiveness of such passions. The two central characters, Catherine and Heathcliff, are fatally flawed characters without moral compunction, characters whose self-absorption and cynicism dominate the story's action and move it toward its inevitable, tragic resolution.

Christopher, John. *White Mountain, The City of Gold and Lead,* and *The Pool of Fire.* 1967. The Tripod trilogy, comprised of these three titles, are well-written science fiction tales. All of the stories have an overall positive moral tone. There are, however, some points that should be addressed in the context of each book (stealing/lying during wartime).

Crane, Stephen. *The Red Badge of Courage.* 1895. This classic war story is a vivid portrayal of a Civil War soldier's initiation into the horrors of battle. The imagery and symbolism serve as a powerful reinforcement of the story's naturalistic theme and provide an excellent opportunity to discuss and evaluate the views of naturalism in light of biblical truth.

Frank, Anne. *The Diary of a Young Girl.* 1952. This true account is a powerful, interesting epiphany story for girls. Some of the more serious issues covered will prove most valuable if followed by guided discussion.

Hardy, Thomas. *The Mayor of Casterbridge*. 1886. This story provides an excellent opportunity for discussing the pessimistic view of life which is a logical outgrowth of man's refusal to acknowledge God and His relationship to man. According to Joyce Kilmer, "In no other writing is Hardy more clearly a fatalist than in *The Mayor of Casterbridge;* in no other book does he urge more unmistakably his belief that men and women are helpless puppets in the hands of mischievous fate, that good-will and courage and honesty are brittle weapons for humanity's defence." Whether or not we agree with Kilmer that this work is Hardy's most fatalistic, we can at least concur that the marks of his fatalism are deeply etched on the Casterbridge characters he creates. The intricate circumstances—and coincidences— that shape this book all point to a dominant theme which is explicitly summarized in the concluding description of the hero-ine's viewpoint: "Her experience had been of a kind to teach her, rightly or wrongly, . . . that happiness was but the occasional episode in a general drama of pain."

————. *Tess of the D'Urbervilles*. 1891. Considered by many to be Hardy's most readable novel, *Tess of the D'Urbervilles* pro-vides a good illustration of the author's pessimistic philosophy and his scorn for what he considered the moral rigidness of Victorian England. Tess, the heroine of the story, is portrayed by Hardy as a victim of fate thrust into one tragic circumstance after another. Through Tess's story, Hardy makes clear his belief that there is no "moral design" which shapes our lives. We are, according to Hardy, pawns in a tragic drama which is played out in utter disregard for individual happiness or betterment. The story provides a good opportunity to discuss the ultimate despair which must result from those who hold such views. Hawthorne's *Scarlet Letter* would provide an interesting contrast to Hardy's book.

Hawthorne, Nathaniel. *The Scarlet Letter.* 1850. In this work Haw-thorne analyzes the effects of sin in the lives of three intriguing Puritan characters. These three, Hester Prynne, Arthur Dimmes-dale, and Roger Chillingworth, weave a dramatic, unforgettable tale. The moral tone of the work is positive; however, due to the poignant theme, this story would prove most valuable if followed by guided discussion and analysis.

Howells, William Dean. *The Rise of Silas Lapham*. 1885. This Howells classic has been called "the first important novel to center on an American businessman and to treat its theme with a realism that was to foreshadow the work of modern writers." The story's central character, Silas Lapham, is a self-made man whose ambition leads him to risk his personal fortune and family happiness for status in a society that scorns him. Unlike many other modern American writers, Howells allows this protagonist to recognize his folly before being destroyed. The book provides an excellent opportunity for discussing the corrupting power of wealth and the social and ethical conflicts which emerge when such corruption goes unchecked.

Hugo, Victor. *The Hunchback of Notre Dame*. 1831. Religious, city, cultural, and criminal life are portrayed in the gothic romance set in medieval times. The drama of the story centers on the faithful hunchback Quasimodo and the innocent, steadfast Esmeralda. There are a few objectionable elements which would need to be addressed.

————. *Les Miserables*. 1862. This intriguing story, set in early nineteenth-century France, contrasts the consequences of repentance and restoration with the effects of bitterness and revenge. Although the overall moral tone of the book is positive, there are a few objectionable elements in the story which should be addressed.

James, Henry. *The Turn of the Screw*. 1898. This is a fascinating psychological tale which provides ample opportunity for discussion of tone and technique. As is characteristic of James, he begins the story with an intriguing situation. A young governess is employed to take charge of a wealthy man's niece and nephew. The man gives the girl only one instruction—take complete charge of the children so that he will not, under any circumstance, have to be disturbed. When the children (seemingly charming, innocent, and polite) and their governess (seemingly competent, sensitive, and loving) first meet, there is every indication that they are perfectly matched. As the story unfolds, however, James weaves an increasingly intricate and mysterious web of circumstances, the resolution of which cannot be easily confined to a single interpretation. Consequently, the novel provides an excellent opportunity for studying and discussing several key literary techniques among which are the importance of viewpoint, the use of foreshadowing, and the function of ambiguity as a literary device in creating this mysterious, unsettling tale.

Knowles, John. *A Separate Peace.* 1960. This psychologically intriguing story is about two very different adolescents. Gene is an introverted, brooding intellectual. His friend, Phineas, is a handsome, idealistic daredevil. On the surface, these schoolboys are the best of friends. As the story unfolds, however, we see the dark struggle that lies beneath the shining surface of their friendship. The story of these two boys can provide valuable discussion on the tragic consequences of jealousy, self-absorption, and self-deception.

Lee, Harper. *To Kill a Mockingbird.* 1960. This story provides an opportunity for discussion of racial prejudice as well as prejudice against the unfamiliar or "abnormal." The overall tone of the story is positive. However, there are some objectionable elements (e.g., attitudes toward religion) which need to be discussed in the context of the story and evaluated in light of biblical truth.

Note: Readers can enjoy each of the three books in the Space trilogy as a story that stands by itself. These books are listed in series order as well as alphabetical order.

Lewis, C. S. *Out of the Silent Planet.* 1938. The biblical allusions and the intense, realistically portrayed struggle between good and evil make Lewis's Space trilogy (including this story and the following two) most valuable when followed by guided discussion. In this first book of Lewis's Space trilogy, Dr. Ransom is kidnapped and finds himself on the way to Malacandra (Mars).

———. *Perelandra.* 1943. In this second book of the trilogy, Lewis recounts the voyage to an unfallen planet (Venus) taken by a Christian and his evil companion. A moral struggle ensues when the two men arrive on the planet and try to convince the inhabitants of their individual viewpoints.

————. *That Hideous Strength.* 1945. This last volume of the trilogy recounts the plan of men who are intent upon turning man into his own god. This book is the culmination of the battle between good and evil which has been carried through the series.

Lipsyte, Robert. *The Contender.* 1967. A good moral tone makes this coming-of-age story a profitable one if followed by guided discussion. Alfred Brooks, a high school dropout, is scared. His job at a local grocery store seems to be a dead end. More frightening, however, is the fact that his best friend is sinking further and further into drug addiction and that a gang of street kids are after him for something he didn't do. So, Alfred begins going to Donatelli's Gym, a boxing club in Harlem that has trained champions. It is at Donatelli's that he learns "it's the effort, not the win, that makes the man."

London, Jack. *Call of the Wild.* 1903. Irving Stone in his noted biography states, "Jack's four intellectual grandparents were Darwin, Spencer, Marx, and Nietzsche." In this classic arctic tale, London illustrates the truth of Irving's observation. A careful analysis and guided discussion of the work are especially valuable in providing concrete illustrations of Darwinian and Nietzschean ideas (e.g., survival of the fittest and the concept of the "superman").

Note: Although all of MacDonald's works are enjoyable and inspirational, those reading them should note that in several of his works for older readers the theological concepts presented (e.g., salvation through faith in the shed blood of Christ) are ambiguous at best and should be addressed when included as part of the story.

MacDonald, George. *The Baronet's Song.* 1879. Edited by Michael R. Phillips, 1983. This is a powerful, inspirational tale about a deaf, mute orphan named Gibby whose talents, courage, and compassion win the hearts of all he meets.

————. *The Baron's Apprenticeship.* 1891. Edited by Michael R. Phillips, 1986. A companion to *The Lady's Confession,* this story recounts the adventures, growth, and amazing discoveries of the bookbinding apprentice Richard Tuke.

————. *The Fight of the Shadow.* Edited by Michael R. Phillips, 1983. Set in Scotland's beautifully wild highlands, the central characters of this spellbinding tale fight to overcome the most frightening evil of all, the evil of a depraved heart.

————. *The Fisherman's Lady.* 1875. Edited by Michael R. Phillips, 1982. A gothic tale set in Scotland during the last century. The charming fisherman Malcolm is the focus of this story of mystery, intrigue, and romance, eventually bringing it to a satisfying conclusion.

————. *The Lady's Confession.* 1879. Edited by Michael R. Phillips, 1986. This is the story of Lady Juliet and her struggle between the compassionate curate Thomas Wingfold and the charming atheist Paul Faber.

————. *The Maiden's Bequest.* 1865. Edited by Michael R. Phillips. 1985. The mutually beneficial friendship between Alec and Annie is the basis for this compelling story set during the nineteenth-century in Scotland.

————. *The Marquis' Secret.* 1877. Edited by Michael R. Phillips, 1982. In this sequel to *The Fisherman's Lady,* the noble Malcolm must save his headstrong sister Florimel from the charms of an ignoble suitor.

————. *A Quiet Neighborhood.* 1866. Edited by Dan Hamilton, 1985. This gothic romance is set in a rural parish of Victorian England. The young vicar Harry Walton quickly wins the affection of his parishoners. But Harry soon discovers that things are not as they seem in his quiet country parish.

————. *The Tutor's First Love.* 1863. Edited by Michael R. Phillips. 1984. Hugh Sutherland slowly drifts away from the kind and noble Elginbrod family who have influenced him through their unshakable faith in God. This is a captivating story of suspense, romance, and adventure.

Melville, Herman. *Billy Budd.* 1924. This compelling story is a testament of Melville's philosophy and an excellent illustration of the use of literary symbols to reinforce theme. Much of Melville's fiction reflects his belief in evil as a powerful force by which men are most often dominated. The theme of *Billy Budd* reflects his belief in the power of man's darker, dominant side; and the characters are symbols which express this theme. Claggert is the embodiment of evil, the one who wears a mask of congeniality to cover his base motivations. In contrast, Billy Budd is the epitome of innocence and good. The third central character of the story, Captain Vere, is the most complex; he is a "maskless man of moderation" and the one who is ultimately forced to resolve the conflict between these good and evil characters.

Orwell, George. *Animal Farm.* 1954. This political satire, written in the guise of an allegory, is a story about animals who overthrow their drunken masters and take over the running of the farm. A discussion and analysis of the work is valuable for studying satire and for showing the inherent weaknesses in a communistic system.

Paton, Alan. *Cry, the Beloved Country.* 1948. A moving tale about the consequences of the political and cultural crises in South Africa. The elegant style and poignant themes merit guided discussion.

Rölvaag, O. E. *Giants of the Earth.* 1927. This is the story of an immigrant Norwegian family in South Dakota. Prairie life meant freedom to Per Hansa and loneliness and depression to his wife Beret. Although this sad tale is an accurate depiction of the hardships of prairie life, the despair inherent in the novel needs to be discussed.

Sienkiewicz, Henryk. *Quo Vadis.* 1896. In this riveting story set during the time of Nero's Rome, Sienkiewicz gives us a picture of the conflict within the Roman Empire, a conflict from which Christianity issued as the leading force in history. The moral tone of the story is above reproach. There are, however, certain objectionable elements presented in conjunction with the degenerate conditions that pervaded historic Rome. These elements should be discussed in the context of the story.

Steinbeck, John. *The Pearl.* 1948. The story is a moving treatise on the innate depravity of man, the corrupting power of wealth, and the misery that can result from these two points. It offers some valuable material for discussion provided by the socio-economic conflict between the rich and the poor. There are some objectionable elements in the story which should be addressed (e.g., references to superstitious practices). Steinbeck's purpose for these references is to give an accurate, vivid reflection of the culture and to use such cultural elements as symbols which reinforce his theme. He accomplishes both of these goals remarkably well. The thematic elements are valuable enough and the objectionable material minimal enough to make this story a good one for guided discussion.

Twain, Mark. *A Connecticut Yankee in King Arthur's Court.* 1889. A twentieth-century Yankee is transported to the middle of King Arthur's court. "This Yankee of mine," Twain states, "is a perfect ignoramus; he is boss of a machine shop, he can build a locomotive or a Colt's revolver, he can put up and run a telegraph line, but he's an ignoramus nevertheless." Regardless of this description, Twain portrays the Yankee's ingenuity as more than a match for the medieval magic and superstition. As is typical, however, beneath the rollicking humor, Twain makes some serious indictments of religion, government, and industrialism.

————. *The Adventures of Huckleberry Finn.* 1884. Huck Finn is one of the most memorable characters in American literature, and his story is one of the most widely read. Twain warns his readers that they will be "persecuted" if they attempt "to find a motive . . . or a moral" in the novel. However, in light of the serious themes Twain presents in Huck's story, his "warning" seems disingenuous at best. Most of these themes are introduced in the first chapter and carefully reinforced throughout the book. They include the belief in the supremacy of individual freedom over the "restrictive" mores of society, the idea that traditional concepts of religion are foolish, and the insistence that man's isolation is what drives him to embrace myriad superstitions (including a belief in God). As is typical of Twain, he cloaks his cynical views in satire. A careful analysis of Huck Finn will reveal not only the vitriolic view of life which lies beneath the surface of the humor but also the inherent flaw in this author's limited perceptions.

Wells, H. G. *The Time Machine.* 1895. Like all of Wells's science fiction tales, this one reflects his political and ethical outlook. This particular work reflects his Fabian socialist position. It also shows some Darwinian influence. Besides pointing out such attitudes and influences, Wells's science fiction provides a valuable study in contrasts. G. K. Chesterton once said that great literature must grow out of a "rich moral soil." It is this richness that Wells's science fiction lacks. This deficiency becomes blatantly apparent when compared with C. S. Lewis's science fiction trilogy. Studying Wells and Lewis together will help students develop an appreciation of and discernment for what good science fiction really is.

―――. *War of the Worlds.* 1898. This book is probably the most famous of Wells's science fiction adventures, and like the others it reflects many of the author's ideas and attitudes. His antipathy for British imperialism and his scorn for "religious zealots" are two of the attitudes reflected in this tale.

Wharton, Edith. *Ethan Frome.* 1911. In this powerful story, Wharton weaves a web of tragic circumstances from which her hero, Ethan Frome, has no hope of escape. Frome's self-deception, his romantic illusions, and his moral indecisiveness all contribute to the final agonizing resolution of the story, a resolution which is heightened by Wharton's deft use of dramatic irony. Like Thomas Hardy and many other modern writers, Wharton shows us a world without God and men without hope.

Biographies and Autobiographies

Note: † indicates a book for young readers, grades 2-6. See annotations, pp.1-116.

Sam, 1722-1803, and John, 1735-1826, Adams
Lee, Susan, and Lee, John.
>†*Sam and John Adams.* 1974.

Gladys Aylward, c. 1900-1970
Howard, Milly.
>†*These Are My People.*
>Bob Jones University Press, 1984.

Hunter, Christine.
>*Gladys Aylward: The Little Woman.* 1970.

Swift, Catherine.
>*Gladys Aylward.* 1989.

Louisa May Alcott, 1832-88
Meigs, Cornelia.
>*Invincible Louisa.* 1933.

Johann Sebastian Bach, 1685-1750
Lee, Robert E.
>*The Joy of Bach.* 1979.

Podojill, Catherine.
>*To God Alone Be the Glory: Johann Sebastian Bach.* 1979.

Clara Barton, 1821-1912
Rose, Mary Catherine.
>†*Clara Barton: Soldier of Mercy.* 1960.

William Whiting Borden, 1747-1887
Taylor, Mrs. Howard.
>*William Borden.* 1988.

Nathaniel Bowditch, 1773-1838
Latham, Jean Lee.
Carry On, Mr. Bowditch. 1955.

David Brainerd, 1718-47
Brainerd, David, ed. Jonathan Edwards.
Autobiography of David Brainerd. 1989.

John Bunyan, 1628-88
Bunyan, John.
Grace Abounding to the Chief of Sinners. 1981.
Dengler, Sandy.
John Bunyan: Writer of Pilgrim's Progress. 1986.
Whyte, Alexander.
Bunyan Characters: Bunyan Himself as Seen in His Grace Abounding. 1981.

Louis Braille, c. 1809-52
Davidson, Margaret.
†*Louis Braille.* 1971.

William Carey, 1761-1834
Clinton, Iris.
Young Man in a Hurry. 1961.
Finnie, Kellsye.
William Carey: Missionary Pioneer. 1986.
Miller, Basil.
William Carey: Father of Modern Missions. 1980.
Walker, F. Deauville.
William Carey. 1980.

Amy Carmichael, 1867-1951
Davis, Rebecca.
With Daring Faith.
Bob Jones University Press, 1987.
Dick, Lois Hoadley.
Amy Carmichael: Let the Little Children Come. 1984.
Elliot, Elisabeth.
A Chance to Die: The Life and Legacy of Amy Carmichael. 1987.
Houghton, Frank.
Amy Carmichael of Dohnavur. 1979.
White, Kathleen.
Amy Carmichael. 1986.

George Washington Carver, c. 1864-1943
Epstein, Sam, and Epstein, Beryl.
†*George Washington Carver.* 1960.

John Chapman, 1774-1845
Kellogg, Steven.
†*Johnny Appleseed.* 1988.

George Rogers Clark, 1752-1818
DeLeeuw, Adele.
†*George Rogers Clark.* 1967.

Fanny Crosby, 1820-1915
Crosby, Fanny.
An Autobiography. 1986.
Dengler, Sandy.
Fanny Crosby: Writer of 8,000 Songs. 1985.
Hustad, Donald P., ed.
Fanny Crosby Speaks Again. 1977.
Loveland, John.
Blessed Assurance: The Life and Hymns of Fanny Crosby. 1978.

Thomas Edison, 1847-1931
Quackenbush, Robert M.,
†*What Has Wild Tom Done Now?* 1981.

Jim Elliot, 1927-56
Elliot, Elisabeth.
> *Through Gates of Splendor.* 1957.
> *Shadow of the Almighty: The Life and Testament of Jim Elliot.*
> 1958.

Michael Faraday, 1791-1867
Ludwig, Charles.
> *Michael Faraday, Father of Electronics.* 1978.

John Foxe, 1516-87
Foxe, John.
> *The Acts and Monuments of These Latter and Perilous Days.*
> 1965.

Jonathan Goforth, 1859-1936
Goforth, Rosalind.
> *Goforth of China.* 1986.

John Hyde, 1892-1912
Bone, Gratia Hyde and Hall, Mary Hyde.
> *Life and Letters of Praying Hyde.* n.d.
McGaw, Francis.
> *John Hyde: Apostle of Prayer.* 1970.
Miller, Basil.
> *Praying Hyde.* 1943.

Bob Jones, Sr., 1883-1968
Johnson, R. K.
> *Builder of Bridges.* 1982.

Adoniram Judson, 1788-1850
Anderson, Courtney.
> *To the Golden Shore: The Life of Adoniram Judson.* 1956.
Bailey, Faith Cox.
> *Adoniram Judson: America's First Foreign Missionary.* 1955.

Ann Hasseltine Judson, 1789-1826
Pittman, E. R.
   Ann Hasseltine Judson of Burma. 1974.

Helen Keller, 1880-1968
Graff, Steward, and Graff, Polly Anne.
   †*Helen Keller: Toward the Light.* 1965.

Johannes Kepler, 1571-1630
Tiner, John Hudson.
   Johannes Kepler: Giant of Faith and Science. 1978.

Esther Ahn Kim, n.d.
Kim, Esther Ahn.
   If I Perish. 1977.

Isobel Kuhn, 1901-57
Canfield, Carolyn.
   One Vision Only. 1959.
Dick, Lois Hoadley.
   Isobel Kuhn. 1987.

John Knox, 1505-72
Martin, Dorothy.
   John Knox: Apostle of the Scottish Reformation. 1982.
Reid, W. Stanford.
   Trumpeter of God: A Biography of John Knox. 1982.

Robert E. Lee, 1807-70
Johnson, William J.
   Robert E. Lee, The Christian. 1976.
Roddy, Lee.
   Robert E. Lee, Christian General and Gentleman. 1977.

C. S. Lewis, 1898-1963
Lewis, C. S.
Surprised by Joy. 1955.
Swift, Catherine.
C. S. Lewis. 1989.

Eric Liddell, 1902-45
Swift, Catherine.
Eric Liddell. 1990.

Abraham Lincoln, 1809-1865
Cavanah, Frances.
†*Abe Lincoln Gets His Chance.* 1959.
Collins, David R.
Abraham Lincoln. 1976.
D'Aulaire, Ingri, and Parin, Edgar.
†*Abraham Lincoln.* 1957.

David Livingstone, 1813-73
Latham, Robert O.
Trail Maker. 1973.
Worchester, J. H.
David Livingstone. n.d.

Kathrine von Bora Luther, 1499-1552
Ludwig, Charles.
Queen of the Reformation. 1986.

Martin Luther, 1483-1546
Bainton, Roland.
Here I Stand: A Life of Martin Luther. 1950.
Benson, Kathleen.
A Man Called Martin Luther. 1980.
Davey, Cyril.
The Monk Who Shook the World. 1960.
D'Aubigne, J. H.
Life and Times of Martin Luther. 1950.
Nohl, Frederick.
Martin Luther: Hero of Faith. 1962.

Alexander Mackay, 1849-90
McFarlan, Donald.
Wizard of the Great Lake. 1975.

Dwight Lyman Moody, 1837-99
Bailey, Faith Cox.
D. L. Moody: The Greatest Evangelist of the Nineteenth Century.
1959.
Fitt, A. P.
Life of D. L. Moody. n.d.
Moody Still Lives. 1936.

George Mueller, 1805-98
Bailey, Faith Cox.
George Mueller. 1958.
Garton, N.
George Mueller and His Orphans. 1963.
Miller, Basil.
George Muller: Man of Faith and Miracles. 1941.
Mueller, George.
Autobiography of George Mueller. 1981.
Pierson, Arthur T.
George Mueller of Bristol. 1971.
Short, Rendle A.
The Diary of George Mueller. 1954.

Andrew Murray, 1828-1917
Choe, Leona.
Andrew Murray: Apostle of Abiding Love. 1978.
Douglas, W. M.
Andrew Murray and His Message. 1981.

John Newton, 1725-1807
Cecil, Richard.
Life of John Newton. 1978.
Newton, John.
Out of the Depths: An Autobiography. 1764.
Pollock, John.
Amazing Grace: John Newton's Story. 1981.
Strom, Kay Marshall.
John Newton: The Angry Sailor. 1984.

Florence Nightingale, 1820-1910
Miller, Basil.
Florence Nightingale: The Lady of the Lamp. 1975.

Haralan Popov, 1907-88
Popov, Haralan.
Tortured for His Faith. 1970. Rev. ed. 1975.

Albert Benjamin Simpson, 1844-1919
Thompson, A. W.
A. B. Simpson: His Life and Work. Rev. ed. 1960.

Mary Mitchell Slessor, 1848-1945
Buchan, James.
The Expendable Mary Slessor. 1981.
Enock, Ester.
Mary Slessor. 1974.
Miller, Basil.
Missionary Heroine of Calabar. 1974.

Charles Haddon Spurgeon, 1834-92
Bacon, Ernest W.
Spurgeon. 1982.
Fullerton, W. Y.
Spurgeon: London's Most Popular Preacher. 1966.
Triggs, Kathy.
Charles Spurgeon. 1984.

John and Betty Stam, 1907-34
English, Schuyler E.
By Life and By Death: Excerpts from the Diary and Letters of John Stam. 1938.
White, Kathleen (Stam).
John and Betty Stam. 1989.

Harriet Beecher Stowe, 1811-96
Ludwig, Charles.
Champion of Freedom. 1987.

Charles Thomas Studd, 1860-1931
Erskine, John T.
Millionaire for God. 1968.
Grubb, Norman.
C. T. Studd. 1972.

William Ashley Sunday, 1862-1935
Ellis, William T.
Billy Sunday. 1959.
Everett, Betty Steele.
Sawdust Preacher: The Story of Billy Sunday. 1987.
Stocker, Fern Neal.
Billy Sunday: Baseball Preacher. 1985.

James Hudson Taylor, 1832-1905
Davey, Cyril.
On the Clouds to China. 1964.
Pollock, J. C.
Hudson Taylor and Maria. 1962.
Taylor, Howard, and Taylor, Mrs. Howard J.
Hudson Taylor: God's Man in China. New ed. 1977.
———. *Hudson Taylor's Spiritual Secret.* New ed. 1989.
Taylor, J. Hudson.
Autobiography of Hudson Taylor. Seventeenth ed., n.d.

Corrie ten Boom, 1892-1983
ten Boom, Corrie.
The Hiding Place. 1971.
————. *Prison Letters.* 1975.

Margaret Thatcher, 1925-
Hole, Dorothy.
Margaret Thatcher: Britain's Prime Minister. 1990.

Harriet Tubman, 1820-1913
Sterling, Dorothy.
†*Freedom Train: The Story of Harriet Tubman.* 1954.

William Tyndale, c. 1494-1536
O'Dell, Scott.
The Hawk That Dare Not Hunt by Day.
Bob Jones University Press, 1987.
Vernon, Louise A.
Bible Smuggler. 1967.

Victoria, Queen 1819-1902
Ludwig, Charles.
Defender of the Faith. 1988.

John Wesley, 1703-91
Davey, Cyril.
Horseman of the King. 1964.
Lean, Garth.
Strangely Warmed. 1979.
Miller, Basil.
John Wesley. 1943.
Spurgeon, Charles Haddon
The Two Wesleys. 1976.
Wood, A. Shevington.
The Burning Heart: John Wesley, Evangelist. 1978.

Susanna Wesley, c. 1669-1741

Dengler, Sandy.
Susanna Wesley: Servant of God. 1987.
Harmon, Rebecca Lamar.
Susanna, Mother of the Wesleys. 1968.
Kirk, John.
Mother of the Wesleys. 1865.

George Whitefield, 1714-70

Whitefield, George.
George Whitefield's Journals. 1960.

John Wycliffe, c. 1329-84

Thomson, Andy.
Morning Star of the Reformation.
Bob Jones University Press, 1988.

Guidelines for Choosing Books

T. S. Eliot once said, "Whether there is such a thing as a harmless book I am not sure: there very likely are books so utterly unreadable as to be incapable of injuring anybody. But it is certain that a book is not harmless merely because no one is consciously offended by it." Eliot's comment implies that there is more to choosing worthy books than simply noting whether a story contains overt objectionable elements. The books we choose for our young people—and ourselves—should possess two characteristics: literary and moral excellence.

What do we mean by literary excellence?

A story is literary if the key elements are artfully expressed and the theme is noteworthy. This definition does not mean that all of our books must be "literary classics." It does mean that the reading material we provide for our children should have literary merit. For example, the central conflict in the story should be compelling and appropriate for the age level for which the story is written. There should also be a variety of characters, and these characters ought to be believable and consistent in the story's context. Although some characters may be flat (or one dimensional) and static (unchanging), such characters should not dominate the story. The central character especially should be fully developed, and he will often be a dynamic character, changing and growing as the story progresses. The action, or plot, should be logical and the resolution of the story believable and satisfying. Finally, the theme or central idea should develop naturally out of these key elements of conflict, character, and plot.

The style, or how a specific author shapes these elements, should also be considered. Sensory images, figurative language, and subtle humor, which are all part of an engaging style, can be present in the simplest of stories. Indeed, these characteristics as well as those mentioned above are what have endeared classics like *Winnie the Pooh, The Velveteen Rabbit, Charlotte's Web,* and *Swiss Family Robinson* to generations of readers.

What do we mean by moral excellence?

As Christians we must recognize that a work of literary excellence is not automatically one of moral excellence. For example, we often reject stories that include offensive language and behavior, no matter how well written; but are we as careful in discerning subtle philosophies that might undermine our Christian faith? How can we be sure we have not overlooked such problems? The first step is to examine how the literary elements listed in the previous section have been presented in the book. What about the central character in the story? This character is usually the one the author intends for the reader to sympathize with and to admire. But is this character truly noble? We can also examine the plot. Does the central conflict reflect an awareness of right and wrong? Does the story's resolution reward the good and punish the evil? Analyzing these elements can help us to distinguish the story's philosophy and enable us to determine if the theme or central idea of the story conflicts with biblical truth.

An equally important aspect in evaluating moral excellence is our approach to specific censorable elements. There are stories that have literary merit and present a moral theme but also include censorable material (e.g., profanity). Should we as Christians simply exclude such books from our libraries and curriculum? As in all other areas of life, we must turn to Scripture for standards we can confidently apply and uphold. In order to formulate this biblical approach and apply scriptural standards, we must first be aware of the common categories of censorable elements. These elements include the following:

1. Profanity (blasphemy whether in statements or epithets; all sacrilege)

2. Scatological realism (specific references to excrement or to the excremental functions)

3. Erotic realism (specific references to physical love between the sexes)

4. Sexual perversion (the portrayal of any sexual relationship or activity—such as adultery, fornication, homosexuality, or incest—other than that which is sanctified by God in marriage)

5. Lurid violence

6. Occultism (Satanism, witchcraft, necromancy, astrology, fortune telling, and the like; a representation of the supernatural powers that oppose God in a way that fascinates the reader or implies the existence of a supernatural order other than the biblical one)

7. Erroneous religious or philosophical assumptions (unbiblical root ideas or attitudes expressed overtly or covertly, explicitly or implicitly, in theme, tone, or atmosphere). These ap-

pear, for example, when a writer invents a fictional world in which no divine presence is felt or moral order is perceptible.

It is not difficult to discern the obvious censurable elements of categories 1-6. However, category 7 is often subtler and more dangerous. For example, Jack London's *Call of the Wild* would appear safe enough in terms of criteria based on only the first six categories. Unfortunately the unbiblical premises in this work are often overlooked or not taken seriously. In discussing censorable elements and in the formulation of policy concerning them, this last category, like the others, requires our serious attention.

Let's begin, however, by identifying the two most commonly held views, the permissivist and exclusivist, and examining them in light of Scripture. Those who hold what may be termed the **permissivist** view allow at least a degree of the objectionable for either of two reasons: (1) the existence in a work of compensating aesthetic qualities; (2) the necessity in art for an honest view of life. These constitute what the courts have called "redeeming social value."

The weakness of the first criterion is that it is too subjective and utilitarian to be an adequate guide for Christians, especially today when aesthetic values rest not on moral principles, which biblical ethics requires, but on the toleration of the social community. The weakness of the second criterion—the necessity for an honest imitation of life—is linked to the first. Ideas of the world and of life vary widely. Every serious secular novelist invents fictional worlds that vindicate his moral and religious preferences. In addition, the Bible makes clear that there are some "realities" we are to flee (I Timothy 6:11; II Tim. 2:22). For the Christian, moral considerations must override the aesthetic and mimetic in literature and life. That which threatens the moral and spiritual life cannot be justified on other grounds. Permissivism, then, elevates human wisdom above the divine.

The **exclusivist** view is held by conscientious pastors, Christian educators, and parents concerned for the moral preservation of their children and for the wholesomeness of their communities. They believe that since evil is evil, any avoidable exposure to it is wrong for even the most praiseworthy of purposes. It follows, they argue, that one should avoid works of literature or discard elements of the curriculum that contain any amount of objectionable elements. A few go further and say that, since the Bible is a sufficient guide in all important matters of life and there is peril in other reading, we *ought not* to read anything else.

The exclusivist position is often based on a misconstruction or misapplication of certain passages of Scripture. Following are two of the most common:

1. "I will set no wicked thing before mine eyes" (Psalm 101:3). This resolution of David may refer to an idol or to some evil device or scheme. It certainly does not refer to all representation of evil, for David read the stories of moral failure in the Pentateuch and, in his capacity as judge, had to scrutinize wrongdoing continually. Sins mentioned in the Bible—for example, David's own adultery with Bathsheba—are wicked, but the *descriptions* of them in Scripture are not wicked. The examples of Scripture, both positive and negative, are good in the sense that they are "written for our learning" (Romans 15:4). "All Scripture is . . . profitable" (II Timothy 3:16), even the parts that reveal most vividly the depths of human degradation. What is represented is evil, but the representation of the evil is valuable for Christian moral understanding. Therefore, it is good.

2. "Finally, brethren, whatsoever things are true, whatsoever things are honest, whatsoever things are just, whatsoever things are pure, whatsoever things are lovely, whatsoever things are of good report; if there be any virtue, and if there be any praise, think on these things" (Philippians 4:8). This grand prescription for mental, moral, and spiritual health expresses the principle that dwelling on good will help to drive out evil. The believer's main subject of meditation should be the Scriptures—for blessing (Psalm 1:2) but also for protection (Proverbs 6:20-24). The biblical commands to center one's mental life on the Scriptures do not exclude those portions in which evil is described, often graphically. On the contrary, those passages, Paul says, were intended to be pondered as negative examples (I Corinthians 10:1-14). The Scriptures use both positive and negative examples to enforce its message. Good literature does also. A person whose mind has been fortified by such examples against the evil in his moral environment will better be able to live in that environment with his mind focused on the things of God.

Our spiritual affinities are with these who hold the exclusivist position, for they are the ones with the sensitive consciences, but we must also consider the implications of this position. The most serious problem with the exclusivist position is that it fails to reconcile the use of censorable elements in Scripture. All seven categories appear in certain ways and to certain degrees in the Bible. The following list is illustrative, but by no means exhaustive:

1. Profanity: "Say we not well that thou art a Samaritan, and hast a devil?" (John 8:48)

2. Scatological realism: Rabshakeh's coarse language (Isaiah 36:12)

3. Erotic realism: Proverbs 5:18-19; Ezekiel 23:20-21; and passages in the Song of Solomon

4. Sexual perversion: the sin of Sodom (Genesis 19); the seduction of Joseph (Genesis 39); the rape of Tamar (II Samuel 13); the liaison in Proverbs 7

5. Lurid violence: Joab's murder of Amasa (II Samuel 20)

6. Occultism: Saul's dealing in necromancy (I Samuel 27)

7. Religious and philosophical assumptions: the misrepresentation of God by Job's three friends (though in no pervasive sense can such assumptions affect any large portion of Scripture)

Obviously the exclusivist view, consistently held, puts the Bible in conflict with itself and lays its advocates open to charges of self-contradiction.

Fortunately there is another position, the **biblical**, which takes the Bible itself as the supreme literary and educational model. It accepts the biblical purpose of moral education as stated in Proverbs 1:4: "To give subtlety to the simple, to the young man knowledge and discretion." It recognizes that the image of God in redeemed man—Christ-likeness—includes moral understanding and that moral understanding requires an awareness of both good and evil and "the end thereof" (Proverbs 14:12). It identifies as spiritually "of full age," or mature, "those who by reason of use have their senses exercised to discern both good and evil" (Hebrews 5:14).

The **biblical position** adopts the method of the Scriptures in teaching moral understanding. The Bible teaches by means of precept and example. Its examples are both positive and negative. The writers of the Old Testament enunciate emphatically the commandments of God and reinforce them with many examples of right behavior and many more examples of behavior to be shunned. They associate consequences with good and evil behavior. New Testament writers draw on these examples, positive and negative, for encouragement and warning.

The Lord Himself made use of negative examples in His teaching, citing the degeneracy of Sodom (Matthew 11:23), Cain's slaying of Abel (Matthew 23:35), the debauchery of Noah's generation (Matthew 24:38), and many other instances of wickedness. Paul's warnings to the Corinthians run nearly the full gamut of human depravity, including incest (I Corinthians 5:1) and homosexuality (I Corinthians 6:9). We regard these accounts of wickedness in the same way that the New Testament writers regarded those recorded in the Old Testament: as "ensamples" given to us for our profit (I Corinthians 10:11; II Peter 2:6). To exclude the negative example from the Christian educational experience is to depart from the educational method of Scripture.

Does this mean that we must accept in our reading and include in our teaching the full range of objectionable elements that the permissivist would allow? Not at all. Following the standard of Scripture controls our choice and handling of material in a way that most pragmatists, let alone permissivists, would find over-restrictive. Although defense attorneys in pornography cases can point to portions of the English Bible that seem to violate the Bible's own admonitions, the Bible is in reality completely self-consistent and purposeful in its presentation of evil. Evil is represented in the Bible in certain ways, for certain purposes, and with certain effects. Understanding the biblical manner of representing evil is a far surer and more workable guide for the conscientious Christian parent or educator than the subjective criteria and arbitrary lists conceived by some conservative moralists, well intentioned as they may be.

A truly biblical position concerning censorable elements is based on the following distinction: if a work of literature treats evil in the same way that it is treated in the Scriptures, we regard it as not only acceptable but also desirable reading for someone of sufficient maturity. If it does not treat evil in the way evil is handled in the Scriptures, its content is not good. Evil in the Bible appears dangerous and repulsive. Reflections of evil appear in the Bible in the form of negative examples so as to create a defense against what is represented or to give hope to the fallen for forgiveness and recovery from sin.

The Scripture gives us three ways of testing literary works with respect to their content.

1. Is the representation of evil purposeful or is it present for its own sake? This is the test of **gratuitousness**. We know that "all scripture is given by inspiration of God, and is profitable for doctrine, for reproof, for correction, for instruction in

righteousness: that the man of God may be perfect, throughly furnished unto all good works" (II Timothy 3:16-17). Nothing in the Scriptures is superfluous or pointless to this high spiritual purpose.

2. Is the representation of evil, if purposeful, present in an acceptable degree? Or is it more conspicuous or vivid than the purpose warrants? This is the test of **explicitness**. No one with a high regard for Scripture would charge it with inappropriateness or excessiveness in its representation of evil. The presentation of evil in the Bible is realistic enough to convince us of its threat as a temptation but not so realistic as to become for us a temptation. Some sins are referred to but not enacted in the text.

3. Is evil presented from a condemning perspective? Is it made to appear both dangerous and repulsive? What is the attitude in the work toward it? For example, if a character in a story steals, are there consequences for this action? Do the noble characters within the story condemn the action? This is the test of **moral tone**. "Woe unto them that call evil good, and good evil," says the Lord through the prophet Isaiah (Isaiah 5:20). A good work of literature does not glorify human weakness or encourage tolerance of sin. It allows evil to appear in a controlled way in order to develop in the reader or hearer a resistance against it. In literature, "vice," wrote Samuel Johnson, "must always disgust." Its purpose is to initiate the reader through "mock encounters" with evil so that evil cannot later deceive him—so that he will be better able to maintain a pure life in an evil world.

These three tests must be considered together. None is sufficient alone to justify the objectionable in a work of literature. Together they work powerfully, because they work biblically, to preserve moral purity while providing for the development of moral understanding and judgment.

There remains the issue of whether works that do not pass the scriptural tests of gratuitousness, explicitness, and moral tone should be completely rejected. We need first to distinguish between educational and recreational reading. As Christians we cannot read for pleasure either works or parts of works whose objectionable elements do not pass the scriptural test. Our enjoyment of a book must be determined by the degree to which its form and content approach the biblical standard. However, the educational purpose requires at times a greater latitude. As students mature, such books may be included as part of our teaching. The purpose for including them is to help young people develop literary and spiritual discernment.

If we are to obey the Lord's commandment to be "wise as serpents" as well as "harmless as doves," we need to know what we are to be wary of. We need to be conscious of events and developments that have a bearing on our service for the Lord and on the well-being of ourselves and our children. But how do we determine which books will most effectively accomplish these educational objectives?

The same scriptural tests apply to evaluating the objectionable *as* literature that pertain to judging the objectionable *in* literature. When determining if an objectionable work or part of a work can function effectively as a negative example, we can put the questions in this way:

1. Is our use of the objectionable material presented only for its own sake, or is it purposeful? This is the criterion of **gratuitousness**.

2. Is the objectionable material too potent to serve well as a negative example? This is the criterion of **explicitness**.

3. Will the objectionable material be presented emphatically as a negative example? That is, will what it portrays appear dangerous and repulsive, regardless of the author's intentions? This is the criterion of **moral tone.**

If we can answer these questions adequately, we are justified, indeed obligated, to expose young people to some material that is repugnant to our Christian morality and theology so that Satan may not take advantage of their naiveté. Such material in the hands of a wise and skillful parent or teacher will create a defense against that which it represents.

Think of teaching literary discernment as inoculation. The moral purpose of Christian teaching is, minimally, to enable the young to escape the infection of evil. There are two ways of escaping an infectious disease: (1) avoiding contact with it and (2) developing a resistance. There are two ways of developing a resistance: (1) inoculation and (2) having a nonfatal case. Having a nonfatal case is not the sort of experience that one can plan; and even if one happens to be successful, it may leave him scarred and disabled. Clearly, inoculation is superior.

There are many biblical examples of this approach. One is found in Proverbs 7. The illustration is intended to inoculate the reader against sexual immorality by providing a vivid account of an adulterous liaison (7:6-27). The reader's ability to profit from this account depends on his maturity. But such instruction is an important part of the young man's defense against one of the most dangerous temptations he will face in the world. The story of the strange woman and the young fool illustrates the method of Scripture, which offers vivid accounts of sin and its consequences, not for titillation of the imagination but "to the intent we should not lust after evil things" (I Corinthians 10:6).

To illustrate the application of this biblical approach to a literary work, let's briefly examine Jack London's *Call of the Wild.* As mentioned earlier, a Darwinian and Nitzschean influence is evident in London's work. Irving Stone, a noted biographer of Jack London commented, "Jack's four intellectual grandparents were Darwin, Spencer, Marx, and Nietzsche. It is Nietzsche's ideas, especially his theory of man, that are most clearly reflected in the *Call of the Wild.* According to Nietzsche, the rise of Christianity with its emphasis on pity, compassion, and mercy had weakened man and thwarted his evolutionary progress. To restore man to the "Darwinian path," Nietzsche proposed that he cast off Christianity by ridding himself of all idealism, destroying his moral nature, and cultivating a ruthless attitude toward life. A careful analysis of *Call of the Wild* will reveal two important details. First, the central character Buck is more than a sled dog. He reasons, feels, and acts with keen awareness. He is, in other words, a symbol of man. Second, his actions clearly outline the Nietzschean process of "man's journey back to the Darwinian path." When Buck is stolen from a domestic environment and thrust into a hostile environment, he quickly loses his idealism—but not his cunning. When the other dogs steal his food, he concludes that a "moral nature is a vain thing and a handicap" in a harsh environment. Thus, he determines to cast aside morality, and he begins to steal, to murder, and to do whatever is necessary to develop a ruthlessness that allows him not only to survive but also to thrive. Eventually, of course, he emerges as "the dominant primordial beast" he was always meant to be. It is important to note that London so skillfully weaves the elements of his story that young readers are often unwittingly drawn to Buck and willingly accept the action of the story and its analysis of life. But guided discussion can thwart the author's intent and, more importantly, help students develop a discernment that will enable them to see the flaws in the logic of such men. The books we have included in our bibliography sections, one for grades 6-8 and another for grades 8-12, titled **"Books for Analysis and Discussion"** are specifically for this purpose.

In conclusion, we must remember that Christian education aims at the moral preservation and development of our young people. This aim requires teaching them to discern and desire good and to recognize and abhor evil, before they encounter the crucial and often subtle moral choices of adulthood. Most often, in literature as in life, good and evil are intertwined. The older the student, the more easily he can separate the strands, categorizing his responses. Christian education has not accomplished its purpose in the mind of the student and prepared him for life until he has learned to discriminate between the good and bad elements of his reading experience and to prefer the one to the other. The Christian parent or teacher must not only judge but also teach judging, if he is to engage in biblical moral education and to succeed in his aims.

Author and Title Index

A

A. B. Simpson: His Life and Work, 152

Aardema, Verna, 1

Aaron and the Green Mountain Boys, 34

Abandoned, 109

Abe Lincoln Gets His Chance, 18, 150

About Owls, 33

About Policemen, 24

About Policemen Around the World, 102

Abraham Lincoln, 94, 130, 150

Across Five Aprils, 132, 133

Acts and Monuments of These Latter and Perilous Days, The, 148

Adam and the Golden Cock, 93

Adam of the Road, 119

Adams, Sam and John, biography of, 51, 145

Adelson, Leone, 1

Adoff, Arnold, 1

Adoniram Judson: America's First Foreign Missionary, 148

Adventures of Huckleberry Finn, The, 143

Adventures of Pinocchio, The, 93

Adventures of Robinson Crusoe, The, 131

Adventures of Tom Sawyer, The, 127

Adventurous Moth, The, 72

Afternoon of the Elves, 126

Agostinelli, Maria Enrica, 1

Alaska in Words and Pictures, 30

Alcott, Louisa May, 117

Alcott, Louisa May, biography of, 120, 145

Aldrich, Bess Streeter, 129

Aldrich, Thomas B., 117

Alexander, Lloyd, 89

Alexander Graham Bell, 61

Alfred, 81

Alice's Adventures in Wonderland, 95

All Aboard the Train, 49

All About Bread, 65

Allamand, Pascale, 1

Allen, Gertrude E., 1

Allen, Jeffrey, 1

Allen, Judy, 2

All in a Suitcase, 62

All in One Day, 39

All in the Woodland Early, 87

All Kinds of Babies, 73

All-of-a-Kind Family, 113

All Ready for Summer, 1

All upon a Stone, 34

Alphabet Symphony, The, 56

Alphabet Tale, The, 34

Alston, Eugenia, 2
Altogether, One at a Time, 102
Amazing Dandelion, The, 73
Amazing Grace: John Newton's Story, 152
Aminal, The, 4
Amos Fortune, Free Man, 124
Amy Carmichael, 147
Amy Carmichael: Let the Little Children Come, 147
Amy Carmichael of Dohnavur, 147
Amy Loves the Rain, 41
Amy Loves the Sun, 41
Andersen, Hans Christian, 2, 89
Anderson, C. W., 2, 3, 89
Anderson, Courtney, 148
Anderson, LaVere, 3
Anderson, Lonzo, 3
Andrew Murray: Apostle of Abiding Love, 151
Andrew Murray and His Message, 151
Andy, 23
Andy and Mr. Wagner, 7
Andy and the Lion, 22
Andy and the School Bus, 7
Andy Buckram's Tin Men, 91
Anglund, Joan Walsh, 3
Angus and the Cat, 29
Angus and the Ducks, 29
Animal Camouflage, 68
Animal Counting Book, 3
Animal Farm, 142
Animal Homes, 67

Animal Houses, 28
Animals in Winter, 5
Animals Keeping Safe, 15
Anna's Garden Song, 77
Anne of Avonlea, 121
Anne of Green Gables, 120
Ann Hasseltine Judson of Burma, 149
Anteater Named Arthur, An, 82
Ants, 9
Ants Are Fun, 62
Appell, Clara and Morey, 3
Apple a Day, An, 64
Applemouse, 79
Apple Tree, 84
Apricot ABC, 58
Are You Listening?, 33
Armstrong, William H., 125
Arnold, Caroline, 4
Arnold, Elliott, 117
Around the World in Eighty Days, 124
Ask Mr. Bear, 29
Astronauts, 37
Attic of the Wind, 54
Austen, Jane, 129
Autobiography, An, 147
Autobiography of David Brainerd, 146
Autobiography of George Mueller, 151
Autobiography of Hudson Taylor, 153
Automobiles for Mice, 27
Away Goes Sally, 93

Aylward, Gladys, biography of, 43, 145

Ayres, Pam, 4

B

Baba, Noboru, 4

Babar Loses His Crown, 23

Baby Animals, 51

Bach, Johann Sebastian, biography of, 145

Bacon, Ernest W., 152

Bailey, Carolyn Sherwin, 4, 89

Bailey, Faith Cox, 148, 151

Bainton, Roland, 150

Baker, Eugene, 4

Balian, Lorna, 4, 5

Balloon, 17

Bambi, 111

Bancroft, Henrietta, 5

Banner in the Sky, 123

Banners at Shenandoah, 130

Bannon, Laura, 5, 89

Barner, Bob, 5

Baronet's Song, The, 140

Baron's Apprenticeship, The, 140

Barr, Cathrine, 5

Barr, Jene, 5, 90

Barrett, Judi, 5

Barrie, Sir James M., 90

Barry: The Bravest Saint Bernard, 38

Bartlett, Janet La Spiza, 40

Bartlett, Margaret Farrington, 6

Bartoli, Jennifer, 6

Barton, Clara, biography of, 71, 145

Basil Brush Finds Treasure, 28

Basketball, 71

Bat Is Born, A, 46

Bats, 70

Bats in the Dark, 48

Bauer, Judith, 6

Baum, L. Frank, 90

Baylor, Byrd, 90

Beach Before Breakfast, The, 51

Beacons of Light: Lighthouses, 35

Beales, Joan, 6

Bear Book, The, 66

Bear by Himself, 40

Bear Called Paddington, A, 9

Bear Mouse, 31

Bears on Hemlock Mountain, The, 21

Bear's Toothache, The, 56

Bearymore, 30

Beastly Circus, A, 64

Beatty, Hetty Burlingame, 6

Beautiful Day for a Picnic, A, 21

Beaver Pond, The, 80

Beavers Live Here, 26

Becker, John, 97

Becky, the Rabbit, 22

Bees and Beelines, 99

Behrens, June, 6, 7

Beim, Jerrold A., 7

Bell, Gina, 7

Bemelmans, Ludwig, 7

Ben and Me, 103

Benchley, Nathaniel, 7

Ben-Hur, 134

Be Nice to Spiders, 37

Benjamin's 365 Birthdays, 5

Bennet, Rowena, 90

Bennett, Rainey, 8

Benson, Kathleen, 150

Berenstain, Michael, 8

Berg, Jean Horton, 8

Bergman, Thomas, 8

Berson, Harold, 8, 9

Beskow, Elsa Maartman, 9

Best-Loved Doll, The, 18

Best of Friends, 114

Beware of a Very Hungry Fox, 86

Bible Smuggler, 154

Big Bear to the Rescue, 57

Big Book of Dogs, The, 52

Big Book of Real Trains, The, 16

Big Dipper, The, 10

Big Frogs, Little Frogs, 59

Biggest Bear, The, 83

Biggest House in the World, The, 53

Biggest Nose, The, 16

Big Red, 119

Big Sister and Little Sister, 88

Big Snow, The, 38

Big Tracks, Little Tracks, 10

Big Yellow Balloon, The, 28

Billy, the Littlest One, 72

Billy and Blaze, 2

Billy Budd, 142

Billy Sunday, 153

Billy Sunday: Baseball Preacher, 153

Bird Life in Wington, 111

Birds at Night, 33

Birds Eat and Eat and Eat, 33

Birds We Know, 32

Bird Talk, 98

Birthday Trombone, The, 39

Bishop, Claire Huchet, 9

Bix, Cynthia Overbeck, 9

Bjorn, Thyra Ferre, 129

Black Arrow, The, 134

Black Jack: Last of the Big Alligators, 106

Blackmore, Richard D., 129

Blades, Ann, 90

Blaze and the Forest Fire, 2

Blaze and the Gray Spotted Pony, 2

Blaze and the Indian Cave, 2

Blaze and the Lost Quarry, 2

Blaze and Thunderbolt, 2

Blaze Finds Forgotten Roads, 2

Blaze Shows the Way, 3

Blessed Assurance: The Life and Hymns of Fanny Crosby, 147

Blind Colt, The, 111

Blind Connemara, The, 89

Blind Men and the Elephant, The, 69

Bloome, Enid, 9

Blueberries for Sal, 55

Blue Bug's Beach Party, 68

Blue Canyon Horse, 92

Blue Fairy Book, 103

Blue Willow, 98

Bobby Bear Finds Maple Sugar, 40

Bobby Bear Goes Fishing, 40

Bobby Bear in the Spring, 40

Bobby Bear's Rocket Ride, 40

Bobby Learns About Woodland Babies, 82

Bolognese, Don, 9

Bond, Michael, 9

Bond, Susan, 9

Bone, Gratia Hyde, 148

Bongiorno, Mary M., 9

Bonsall, Crosby, 10

Boo, 51

Borack, Barbara, 10

Borden, William Whiting, biography of, 145

Bottom of the Sea, The, 98

Bowditch, Nathaniel, biography of, 120, 146

Box with Red Wheels, The, 65

Boyhood of Ranald Bannerman, The, 120

Boy Who Walked off the Page, The, 54

Boy with a Pack, 120

Braille, Louis, biography of, 23, 146

Brainerd, David, 146

Brainerd, David, autobiography of, 146

Brandenberg, Aliki, 10

Brandenberg, Franz, 10

Brandt, Keith, 10

Branley, Franklyn M., 10, 11, 90, 91

Brave Baby Elephant, 48

Brave Cowboy, The, 3

Bravest Dog Ever, The, 77

Brave the Wild Trail, 101

Brecht, Edith, 91

Breinburg, Petronella, 12

Brian Wildsmith's ABC, 85

Brian Wildsmith's Wild Animals, 86

Bridge, The, 108

Bridwell, Norman, 12

Brierley, Louise, 12

Bright, Robert, 12

Brighty of the Grand Canyon, 100

Brinckloe, Julie, 12

Brink, Carol R., 91

Broekel, Ray, 12

Bronson, Wilfrid S., 91

Brontë, Charlotte, 129

Brontë, Emily, 136

Bronze Bow, The, 122

Brothers, Aileen, 12

Brower, Pauline, 7

Brown, Liane I., 130

Brown, Marc, 12

Brown, Marcia, 13

Brown, Margaret Wise, 13

Brown, Myra Berry, 13

Browning, Elizabeth Barrett, 130

Bruna, Dick, 13

Bruningham, John, 15

Brustlein, Janice, 13, 14

Buchan, James, 152

Buckley, Helen E., 14

Budd, Lillian, 14

Budney, Blossom, 14

Buff, Mary and Conrad, 14

Buffy the Barn Owl, 15

Bug City, 45

Builder of Bridges, 148

Building a House, 70

Bulla, Clyde Robert, 14

Bun: A Tale from Russia, The, 13

Bunting, Eve, 14

Bunyan, John, 15, 146

Bunyan, John, biography of, 146

Bunyan Characters: Bunyan Himself as Seen in His Grace Abounding, 146

Burnett, Frances H., 92

Burnford, Sheila, 118

Burning Heart: John Wesley, Evangelist, The, 154

Burton, Hester, 92

Burton, Jane, 15

Burton, Virginia Lee, 15

Busch, Phyllis S., 16

Busy Trains, 53

Butternut Bill and the Bear, 54

Butternut Bill and the Bee Tree, 54

Buttons at the Zoo, The, 54

Buxbaum, Susan Kovacs, 15

Buzztail: The Story of a Rattlesnake, 106

Buzzy Bear and the Rainbow, 57

Buzzy Bear's Winter Party, 57

Byars, Betsy, 16, 118

By Life and by Death: Excerpts from the Diary and Letters of John Stam, 153

By Secret Railway, 109

By the Shores of Silver Lake, 115

C

Caddie Woodlawn, 91

Cake Story, The, 86

Calhoun, Mary, 16

Calico Bush, 97

Calico Cat Meets Bookworm, 19

Call It Courage, 122

Call of the Wild, 140

Cameron, Elizabeth, 16

Canfield, Carolyn, 149

Canfield, Dorothy, 92

Cannonball Simp, 15

Caple, Kathy, 16

Captains Courageous, 133

Captive Treasure, 43

Carême, Maurice, 16

Carey, William, biography of, 146

Carle, Eric, 16, 17

Carlisle, Jane, 17

Carlisle, Norman and Madelyn, 17

Carmichael, Amy, biography of, 118, 147

Carnival of the Animals, 72

Carolina's Courage, 87

Carpenter, A, 29

Carrick, Donald, 17

Carroll, Lewis.
  See Dodgson, Charles

Carrot Seed, The, 51

Carry On, Mr. Bowditch, 120, 145

Carver, George Washington, biography of, 26, 147

Case of the Cat's Meow, The, 10

Case of the Hungry Stranger, The, 10

Casey, Denise, 17

Casper, the Caterpillar, 30

Cat and Mrs. Cory, The, 98

Catastrophe Cat, 64

Catch the Wind!, 35

Cathedral, 120

Catherall, E. A., 17

Cats Know Best, 26

Catton, Bruce, 130

Caudill, Rebecca, 18

Cavanah, Frances, 18, 150

Cave, Ron Joyce, 18

Cecil, Richard, 152

Cervantes, Miguel de, 130

Chald, Dorothy, 18

Chalk Box Story, The, 30

Chameleon Was a Spy, 57

Champion of Freedom, 133, 153

Chance to Die: The Life and Legacy of Amy Carmichael, A, 147

Chandler, Edna Walker, 18, 19

Chandoha, Walter, 19

Chapin, Cynthia, 19, 90

Chapman, John, biography of, 49, 147

Charles, Donald, 19

Charles Spurgeon, 152

Charlie Needs a Cloak, 24

Charlie the Tramp, 41

Charlotte's Web, 114

Chester, 41

Chicken Book, The, 86

Chicken Little Count-to-Ten, 32

Child, Lydia Maria, 19

Child's Book of Manners, A, 63

Child's Book of Seasons, A, 45

Child's Garden of Verses, A, 77

Choe, Leona, 151

Choo Choo, 15

Chrisman, Arthur Bowie, 92

Christmas Carol, A, 118

Christmas on the Mayflower, 100

Christopher, John, 136

Church, Jeffrey, 66

Circus Baby, The, 66

Citrus Fruits, 82

City-Country ABC, The, 83

City Night, 70

City of Gold and Lead, The, 136

Clara Barton: Soldier of Mercy, 71, 145

Clark, Ann Nolan, 92

Clark, George Rogers, biography of, 23, 147

Claverie, Jean, 19

Clean Brook, The, 6

Clear for Action, 120

Cleary, Beverly, 93

Clifford, Eth, 125

Clifford, the Small Red Puppy, 12

Clinton, Iris, 146

Cloud Book, The, 24

Clouds, 63

cluck baa, 15

Coatsworth, Elizabeth, 19, 93

Cock, the Mouse, and the Little Red Hen, The, 51

Coles, Peter, 19

Collier, Ethel, 19, 20

Collins, David R., 130, 150

Collodi, Carlo, 93

Colonial Farm, 7

Color, 67

Columbus Day, 74

Come Summer, Come Winter, 74

Come Visit a Prairie Dog Town, 2

Compere, Mickie, 20

Complete Peterkin Papers, The, 99

Conford, Ellen, 20

Conklin, Gladys, 20

Connecticut Yankee in King Arthur's Court, A, 143

Contender, The, 140

Cooper, James Fenimore, 130

Corduroy, 30

Cotton, 38

Count of Monte Cristo, The, 131

Country Noisy Book, The, 13

Country School, 7

Courage by Darkness, 109

Courage of Sarah Noble, The, 21

Cowboy Book, The, 21

Cowboys, 38, 57, 76

Cowboy Sam and Big Bill, 18

Cowboy Sam and Porky, 18

Cowboy Sam and Shorty, 19

Cowboy Small, 51

Coyote Cry, 90

Craft, Ruth, 20

Craig, Janet, 20

Crane, Stephen, 136

Cranes in My Corral, 101

Cranky Blue Crab, The, 83

Crawford, Mel, 21

Credle, Ellis, 21

Cretan, Gladys, Y., 21

Cricket in Times Square, The, 112

Cristini, Ermanno, 21

Crosby, Fanny, 147

Crosby, Fanny, biography of, 147

Crown and Jewel, 108

Cry, the Beloved Country, 142

Cue for Treason, 123

Curious George Goes to the Hospital, 70

Curry, Nancy, 21

D

D. L. Moody: The Greatest Evangelist of the Nineteenth Century, 151

Dalgliesh, Alice, 21, 93

Dallinger, Jane, 22

Dan Frontier, 45

Dan Frontier, Trapper, 45

Dan Frontier and the Big Cat, 45

Dandelion, 31

Dandelions, 68

Dangerous Game, A, 108

Daniel of Babylon, 133

Darby, Gene, 22

Darkness in Daytime, 90

Darros, Arthur, 22

D'Aubigne, J. H., 150

Daugherty, James, 22

D'Aulaire, Ingri and Edgar Parin, 22, 94, 150

Davey, Cyril, 150, 153, 154

David Copperfield, 131

David Livingstone, 150

Davidson, Margaret, 23, 146

Davis, Mary Octavia, 23

Davis, Rebecca, 118, 147

Davis, Tim, 23

Dawn Wind, 122

Day, Jennifer W., 23

Day in the Life of a Firefighter, A, 76

Day of the Wind, The, 66

Day We Saw the Sun Come Up, The, 37

Dead Tree, The, 80

DeAngeli, Marguerite, 93, 94

Dearmin, Jennie T., 65

Dear Terry, 114

De Brunhoff, Laurent, 23

Deep Dives of Stanley Whale, The, 7

Deep in the Forest, 80

Deer in the Pasture, The, 17

Deerslayer, The, 130

Defender of the Faith, 133, 154

Defoe, Daniel, 131

DeJong, Meindert, 94

DeLeeuw, Adele, 23, 147

Delton, Judy, 23

Dempsey, Michael W., 24

Dengler, Sandy, 146, 147, 155

Dennis, Wesley, 23

Denny's Friend Rags, 78

DePaola, Tomie, 23, 24

Department Store, 35

DeRegniers, Beatrice Schenk, 24

Derwood, Inc., 108

Deserts, 68

Devlin, Wende and Harry, 24

Diary of a Young Girl, The, 136

Diary of George Mueller, The, 151

Dick, Lois Hoadley, 131, 147, 149

Dickens, Charles, 118, 131

Dickinson, Terence, 24

Did You Carry the Flag Today, Charley?, 18

Dillon, Ina K., 24

Discovering Trees, 30

Dixon, Annabelle, 24

Dobry, 112

Dodge, Mary Mapes, 95

Dodgson, Charles [pseud. Lewis Carroll], 95

Dog from Nowhere, The, 19

Dolch, Edward W. and Marguerite P., 24, 25

Domanska, Janina, 25

Donkey-donkey, 25

Don Quixote, 130

Door in the Wall, The, 93

Douglas, W. M., 151

Down, Down the Mountain, 21

Down Comes the Leaves, 5

Down the River Without a Paddle, 85

Do You Know About Stars?, 31

Do You Suppose Miss Riley Knows?, 21

Do You Want to Be My Friend?, 17

Dr. Trotter and His Big Gold Watch, 35

Dresser, Elizabeth, 38

Drop of Blood, A, 74

Drummer Hoff, 26

DuBois, William Péne, 25, 95

Duchess Bakes a Cake, The, 48

Ducks Don't Get Wet, 36

Dugan, William, 25

Duke Decides, 123

Dumas, Alexandre, 131

Dusty, 51

Duvoisin, Roger, 25, 28

E

Eagle of the Ninth, 122

Ear Book, The, 65

Early Morning in the Barn, 78

Ears and Hearing, 19

Ears Are for Hearing, 74

Eats: Poems, 1

Eat Your Peas, Louise, 76

Eberle, Irmengarde, 26

Ed Emberley's Great Thumbprint Drawing Book, 26

Edison, Thomas, biography of, 20, 69, 147

Edmonds, Walter D., 95

Edwardian Summer, An, 36

Edwards, Julie, 96

Eggleston, Edward, 118

Eight Cousins, 117

Eisler, Colin, 26

Elephant Book, The, 63

Elephant's Child, The, 101

Elephants of Africa, 20

Elevator/Escalator Book, The, 5

Eleven Cats in a Bag, 4

Elgin, Kathleen, 96

Eliot, George, 131

Elkin, Benjamin, 26
Elliot, Elisabeth, 147, 148
Elliot, Jim, biography of, 148
Ellis, William T., 153
Emberley, Barbara, 26
Emberley, Ed, 26
Emberley, Rebecca, 26
Emert, Phyliss Raybin, 26
Emily's Autumn, 81
Emma, 129
Emperor Penguins, The, 60
Endless Steppe, The, 132
English, Schuyler E., 153
Enock, Ester, 152
Enright, Elizabeth, 96
Epstein, Sam and Beryl, 26, 147
Eric Liddell, 150
Erskine, John T., 153
Esbensen, Barbara Juster, 27
Estes, Eleanor, 96, 97
Ethan Frome, 144
Ets, Marie Hall, 27
Euphonia and the Flood, 16
Evans, Eva Knox, 27
Evan's Corner, 41
Everett, Betty Steele, 153
Everyday Animals, 1
Everyday Turtles, Toads, and Their Kin, 1
Every Perfect Gift, 133
Expendable Mary Slessor, The, 152
Exploring the Sky by Day, 24

F

Facts and Fictions of Minna Pratt, The, 126
Fairclough, Chris, 27
False Coin, True Coin, 131
Fanny Crosby: Writer of 8,000 Songs, 147
Fanny Crosby Speaks Again, 147
Faraday, Michael, biography of, 148
Farley, Walter, 27
Farm Animals, 43
Farmer, The, 51
Farmer Boy, 115
Farmer in the Dell, The, 27
Farming, 35
Far Out the Long Canal, 94
Father's Arcane Daughter, 102
Father's Promise, A, 101
Fatio, Louise, 27, 28
Faulkner, Georgene, 97
Favorite Poems Old and New, 28
Feathered Ones and Furry, 28
Felder, Eleanor, 28
Fenner, Phyllis, 97
Fenton, Edward, 28
Ferris, Helen, 28
Fiammenghi, Gioia, 61
Field, Rachel, 97
Fife, Dale, 97
Fight of the Shadow, The, 141
Find Out by Touching, 75
Finnie, Kellsye, 146

Fire Engine Book, The, 87
Fire Engines, 77
Fire Fighters, 12
Firefly Named Torchy, A, 82
Firmin, Peter, 28
First Four Years, The, 115
First Train, The, 81
Fir Tree, The, 89
Fish Book, The, 57
Fisher, Aileen, 28, 29
Fisher, Leonard Everett, 29
Fisherman's Lady, The, 141
Fish Is Fish, 53
Fitt, A. P., 151
Five Chinese Brothers, The, 9
Flack, Marjorie, 29
Flags, 79
Flash, Crash, Rumble, and Roll, 10
Fleischman, Paul, 118
Flickertail, 4
Flight of the Snow Goose, The, 31
Flip, 23
Flip and the Morning, 23
Floating and Sinking, 11
Flocks of Birds, 88
Florence Nightingale: The Lady of the Lamp, 152
Florian, Douglas, 29, 30
Flower Grows, A, 70
Flowers, Fruits, Seeds, 84
Fly Went By, A, 55
Foal for You, A, 19

Follow the Water from Brook to Ocean, 22
Forbes, Esther, 125
Forest Folk, 14
Foster, Celeste K., 30
Foster, Doris VanLiew, 30
Four-Story Mistake, The, 96
Fourth of July Raid, 100
Fox, Charles Philip, 30
Fox Book, The, 66
Fox Eyes, 13
Foxe, John, 148
Foxe, John, biography of, 148
Foxie, the Singing Dog, 22
Fradin, Dennis B., 30
François, Paul, 30
Frank, Anne, 136
Freedom Train: The Story of Harriet Tubman, 113, 154
Freeman, Don, 30, 31
Freeman, Mae Blacker, 31
Freschet, Berniece, 31
Fresh Cider and Pie, 10
Friend Is Someone Who Likes You, A, 3
Friendly Prairie Dog, The, 17
Friskey, Margaret, 32
Fritz, Jean, 32
Frog and Toad Are Friends, 54
Froman, Robert, 98
From Anna, 104
From the Mixed-Up Files of Mrs. Basil E. Frankweiler, 102
From This to That, 46
Fullerton, W. Y., 152

Funny Thing, The, 32

G

Gág, Wanda, 32

Galdone, Paul, 33

Gambill, Henrietta, 33

Gannett, Ruth S., 98

Gans, Roma, 33, 98

Gardiner, John Reynolds, 98

Garelick, May, 33, 34

Garten, Jan, 34

Garton, N., 151

Gates, Doris, 98

Gauch, Patricia Lee, 34

Gay, Zhenya, 34

Gee, Mable, 9

Gelman, Rita Golden, 15

Gentle Ben, 121

George, Jean Craighead, 34, 119

George Mueller, 151

George Mueller and His Orphans, 151

George Mueller of Bristol, 151

George Muller: Man of Faith and Miracles, 151

George Rogers Clark, 23, 147

George Washington Carver, 26

George Whitefield's Journals, 155

Georgiady, Nicholas, 34

Georgiou, Constantine, 34

Gergely, Tibor, 13, 34

Gertie Groundhog, 43

Giambarba, Paul, 35

Giant, The, 95

Giants of the Earth, 142

Gibbons, Gail, 35

Giesen, Rosemary, 79

Giff, Patricia Reilly, 35

Gift of Hawaii, The, 5

Giggly-Wiggly, Snickety-Snick, 78

Gilbert, Helen Earle, 35

Gilroy, Ruth G. and Frank, 36

Gingerbread Man, The, 36

Gingercat's Catch, 5

Ginger Pye, 96

Gladys Aylward, 145

Gladys Aylward: The Little Woman, 145

Glendinning, Sally, 36

Glenn Learns to Read, 3

Gloomy Gus, 109

Go, Team, Go, 123

Go and Hush the Baby, 16

God's Care Is Everywhere, 83

Goffstein, M. B., 36

Goforth, Jonathan, biography of, 148

Goforth, Rosalind, 148

Goforth of China, 148

Golden Key, The, 107

Goldin, Augusta, 36, 98, 99

Goldman, Ethel, 36

Goldsmith, Oliver, 132

Gone-Away Lake, 96

Good Friends, The, 30

Good Master, The, 121

Good Morning, Mr. Sun, 68

Good Morning, Teacher, 5

Goodall, John S., 36

Good-bye, Mr. Chips, 132

Goodbye, My Lady, 122

Goodnight, Goodnight, 70

Goodnight Moon, 13

Goodnight Owl!, 45

Goor, Ron and Nancy, 37

Goose That Was a Watchdog, The, 40

Gordon Goes Camping, 12

Goudey, Alice E., 37

Grace Abounding to the Chief of Sinners, 146

Graff, Steward and Polly Anne, 37, 149

Graham, Margaret Bloy, 37

Graham, Mary Stuart, 37

Grahame, Kenneth, 99

Gramatky, Hardie, 37

Grand Canyon, 58

Grandparents Around the World, 69

Grandpa, 10

Grandpa's Gizmos, 58

Gravity Is a Mystery, 11

Gray, Elizabeth Janet, 119

Great Big Animal Book, The, 37

Great Big Enormous Turnip, The, 79

Great Expectations, 131

Great Gilly Hopkins, The, 127

Great Stone Face and Other Tales of the White Mountains, The, 132

Green, Ivah, 37

Greene, Carol, 37, 38

Green Fairy Book, 103

Gregory, O. B., 38

Grubb, Norman, 153

Guess What Grasses Do, 70

Guggenmos, Josef, 38

Guide Dogs, 26

Guilfoile, Elizabeth, 38

Gulick, Peggy, 38

H

Hader, Berta and Elmer, 38

Hailstone and Halibut Bones, 64

Hale, Edward Everett, 132

Hale, Lucretia, 99

Haley, Gail E., 38

Hall, Donald, 38

Hall, James N., 133

Hall, Lynn, 38

Hall, Mary Hyde, 148

Hamsa, Bobbie, 39

Hankin, Rebecca, 39

Hans Brinker and the Silver Skates, 95

Happy Birthday Present, The, 40

Happy Lion, The, 27

Happy Lion's Treasure, The, 27

Happy Owls, The, 66

Hardy, Thomas, 137

Hare and the Tortoise, The, 39

Harmon, Rebecca Lamar, 155

Harriet Goes to the Circus, 56

Harris, Beth Coombe, 99
Harry the Dirty Dog, 87
Hartelius, Margaret, 39
Harvey, Fran, 39
Haunt-Fox, 102
Hautiz, Esther, 132
Have You Seen My Brother?, 38
Have You Seen My Duckling?, 78
Have You Seen Trees?, 64
Hawes, Judy, 39, 99
Hawkinson, John and Lucy (Ozone), 39
Hawkinson, Lucy (Ozone), 39
Hawk That Dare Not Hunt by Day, The, 121, 154
Hawthorne, Nathaniel, 132, 137
Hayes, Ann, 39
Hayes, Geoffrey, 40
Hays, Wilma Pitchford, 40, 100
Hazen, Barbara Shook, 40
Hear Your Heart, 75
Hector Penguin, 28
Hefter, Richard, 40
Heide, Florence Parry, 40
Heidi, 112
Heilbroner, Joan, 40
Hein, Lucille, 40
Helen Keller: Toward the Light, 37, 149
Helmrath, Marilyn Olear, 40-41
Henny-Penny, 77
Henriod, Lorraine, 41
Henry, Marguerite, 41, 100, 126

Henry Explores the Mountains, 79
Henry Possum, 8
Here Comes the Strikeout, 49
Here I Stand: A Life of Martin Luther, 150
Here's Benjie!, 83
Her Majesty Grace Jones, 103
Herman and the Bears Again, 62
Hess, Donna, 101, 132
Hidden Life of the Desert, The, 85
Hidden Life of the Forest, The, 51
Hidden Messages, 81
Hide and Seek Day, 87
Hiding Place, The, 154
Hill, Elizabeth Starr, 41
Hilton, James, 132
Hippo with Feathers, A, 69
Hitty—Her First Hundred Years, 97
Hoban, Julia, 41
Hoban, Russell, 41
Hobbit, The, 134
Hoff, Syd, 41-42
Hoffman, E. T. A., 42
Hoffman, Mary, 42
Hogrogian, Nonny, 42
Hold My Hand, 88
Hole, Dorothy, 132, 154
Holl, Adelaide, 42
Holland, Joyce, 43
Holland, Rowena, 43

Holling, Holling Clancey, 100

Holmgren, Virginia C., 43

Holsclaw, Cora, 12

Holt, P. N., 17

Homer Price, 105

Homes, 64

Honker: The Story of a Wild Goose, 106

Hoosier Schoolmaster, The, 118

Hop-High, the Goat, 89

Horse and His Boy, The, 104

Horse in Harry's Room, The, 42

Horseman of the King, 154

Horses, Horses, Horses, 97

Horwitz, Joshua, 43

Hot and Cold, 76

Hough, Charlotte, 43

Houghton, Frank, 147

House of Sixty Fathers, The, 94

House of the Seven Gables, The, 132

House That Jack Built, The, 65

How, Hippo!, 13

Howard, Milly, 43, 101, 145

How a Seed Grows, 48

How Big Am I?, 40

How Big Is a Foot?, 62

How Can I Find Out?, 9

How Does It Feel to Be a Tree?, 62

Howe, Caroline Walton, 44

Howells, William Dean, 138

How Fletcher Was Hatched!, 24

How Many Teeth?, 75

How My Garden Grew, 70

How You Talk, 75

Hudson Taylor: God's Man in China, 153

Hudson Taylor and Maria, 153

Hudson Taylor's Spiritual Secret, 153

Hue and Cry, 135

Hugo, Victor, 138

Human Body: The Ear, The, 96

Hummingbirds in the Garden, 33

Humpback Whales, 64

Humphrey, Jack W. and Sandra Altheide, 44

Hunchback of Notre Dame, The, 138

Hundred Angels Singing, A, 81

Hundred Dresses, The, 96

Hundreds and Hundreds of Strawberries, 19

Hungry Sharks, 83

Hunt, Irene, 132

Hunter, Christine, 145

Hunter, Ilene, 44

Hurd, Edith Thatcher, 44, 45

Hurley, William, 45

Hurrah for Maxie, 38

Hurricane, 85

Hustad, Donald P., ed., 147

Hutchins, Pat, 45

Hyde, Dayton O., 101

Hyde, John, biography of, 148

I

I Can Be a Carpenter, 52

I Can Be a Fire Fighter, 39

I Can Be a Nurse, 6
Icebergs, 33
Ichikawa, Satomi, 45
I Feel the Same Way, 61
If Everybody Did, 78
If I Perish, 149
If I Were a Cricket, 60
I Know a Newspaper Reporter, 41
I Know Something You Don't Know, 1
I Learn to Read About Jesus, 71
I Like Cats, 24
I Like Fruit, 36
I Like the Library, 70
I Like Trains, 86
I Love You, Mary Jane, 5
I'm Going on a Bear Hunt, 76
I'm Tired of Lions, 34
Impossible, Possum, 20
In a Meadow Two Hares Hide, 6
Inch by Inch, 53
Incredible Journey, The, 118
Indian Two Feet and His Eagle Feather, 32
Indian Two Feet and His Horse, 32
Indian Two Feet and the Grizzly Bear, 32
In My Garden, 21
In My Mother's House, 92
In My Uncle's House, 110
In Search of Honor, 132
Inspector Peckit, 31

In Spite of All the Terror, 92
In the Forest, 27
In the Middle of the Night, 28
In the Night, 75
In the Woods, 24
Invincible Louisa, 120, 145
Ipcar, Dahlov, 45
Ira Sleeps Over, 82
Iron Duke, 134
Irving, Washington, 133
Island of the Blue Dolphins, 121
Island Time, 51
Isobel Kuhn, 149
Israel, Laurie, ed., 46
It's Nesting Time, 33
Ivanhoe, 134
I Want to Be a Forester, 4
I Want to Be a Service Station Attendant, 4
I Want to Read, 86

J

James, Henry, 138
James, Will, 119
Jane Eyre, 129
Jarrell, Randall, 46
Jefferies, Madeleine Milner, 46
Jennings, Terry, 46
Jennison, Keith W., 46
Jenny Wren, 114
Jimmie, the Youngest Errand Boy, 47
Jimmy and Joe Get a Hen's Surprise, 36
Joey and Patches, 47

Joey Kangaroo, 59

Johannes Kepler: Giant of Faith and Science, 149

John and Betty Stam, 153

John Bunyan: Writer of Pilgrim's Progress, 146

John Hyde: Apostle of Prayer, 148

John Knox: Apostle of the Scottish Reformation, 149

John Newton: The Angry Sailor, 152

John Wesley, 154

Johnny Appleseed, 49, 147

Johnny Lion's Bad Day, 44

Johnny Lion's Book, 44

Johnny Lion's Rubber Boots, 44

Johnny Maple-Leaf, 80

Johnny Tremain, 125

Johnson, Crockett, 46, 47

Johnson, Gladys O., 47

Johnson, Hannah Lyons, 47

Johnson, Helen Lossing, 47

Johnson, Jean, 47

Johnson, Margaret S., 47

Johnson, R. K., 148

Johnson, Sylvia, 47

Johnson, William J., 149

Johnston, Johanna, 48

Jones, Bob, 133

Jones, Bob, Sr., biography of, 148

Jordan, Helene J., 48

Jo's Boys, 117

Joslin, Sesyle, 48

Journeyman, The, 135

Journey to the Center of the Earth, 124

Joyful Noise: Poems for Two Voices, 118

Joy of Bach, The, 145

Judson, Adoniram, biography of, 148

Judson, Ann Hasseltine, biography of, 149

Judson, Marilyn, 44

Jungle Book, The, 119

Jungle Sounds, 26

Junk Day on Juniper Street and Other Easy to Read Stories, 61

Just Awful, 84

Juster, Norton, 119

Justin Morgan Had a Horse, 100

Just-in-Time Joey, 74

Just Me, 27

Just Me and My Dad, 57

Just One Me, 12

Just So Stories, 101

K

Kahl, Virginia, 48

Kandoian, Ellen, 48

Kangaroo, 73

Karen's Opposites, 69

Kate, 105

Katey, 46

Katie Kittenheart, 108

Katy and the Big Snow, 15

Kauffman, Lois, 48

Kaufmann, John, 48, 101

Kavik, the Wolf Dog, 110

Keats, Ezra Jack, 48, 49

Keith, Harold, 119

Keller, Helen, biography of, 37, 149

Kellogg, Steven, 49, 147

Kelly, Eric, 126

Kepler, Johannes, biography of, 149

Kesselman, Wendy, 49

Kessler, Ethel, 49

Kessler, Leonard, 49

Kick, Pass, and Run, 49

Kickapoo, 58

Kidnapped, 134

Kim, Esther Ahn, 149

Kim, Esther Ahn, biography of, 149

Kincaid, Doug, 19

Kind of Secret Weapon, A, 117

King for Brass Cobweb, A, 83

King Krakus and the Dragon, 25

King Lion and His Cooks, 12

King of the Wind, 126

King Robert the Resting Ruler, 64

King's Choice, The, 74

King's Fifth, The, 121

Kingsley, Charles, 133

Kipling, Rudyard, 101, 119, 133

Kirk, John, 155

Kirkland, Wallace, 49

Kirkpatrick, Rena K., 49

Kishida, Eriko, 50

Kiss Is Round, A, 14

Kittens Are Like That, 66

Kjelgaard, Jim [James Arthur], 102, 119

Knight, David C., 50

Knight, Eric M., 102

Knightly, Rosalinda, 50

Knight's Fee, 122

Knowles, John, 139

Knox, John, biography of, 149

Konigsburg, E. L., 102

Krauss, Ruth, 50

Kuchalla, Susan, 50

Kuhn, Dwight, 50

Kuhn, Isobel, biography of, 149

Kumin, Maxine, 50

Kuskin, Karla, 50

L

Lad: A Dog, 113

Ladybug, 106

Lady's Confession, The, 141

Lamb, Charles and Mary, 102

Lamont, Bette, 50

Landin, Les, 102

Land Transport Around the World, 77

Lang, Andrew, 103

Langner, Nola, 50

Langton, Jane, 103

Lantern Bearers, 122

Lantern in Her Hand, A, 129

Lasky, Kathryn, 51

Lassie Come-Home, 102

Last Battle, The, 104

Last Little Cat, The, 94

Last of the Mohicans, The, 130

Latham, Jean Lee, 120, 146

Latham, Robert O., 150

Lawson, Robert, 103

Leaf, Munro, 51

Lean, Garth, 154

LeBar, Mary, 51

Lee, Harper, 139

Lee, Robert E., 145

Lee, Robert E., biography of, 149

Lee, Susan and John, 51, 145

Lefèvre, Félicité, 51

Legend of Sleepy Hollow, The, 133

Leister, Mary, 51

Lenski, Lois, 51, 52

Lentil, 55

Les Miserables, 138

Le Tord, Bijou, 52

Let's Bake Bread, 47

Let's Find Out About Names, 67

Let's Find Out About Weather, 51

Let's Look at the Birds, 65

Let's Look at Whales, 65

Let's Visit a Printing Plant, 63

Lewis, C. S., 104, 139, 140, 150

Lewis, C. S., biography of, 150

Lewis, Jean, 52

Liddell, Eric, biography of, 150

Life and Letters of Praying Hyde, 148

Life and Times of Martin Luther, 150

Life Cycle of an Ant, The, 79

Life of D. L. Moody, 151

Life of John Newton, 152

Liffring-zug, Joan, 52

Lighthouse at Dangerfield, The, 35

Lighthouse Book, The, 8

Light Princess, The, 107

Like Nothing at All, 28

Lillegard, Dee, 52

Lincoln, Abraham, biography of, 18, 94, 130, 150

Lindgren, Astrid, 104

Lindman, Maj, 53

Linn, Margot, 53

Linton, Margaret, 79

Lion, the Witch, and the Wardrobe, The, 104

Lion and the Bird's Nest, The, 50

Lionni, Leo, 53

Lippman, Peter, 53

Lipsyte, Robert, 140

Lisle, Janet Taylor, 126

Little, Jean, 104-5

Little Airplane, The, 51

Little Auto, The, 52

Little Bear, 60

Little Bear Learns to Read the Cookbook, 13

Little Bear's Friend, 60

Little Bear's Visit, 60

Little Black, a Pony, 27

Little Blue and Little Yellow, 53

Little Boy Who Lives Up High, 39

Littledale, Freya and Harold, 53

Little Dog Tim, 77

Little Ego, 36

Little Engine That Could, The, 67

Little Fellow, The, 41

Little Fire Engine, The, 52

Little Fox, The, 91

Little Frightened Tiger, 56

Little Goat in the Mountains, The, 1

Little Green Frog, The, 99

Little House, The, 15

Little House in the Big Woods, 115

Little House on the Prairie, 115

Little Island, The, 56

Little Match Girl, The, 89

Little Men, 117

Little Navajo Bluebird, 92

Little Pig in the Cupboard, The, 14

Little Raccoon and No Trouble at All, 61

Little Raccoon and Poems from the Woods, 61

Little Raccoon and the Thing in the Pool, 61

Little Red Caboose, The, 68

Little Red Hen, The, 8

Little Red Lighthouse and the Great Gray Bridge, The, 78

Little Red Riding Hood, 13

Little Sailboat, The, 52

Little Seal with Meal Appeal, The, 70

Littlest House, The, 21

Little Toot, 37

Little Train, The, 52

Little Wild Horse, 6

Little Women, 117

Little Wood Duck, The, 85

Little Wooden Farmer, The, 21

Livingston, Myra Cohn, 54

Livingstone, David, biography of, 150

Llamas on the Loose, 109

Lobel, Arnold, 54

Lofting, Hugh, 105

London, Jack, 140

Long Ago in Colonial Days, 48

Longfellow, Henry Wadsworth, 54

Look at Flowers, 49

Look Through My Window, 105

Lorna Doone, 129

Louis Braille, 23, 146

Loveland, John, 147

Low, Elizabeth, 105

Lowitz, Sadyebeth and Anson, 54

Lowry, Lois, 105

Lucht, Irmgard, 38

Lucky Ladybugs, 20

Lucky Little Porcupine, The, 57

Ludwig, Charles, 133, 148, 150, 153-54

Luna: The Story of a Moth, 106

Lund, Doris Herold, 54

Luther, Kathrine von Bora, biography of, 150

Luther, Martin, biography of, 150

M

McCain, Murray, 54

McCall, Edith, 54

McCauley, David, 120

McClintock, Marshall, 55

McCloskey, Robert, 55, 105

McClung, Robert M., 55, 106-7

MacDonald, George, 107, 120, 140-41

MacDonald, Golden, 56

McFarlan, Donald, 151

McGaw, Francis, 148

McGinley, Phylis, 107

McGovern, Ann, 56

MacGregor, Ellen, 56, 108

Machentanz, Sara and Fred, 56

Mackay, Alexander, biography of, 151

MacLachlan, Patricia, 56, 126

McMillan, Bruce, 56

McPhail, David, 56

Madeline, 7

Maestro, Betsy and Giulio, 56-57

Magician's Nephew, The, 104

Maiden's Bequest, The, 141

Make Way for Ducklings, 55

Man Called Martin Luther, A, 150

Mandy, 96

Manners Can Be Fun, 51

Manners Zoo, The, 9

Mansfield Park, 129

Man Without a Country, The, 132

Many Is How Many?, 67

Many Moons, 113

Marble Faun, The, 132

Marc and Pixie and the Walls in Mrs. Jones's Garden, 28

Margaret Thatcher: Britain's Prime Minister, 132, 154

Margolis, Richard J., 57

Marino, Dorothy, 57

Mark of the Horse Lord, The, 123

Marquis' Secret, The, 141

Martin, Dick, 57

Martin, Dorothy, 149

Martin, Patricia Miles, 57

Martini, Teri, 57

Martin Luther: Hero of Faith, 150

Mary Alice, Operator Number Nine, 1

Mary of Mile 18, 90

Mary Poppins, 113

Mary Slessor, 152

Mason, Miriam E., 108

Massi, Jeri, 108-9

Massie, Diane Redfield, 57

Matchlock Gun, The, 95

Mayer, Marianna, 57
Mayer, Mercer, 57
Mayor of Casterbridge, The, 137
Meader, Stephen W., 120
Meadowcroft, Enid L., 109
Me and My Flying Machine, 57
Means, Florence Crannell, 109
Medallion, 114
Meek, Pauline Palmer, 58
Meet the Orchestra, 39
Meigs, Cornelia, 120, 145
Melindy's Medal, 97
Mell, Jan, 58
Melville, Herman, 142
Men Against the Sea, 133
Menken, John, 58
Men of Iron, 121
Mesa Verde National Park, 69
Message to Hadrian, 123
Mice of the Herring Bone, 23
Michael Faraday, Father of Electronics, 148
Michael Is Brave, 14
Mike Mulligan and His Steam Shovel, 15
Miklowitz, Gloria D., 58
Miles, Miska, 58, 59, 109
Miller, Basil, 146, 148, 151-52, 154
Miller, Edna, 59
Miller, Natalie, 59
Miller, Patricia K., 59-60
Millionaire for God, 153
Millions of Cats, 32

Milne, A. A., 60
Minarik, Else Holmelund, 60
Mio, My Son, 104
Miracles on Maple Hill, 112
Miss Hickory, 89
Missing Maple Syrup Sap Mystery, The, 35
Missionary Heroine of Calabar, 152
Mississippi Possum, 58
Miss Pickerell Goes to Mars, 108
Misty of Chincoteague, 100
Mitten, The, 80
Mittens, 62
Mixed-Up Chameleon, The, 17
Mizumura, Kazue, 60
Mock, Dorothy, 60
Moffats, The, 97
Monk Who Shook the World, The, 150
Montgomery, Elizabeth Rider, 61
Montgomery, L. M., 120-21
Moody, Dwight Lyman, biography of, 151
Moody Still Lives, 151
Moon Flights, 30
Moon Seems to Change, The, 10
Moon Singer, The, 14
Moore, Lilian, 61
Moose Is Not a Mouse, A, 8
More All-of-a-Kind Family, 113
Morey, Walt, 109-10, 121

Morning Star of the Reformation, 134, 155
Morris, Robert A., 61
Morrison, Bill, 62
Morse, Flo, 62
Morse, Samuel French, 62
Mother of the Wesleys, 155
Mother Owl, The, 44
Mother Raspberry, 16
Mott, Evelyn Clarke, 62
Mountain Born, 116
Mouse and the Motorcycle, The, 93
Mousekin's Christmas Eve, 59
Mousekin's Family, 59
Mowat, Farley, 110
Mr. Key's Song, 54
Mr. Peaceable Paints, 84
Mr. Pine's Mixed-up Signs, 49
Mr. Plum and the Little Green Tree, 35
Mr. Revere and I, 103
Mr. Zip and the U.S. Mail, 5
Mrs. Frisby and the Rats of NIMH, 110
Mueller, George, 151
Mueller, George, biography of, 151
Murray, Andrew, biography of, 151
Mushrooms and Molds, 98
Muskrat, Muskrat, Eat Your Peas!, 86
Mutiny on the Bounty, 133
Myers, Bernice, 62

My Father's Dragon, 98
My Five Senses, 10
My Hands, 10
Myller, Rolf, 62
My Mother and I, 29
My Plant, 86
My Red Umbrella, 12
Myrick, Mildred, 62
My Side of the Mountain, 119
My Very Special Friend, 40

N

Napping House, The, 86
Nathan Hale, 81
Nature's Lumberjack, 66
Naylor, Phyllis Reynolds, 127
Neigoff, Anne, 62
Nest, The, 34
Newberry, Clare Turlay, 62
New Boy in Dublin, 14
New Coat for Anna, A, 87
New House, New Town, 62
Newton, John, 152
Newton, John, biography of, 152
Nicholas, Charles, 63
Nicholas Nickleby, 131
Night Animals, 73
Night Flight, 134
Nightingale, Florence, biography of, 152
Nightingale, The, 89
Night in the Country, 7
Night Markets: Bringing Food to a City, 43

Niizaka, Kazuo, 63
Noah's Ark, 76
Nohl, Frederick, 150
Noisy Book, The, 13
Noisy Gander, 58
No Measles, No Mumps for Me, 75
Nordhoff, Charles, 133
North, South, East, and West, 11
North of Danger, 97
Noses and Toes, 40
Now I Know What's Under the Ocean, 20
Number the Stars, 105
Numeroff, Laura Joffe, 63
Nutcracker, The, 42
Nye, Julie, 110, 133

O

O'Brien, Robert C., 110
Octopus, 74
Oda, Hidetomo, 63
Odd One Out, 65
O'Dell, Scott, 121, 154
Odor, Ruth Shannon, 63
Oetting, Rae, 63
Old Woman and Her Pig, The, 33
Oliver Twist, 131
Olympics, 30
Once in a Wood: Ten Tales from Aesop, 63
Once There Was a Tree, 16
Once upon a Mountain, 9
Once We Went on a Picnic, 29

One, Two, Three for Fun, 77
One Fine Day, 42
One Fish, Two Fish, Red Fish, Blue Fish, 73
O'Neil, Catherine, 63
O'Neill, Mary, 64
One Morning in Maine, 55
One Vision Only, 149
On the Banks of Plum Creek, 115
On the Clouds to China, 153
On the Farm, 25
On Yonder Mountain, 43
Oppenheim, Joanne, 64
Orczy, Baroness Emmuska, 133
Orderly Cricket, The, 63
Orlowsky, Wallace, 64
Orton, Helen Fuller, 110
Orwell, George, 142
Oscar Otter, 7
Otto in Africa, 25
Our Country's Flag, 34
Out of the Depths: An Autobiography, 152
Out of the Silent Planet, 139
Over, Under, and All Around, 79
Over the River and Through the Wood, 19
Owl and the Woodpecker, The, 85
Owl Moon, 87
Owls in the Family, 110
Ox-Cart Man, 38
Oxygen Keeps You Alive, 91

P

Paddle-to-the-Sea, 101

Panek, Dennis, 64

Papa Like Everyone Else, A, 113

Papa's Wife, 129

Pape, Donna Lugg, 64

Parade Starts at Noon, The, 58

Parin, Edgar, 22, 94, 150

Parish, Peggy, 64

Parr, Letitia, 64

Parrot Book, The, 34

Parson, Virginia, 64

Patent, Dorothy Hinshaw, 64

Paterson, Katherine, 127

Pathfinder, The, 130

Patterson, Geoffrey, 65

Paton, Alan, 142

Paul Revere's Ride, 54

Paulossie, An Eskimo Boy, 78

Peanut, 73

Pearl, The, 143

Pearson, Violet T., 83

Peck, Helen E., 65

Peek-a-boo, 49

Peet, Bill, 65

Pelle's New Suit, 9

Penny, Malcolm, 65

People on Long Ago Street, The, 14

Peppé, Rodney, 65

Perelandra, 139

Perera, Thomas Biddle, 64

Periwinkle, 25

Perkins, Al, 65

Perry, Phyllis J., 65

Persuasion, 129

Peter and the Wolf, 69

Peter Pan, 90

Peter's Chair, 48

Petersham, Maud and Miska, 65-66

Peterson, Hans, 66

Peterson, Willis, 66

Petunia, I Love You, 25

Pfloog, Jan, 66

Phantom Tollbooth, The, 119

Piatti, Celestino, 66

Picking and Weaving, 52

Pickle Things, 12

Pierce, Robert, 66

Pierson, Arthur T., 151

Pigs and Pirates, 82

Pilgrim's Progress, 15

Pink Pig, 43

Pinkston, William S., Jr., 67

Pinto's Journey, 91

Pioneers, The, 130

Pip Camps Out, 13

Piper, Watty, 67

Pirates' Bridge, The, 37

Pitcairn's Island, 133

Pitt, Valerie, 67

Pittman, E. R., 149

Plain Princess, The, 107

Planets in Our Solar System, The, 11

Play with Me, 27

Pocket Change, 83
Pocketful of Cricket, A, 18
Pocketful of Seasons, A, 30
Podendorf, Illa, 67, 68
Podojill, Catherine, 145
Poems for Galloping, 69
Poems for Weather Watching, 46
Pohl, Kathleen, 68
Poisons Make You Sick, 18
Polgreen, John and Cathleen, 68
Police, 12
Policeman Small, 52
Police Officers, A to Z, 47
Pollock, J. C., 153
Pollock, John, 152
Ponies of Mykillengi, 3
Pony for Three, 3
Pool of Fire, The, 136
Popov, Haralan, 152
Popov, Haralan, biography of, 152
Possum, 55
Post Office Cat, The, 38
Potatoes, 81
Potter, Beatrix, 68
Potter, Marian, 68
Poulet, Virginia, 68
Powell, Elsa, 68
Powzyk, Joyce, 68
Prairie, The, 130
Praying Hyde, 148
Preston, Edna M., 8
Pride and Prejudice, 129

Prince Caspian: The Return to Narnia, 104
Princess and Curdie, The, 107
Princess and the Goblin, The, 107
Princess and the Lion, The, 93
Prison Letters, 154
Prokofiev, Sergei S., 69
Provensen, Alice and Martin, 69
Pudgy, the Beaver, 22
Puff, 86
Pulling Together, 83
Puppies Are Like That, 66
Pyle, Howard, 121

Q

Quackenbush, Robert M., 69, 147
Quackenbush, Robert M., ed., 69
Queen of the Reformation, 150
Question of Yams, A, 69
Quiet! There's a Canary in the Library, 31
Quiet Neighborhood, A, 141
Quigley, Lillian, 69
Quo Vadis, 142

R

Rabbit Garden, 59
Rabbit Hill, 103
Rabbit Seeds, 52
Rabbits' World, The, 72
Radlawer, Ruth, 69
Rain and Hail, 11

Rainbow of My Own, A, 31
Rain Drop Splash, 80
Rain Rain Rivers, 75
Rains Will Come, The, 109
Raminagrobis and the Mice, 9
Rand, Joyce, 69
Randy's Dandy Lions, 65
Ransome, Arthur, 111
Rawlings, Marjorie Kinnan, 121
Ray and Stevie on a Corn Belt Farm, 52
Raynor, Dorka, 69
Rebecca of Sunnybrook Farm, 114
Red Badge of Courage, The, 136
Redbird: The Story of a Cardinal, 106
Red Fairy Book, 103
Refuge, 130
Reid, J. Calvin, 111
Reid, W. Stanford, 149
Reluctant Dragon, The, 99
Remembering Box, The, 125
Renegade in the Hills, 113
Repp, Gloria, 69, 111, 134
Rey, Hans A. and Margaret, 70
Rice, Eve, 70
Rich, Louise Dickinson, 111
Rickie, 23
Rifles for Watie, 119
Right-Hand Man, 116
Riley, Jane, 70
Rinkoff, Barbara, 70
Ripper, Charles L., 70

Rise of Silas Lapham, The, 138
Rivers, 17
Roar and More, 51
Robbie and the Sled Dog Race, 56
Robbins, Ken, 70
Robert E. Lee, Christian General and Gentleman, 149
Robert E. Lee, The Christian, 149
Rockets and Satellites, 11
Rockwell, Anne, 70, 71
Rockwell, Harlow, 70, 71
Roddy, Lee, 149
Roller Skates, 112
Roll of Thunder, Hear My Cry, 127
Rölvaag, O. E., 142
Romanek, Enid Warner, 71
Romano, Louis, 34
Rootabaga Stories, 112
Roots Are Food Finders, 91
Rose, Mary Catherine, 71, 145
Rosebud, 26
Rose in Bloom, 117
Rosenthal, Bert, 71
Rossetti, Christina G., 71
Rounds, Glen, 111
Ruby Throat: The Story of a Hummingbird, 55
Rudin, Ellen, 71
Rumble-Seat Pony, The, 3
Runaway Giant, The, 42
Runaway Princess, The, 43
Runaway Stallion, 110

Runner for the King, 90
Runyon, Leilah E., 71
Rylant, Cynthia, 71

S

St. John, Patricia, 111
Saint-Saëns, Camille, 72
Salt, 98
Salten, Felix, 111
Sam and John Adams, 51, 145
Sammy the Seal, 42
Sam the Minuteman, 8
Sandburg, Carl, 112
Sandy, the Swallow, 22
Sapienza, Marilyn, 72
Sarah Plain and Tall, 56
Sarah Somebody, 76
Sarah Whitcher's Story, 87
Sargent, Robert, 72
Saturdays, The, 96
Saturday Walk, 86
Sawdust Preacher: The Story of Billy Sunday, 153
Sawyer, Ruth, 112
Scarlet Letter, The, 137
Scarlet Pimpernel, The, 133
Schaaf, Peter, 72
Schackburg, Richard, 72
Schlein, Miriam, 72
Schneider, Nina, 72
Schwartz, Alvin, 73
Schwartz, Elizabeth, 73
Scott, Sir Walter, 134
Scout, 110
Seahorse, 61

Sea Star, 100
Secret Garden, The, 92
Secret Hiding Place, The, 8
Secret of the Golden Cowrie, The, 111
Seeds, 46
Seeds by Wind and Water, 48
Seeing in Special Ways, 8
See the First Star, 76
Selden, George, 112
Seligman, Iran L., 59, 60
Selsam, Millicent E., 73
Sense and Sensibility, 129
Separate Peace, A, 139
Seredy, Kate, 112, 121
Serraillier, Ian, 121
Serventy, Vincent, 73
Seuling, Barbara, 73
Seuss, Dr., 73-74
Seven Days of Creation, The, 29
Several Tricks of Edgar Dolphin, The, 8
Shadow Book, The, 24
Shadow of the Almighty: The Life and Testament of Jim Elliot, 148
Shadows and More Shadows, 67
Shannon, Monica, 112
Shannon, Terry, 74
Shaw, Evelyn, 74
Shawn's Red Bike, 12
Sheehan, Angela, 24
Shen of the Sea: Chinese Stories for Children, 92

Sheriff at Waterstop, 113
Shiloh, 127
Shine, Sun!, 37
Shivkumar, K., 74
Short, Rendle A., 151
Shortall, Leonard, 74
Showers, Paul, 74, 75
Shrimps, 39
Shulevitz, Uri, 75
Sienkiewicz, Henryk, 142
Signs, 37
Silas Marner, 131
Silcott, Philip B., 76
Silence over Dunkerque, 123
Silent Concert, The, 51
Silver Branch, The, 123
Silver Chair, The, 104
Silver Sword, The, 121
Simon, 123
Simon, Norma, 76
Simon, Seymour, 76
Simple Folk Instruments to Make and to Play, 44
Simpson, Albert Benjamin, biography of, 152
Singing Tree, The, 112
Sivulich, Sandra Stroner, 76
Six Foolish Fishermen, 26
Sleepy Time, 27
Slessor, Mary Mitchell, biography of, 152
Slobodkin, Florence and Louis, 76
Smallest Boy in the Class, The, 7

Smiling Dragon, The, 65
Smith, Betsy, 76
Smith, Robert Paul, 76
Smoke Above the Lane, 94
Smoky, 119
Snipp, Snapp, Snurr and the Red Shoes, 53
Snipp, Snapp, Snurr and the Seven Dogs, 53
Snow, Pegeen, 76
Snow Day, 57
Snow Dog, 102
Snow Is Falling, 11
Snowshoe Paws, 47
Snow Time, 72
Snowy Day, The, 48
Snug in the Snow, 105
Sod House, The, 93
Some Are Small, 25
Some Summer!, 114
Song of the Day Birds and the Night Birds, The, 45
Sonnets from the Portugese, 130
Soo Ling Finds a Way, 6
Sorensen, Virginia, 112
Sound Friendships, 124
Sounder, 125
Speare, Elizabeth George, 122
Spelling Window, The, 84
Sperry, Armstrong, 122
Spiders, 22
Spider Silk, 36
Spiderweb for Two, 96
Spier, Peter, 76

Spike: The Story of a Whitetail Deer, 55
Splash! All About Baths, 15
Spring Begins in March, 105
Spurgeon, 152
Spurgeon, Charles Haddon, 154
Spurgeon, Charles Haddon, biography of, 152
Spurgeon: London's Most Popular Preacher, 152
Spyri, Johanna, 112
Squeaky, the Squirrel, 22
Squeeze a Sneeze, 62
Stam, John and Betty, biography of, 153
Stam, Kathleen, 153
Standiford, Natalie, 77
Stanek, Muriel, 77
Star Island Boy, 111
Star of Light, 111
Star of Wild Horse Canyon, 14
Star-Spangled Banner, The, 77
Stay Safe, Play Safe, 73
Steam Train Ride, 62
Steele, Mary Q., 77
Steele, Philip, 77
Steig, William, 77
Steinbeck, John, 143
Stephen, R. J., 77
Sterling, Dorothy, 113, 154
Stevenson, Robert Louis, 77, 122, 134
Stewart, Elizabeth Laing, 77
Stobbs, William, 77
Stocker, Fern Neal, 153

Stokes, Bill, 77
Stolen Years, The, 134
Stone Fox, 98
Stone Soup, 72
Stop, Look, and Listen for Trains, 18
Storm Book, The, 88
Stormy, Misty's Foal, 100
Story About Ping, The, 29
Story of a Bad Boy, The, 117
Story of Dr. Dolittle, The, 105
Story of the Star-Spangled Banner, The, 59
Story of the Statue of Liberty, The, 59
Stover, Jo Ann, 78
Stowe, Harriet Beecher, biography of, 133, 153
Straight Hair, Curly Hair, 36, 99
Strange Disappearance of Arthur Cluck, The, 8
Strangely Warmed, 154
Streamlined, 101
Street, James, 122
Stripe: The Story of a Chipmunk, 55
Stripes and Spots, 46
Strom, Kay Marshall, 152
Studd, Charles Thomas, biography of, 153
Sugaring Time, 51
Summer Noisy Book, The, 13
Summer of the Swans, The, 118
Sun: Our Nearest Star, The, 11

Sunday, William Ashley, biography of, 153

Sunlit Sea, The, 99

Sunshine Makes the Seasons, 91

Sun Up, 80

Supraner, Robyn, 78

Surprised by Joy, 150

Surprise for Mother, 52

Susanna, Mother of the Wesleys, 155

Susanna Wesley: Servant of God, 155

Sutcliff, Rosemary, 122-23

Suteyev, V., 78

Svea: The Dancing Moose, 3

Swallows and Amazons, 111

Swallows Come Home, 43

Swift, Catherine, 145, 150

Swift, Hildegarde H., 78

Swim, Little Duck, 59

Swim, Robert C., 78

Swing Around the Sun, 27

Swiss Family Robinson, The, 124

Sylvester and the Magic Pebble, 77

T

Tafuri, Nancy, 78

Take a Trip to Holland, 27

Talbot, Winifred, 78

Tale of Peter Rabbit, The, 68

Tale of Two Cities, A, 131

Tales from Shakespeare, 102

Talk About School, 71

Taste and Smell, 19

Taylor, Howard, and Mrs. Howard J., 153

Taylor, J. Hudson, 153

Taylor, James Hudson, biography of, 153

Taylor, Mark, 79

Taylor, Mildred D., 127

Taylor, Mrs. Howard, 145

Taylor, Sydney, 113

Teddy, 71

Teddy Bear's Bird and Beast Band, 44

Teddy, 71

Tell Me Some More, 10

ten Boom, Corrie, 154

ten Boom, Corrie, autobiography of, 154

Ten Brothers with Camels, 21

Ten Copycats in a Boat and Other Riddles, 73

Terhune, Albert Payson, 113

Terry, Trevor, 79

Tess of the D'Urbervilles, 137

Tester, Sylvia Root, 79

Thanksgiving Story, The, 21

Thank You, God, for Water, 60

That Hideous Strength, 140

Thatcher, Margaret, biography of, 132, 154

Theodore Turtle, 56

"There Are Rocks in My Socks," Said the Ox to the Fox, 79

These Are My People, 101, 145

They Didn't Use Their Heads, 78

Thief in the Attic, The, 84

Thimble Summer, 96

Things to Do with Water, 68

This Little Pig, 59

Thomas Alva Edison, Inventor, 20

Thomas, Patricia, 79

Thomas, Ulrich, 79

Thompson, A. W., 152

Thompson, Brenda, 79

Thomson, Andy, 113, 134, 155

Three Billy Goats Gruff, The, 79

Three Kittens, 78

Three Little Pigs, The, 19

Three Musketeers, The, 131

Three Pigs, The, 79

Through Gates of Splendor, 148

Through the Looking Glass, 95

Thunderhoof, 42

Thurber, James, 113

Thy Friend, Obadiah, 80

Tiger: The Story of a Swallowtail Butterfly, 106

Time for Jody, 49

Time Machine, The, 144

Time of Wonder, 55

Timmy Tiger's New Coat, 63

Timothy's Forest, 53

Tiner, John Hudson, 149

Tiny Seed, The, 16

Titus Tidewater, 81

To God Alone Be the Glory: Johann Sebastian Bach, 145

To Kill a Mockingbird, 139

To the Golden Shore: The Life of Adoniram Judson, 148

Tolkien, J. R. R., 134

Tolstoy, Alexei, 79

Tommy's Pets, 25

Toolbox, The, 71

Too Many Rabbits, 64

Tortured for His Faith, 152

Touch and Feel, 19

Trail Maker, 150

Trains, 35

Travel by Land, 6

Traveling Ball of String, The, 16

Travers, P[amela] L., 113

Trease, Geoffrey, 123

Treasure in the Little Trunk, The, 110

Treasure in the Yukon, 109

Treasure Island, 122

Treasure of Pelican Cove, The, 43

Treasures of the Snow, 111

Treat Truck and the Big Rain, 44

Tree for Peter, A, 112

Tree Is a Plant, A, 14

Tree Is Nice, A, 81

Trees, 46

Tresselt, Alvin, 80

Triggs, Kathy, 152

Trip to the Doctor, 53

Truck and Bus Book, The, 25

Trumpeter of God: A Biography of John Knox, 149

Trumpeter of Kracow, The, 126

Trumpet of the Swan, The, 114

Truthful Harp, The, 89

Tubman, Harriet, biography of, 113, 154

Tunis, John R., 123, 134

Turkle, Brinton, 80

Turner, Dorothy, 81

Turn of the Screw, The, 138

Turtle, The, 63

Turtle Pond, 31

Tutor's First Love, The, 141

Twain, Mark, 127, 143

24 Hours in a Forest, 84

Twenty Thousand Leagues Under the Sea, 124

Twenty-One Balloons, 95

Two Collars, The, 108

Two Good Friends, 23

Two Logs Crossing, 95

Two Piano Tuners, 36

Two Wesleys, The, 154

Tyndale, William, biography of, 121, 154

U

Udry, Janice May, 81

Ugliest Sweater, The, 63

Ugly Duckling, The, 2

Ullman, James Ramsey, 123

Umbrella, 87

Uncle Fonzo's Ford, 109

Understood Betsy, 92

Under the Lemon Tree, 45

Under the Sun, 48

Up a Road Slowly, 133

Up in the Air, 54

Upside Down, 46

Usborne Guide to Stamps and Stamp Collecting, 2

V

VanClief, Sylvia W., 40

Vandevenne, Jean, 114

VanGelder, Richard G., 5

Van Woerkom, Dorothy, 81

Vegetables, 82

Verleyen, Cyriel, 81

Verne, Jules, 124

Vernon, Louise A., 154

Veronica and the Birthday Present, 25

Veronica's Smile, 25

Verrier, Suzanne, 81

Very Busy Spider, The, 17

Very Hungry Caterpillar, The, 17

Very Like a Star, 84

Very Quiet Cricket, The, 17

Vessel, Matthew F., 86

Vicar of Wakefield, The, 132

Victoria, Queen, biography of, 133, 154

Violin Close Up, The, 72

Visit to the Bakery, A, 87

Voelker, Joyce, 114

Voight, Virginia, 81

Voorhees, Carolyn, 82

Voyage of the Dawn Treader, The, 104

Voyages of Dr. Dolittle, The, 105

Vulcan: The Story of a Bald Eagle, 107

W

Waber, Bernard, 82

Wackerbarth, Marjorie, 82

Wait and See, 84

Wake, Susan, 82

Wake Up, City!, 80

Wake Up, Farm!, 80

Walk in the Desert, A, 4

Walk in the Woods, A, 49

Walker, Barbara, 82

Walker, F. Deauville, 146

Walk in the Woods, A, 49

Wallace, Lew, 134

Walley, Susan, 114

Walter, Frances, 83

Walters, Marguerite, 83

Walter the Lazy Mouse, 29

Wannamaker, Bruce, 83

Ward, Lynd, 78, 83

War of the Worlds, 144

Warrior Scarlet, 123

Washington's Breakfast, 32

Watch Honeybees with Me, 39

Watch Out, Ronald Morgan, 35

Watch Out for the Chicken Feet in Your Soup, 24

Water, 24

Waters, John F., 83

Water We Drink!, The, 9

Watkins, Dawn, 83, 84, 114, 135

Watson, Jane Werner, 84

Watts, Barrie, 84

We Are Helpers, 51

Weather, 46

Web in the Grass, The, 31

Web of Traitors, 123

Weeds and Wildflowers, 68

Weisgard, Leonard, 56, 84

Wells, H. G., 144

Wesley, John, biography of, 154

Wesley, Susanna, biography of, 155

Westward, Ho!, 133

Wexler, Jerome, 84

Whaler 'Round the Horn, 120

Wharton, Edith, 144

What About Trucks?, 18

What Happens to a Hamburger, 75

What Has Wild Tom Done Now?, 69, 147

What I Like About Toads, 39

What Is a Bird?, 23

What Is a Turtle?, 22

What Is Big?, 86

What Is Pink?, 71

What Makes Day and Night, 11

What Makes It Rain?, 10

What Sadie Sang, 70

What's It Like to Be a Nurse?, 6

What's It Like to Be an Airline Pilot?, 6

What's That Noise?, 48

What the Moon Is Like, 11

What Will the Weather Be?, 90

Wheat, 47

Wheel on the Chimney, 13

Wheel on the School, The, 94

When an Animal Grows, 73

When Animals Are Babies, 73

When Dad Fills in the Garden Pond, 4

When I Am Big, 76

When Insects Are Babies, 20

When I Was Young in the Mountains, 71

When Joy Came: The Story of the First Christmas, 58

When Peter Was Lost in the Forest, 66

When Sea and Sky Are Blue, 64

When We Were Very Young, 60

When Will It Snow?, 42

When Winter Comes, 30

Where Am I?, 7

Where Do Bears Sleep?, 40

Where Does Everyone Go?, 29

Where Does the Butterfly Go When It Rains?, 34

Where Does Your Garden Grow?, 36

Where Is Duckling Three?, 38

Where the Brook Begins, 6

While Susie Sleeps, 72

Whistle for Willie, 49

White, E. B., 114

White, Kathleen, 147, 153

Whitefield, George, 155

Whitefield, George, biography of, 155

White Mountain, 136

White Stag, The, 112

Whitney, Alama Marshak, 84

Who Goes There in My Garden?, 20

Who Likes It Hot?, 34

Who Will Wash the River?, 64

Who Works Here?, 4

Why Am I Different?, 76

Why Does It Rain?, 39

Whyman, Kathryn, 85

Why Mosquitoes Buzz in People's Ears, 1

Why So Sad, Little Rag Doll?, 82

Whyte, Alexander, 146

Wiese, Kurt, 9, 85

Wiesner, David, 85

Wiest, Robert and Claire, 85

Wiewandt, Thomas A., 85

Wiggin, Kate Douglas, 114

Wilder, Laura Ingalls, 115

Wildsmith, Brian, 85, 86

William Borden, 145

William Carey, 146

William Carey: Father of Modern Missions, 146

William Carey: Missionary Pioneer, 146

Williams, Connie, 116

Williams, Garth, 86

Will Spring Be Early or Will Spring Be Late?, 47

Wilson, Sarah, 86
Wind Blew, The, 45
Wind in the Willows, The, 99
Wing, Henry, 86
Wings and Wheels, 19
Winnie-the-Pooh, 60
Winter Bear, The, 20
Winter's Coming, 14
Witch of Blackbird Pond, The, 122
With Daring Faith, 118, 147
With Wings as Eagles, 67
Wizard of Oz, The, 90
Wizard of the Great Lake, 151
Wolcott, Patty, 86
Wonder-Fish from the Sea, 38
Wonders of Nature, 84
Wondriska, William, 86
Wong, Herbert H., 86
Wood, 85
Wood, A. Shevington, 154
Wood, Audrey, 86
Wool, 24
Woolley, Catherine, 86
Worchester, J. H., 150
Working with Water, 17
Wright, Betty Ren, 86
Wright, Ethel, 86
Wuthering Heights, 136
Wycliffe, John, biography of, 155

Wyss, Johann David, 124

X

X Marks the Spot, 28

Y

Yankee Doodle, 72
Yashima, Taro, 87
Yates, Elizabeth, 87, 116, 124, 135
Yearling, The, 121
Yellow Fairy Book, 103
Yertle the Turtle and Other Stories, 74
Yolen, Jane, 87
Yonie Wondernose, 94
You Can Catch Fish, 77
You Can Find a Snail, 60
Younger, Jesse, 87
Young Man in a Hurry, 146
Your First Garden Book, 12
Your Pet Lion, 39

Z

Zebra, 42
Ziefert, Harriet, 87
Ziegler, Sandra, 87
Zion, Gene, 87
Zoli's Legacy I: Inheritance, 135
Zoli's Legacy II: Bequest, 135
Zolotow, Charlotte, 88
Zoo, Where Are You?, 56